Praise for *Brink of Chaos*

When one adds up the total number of all the books in circulation that have been authored by Tim LaHaye, you quickly see that he is one of the most read authors in the entire world! Few can compare. There is a reason for that. What he writes, matters. Once again, he has written a compelling novel on the end times. Fast-paced, filled with action and adventure, and an accurate biblical portrayal, you won't be able to put it down.

Jim Garlow, pastor, Skyline Church, San Diego
and chairman of ReAL, Washington, DC

Praise for Other Books in The End Series

Dr. Tim LaHaye writes about the future with the kind of gripping detail that others would use to describe the past. I've been reading Tim LaHaye's books for over thirty years, but *Thunder of Heaven* may be his best yet!

Mike Huckabee, former Arkansas governor

Tim LaHaye's books always entertain, educate, and thrill, but *Thunder of Heaven* takes it to a new level. I never thought the End of Days would cost me so much sleep!

Glenn Beck, number one *New York Times* bestselling author

Tim LaHaye writes about the prophetic future with such accuracy and passion that once you get started reading what he has written, you do not put the book away until it is finished! In our generation, he has led the way back to a proper appreciation of the prophetic writings of Scripture. Everywhere I go, I meet someone who has read one of Tim's books and been blessed by it. This book will continue that tradition!

Dr. David Jeremiah, senior pastor of Shadow Mountain
Community Church, founder and CEO of Turning Point

Other Books by Tim LaHaye

The End Series

Edge of Apocalypse

Thunder of Heaven

Brink of Chaos

Revelation Unveiled

Finding the Will of God in a Crazy, Mixed-Up World

How to Win Over Depression

Anger Is a Choice (Tim LaHaye and Bob Phillips)

*The Act of Marriage: The Beauty of Sexual Love
(Tim and Beverly LaHaye)*

*The Act of Marriage after 40: Making Love for Life
(Tim and Beverly LaHaye with Mike Yorkey)*

#1 *NEW YORK TIMES* BESTSELLING AUTHOR

TIM LaHAYE
& CRAIG PARSHALL

A JOSHUA JORDAN NOVEL

BRINK OF
CHAOS

THE END SERIES

ZONDERVAN®

ZONDERVAN.com/
AUTHORTRACKER
follow your favorite authors

ZONDERVAN

Brink of Chaos
Copyright © 2012 by Tim LaHaye

This title is also available as a Zondervan ebook. Visit www.zondervan.com/ebooks.

This title is also available in a Zondervan audio edition. Visit www.zondervan.fm.

Requests for information should be addressed to:
Zondervan, *Grand Rapids, Michigan 49530*

Library of Congress Cataloging-in-Publication Data

LaHaye, Tim F.
      Brink of chaos / Tim LaHaye and Craig Parshall.
          p.   cm. — (The end series ; 3)
      ISBN 978-0-310-31881-1 (softcover)
      1. End of the world — Fiction. I. Parshall, Craig, 1950 - II. Title.
PS3562.A315B75 2012
813'.54 — dc3   2011019479

Published in association with the literary agency of WordServe Literary Group, Ltd., 10152 S. Knoll Circle, Highlands Ranch, CO 80130.

Cover design: James Hall
Cover photography: 123RF®
Interior design: Christine Orejuela-Winkelman
Editorial team: Sue Brower, Nicci Jordan Hubert, Bob Hudson, and Samantha Vanderberg

Printed in the United States of America

12 13 14 15 16 17 18 /DCI/ 22 21 20 19 18 17 16 15 14 13 12 11 10 9 8 7 6 5 4 3 2 1

*To all those who see
the chaotic events in the Middle East
as a fulfillment of End Times Bible Prophecy
and want to be ready when it happens*

BRINK OF
CHAOS

PROLOGUE

In the Near Future

"Joshua."

The voice called to him so powerfully that it reverberated in his chest as if he were standing on the thundering edge of Niagara Falls.

"Joshua Jordan."

For a split second he couldn't feel his heart beating. When he sensed it thumping again, he tried to speak, fumbling for the words. When he was finally able to reply, the words caught in his throat. "Here. Yes. I'm here."

The darkness began to part, first at the edges. Then there was the flood of illumination, an ocean of light like nothing he had ever seen. He had seen the northern lights a few times, years before, when he was stationed in Alaska. The night sky had lit up with a shimmering, iridescent band. Sweeping waves of color had rippled across the night sky like translucent ribbons.

But that was nothing compared to this. What he saw now was … indescribable. He tried to catch his breath.

Am I in the air?

Yes, there was the sensation of flying.

Airborne.

But flying had been his life, hadn't it? Piloting test planes for the Air Force. Flying a series of combat missions in Iraq and advanced U-2 spy-plane flights over Iran. Shaking hands with a president.

Finishing his MIT degree and his defense-contracting work on fighter jets at his own tech company, Jordan Technologies, and his spectacular business success and impressive financial fortune that quickly followed. And later his creation of the ultimate missile defense system, Return to Sender — RTS. And the incredible turn of events that led to another meeting with yet another president, and his reluctant defiance of Congress and his having to face down a court order from a federal judge to protect his country. And then those political, legal, and personal hurricanes that resulted from all of that. But all the time, at the center of it all, flying machines. Those designs and schematics of his for devices that utilized the rules of engineering, physics, thrust, and avionics to blast through the air. Inventions of speed and deadly accuracy. Made of steel, electrical wire, computer chips, and lasers. The genius of man.

But this was different. What Joshua was experiencing now, his journey upward as he defied gravity, this was beyond the ability of man. Beyond all physics. Beyond nature. Somewhere a golden note sounded like the chorus of a thousand trumpets, and it filled the sky with sound. Thrilling, thrilling. His heart beat faster. Then he looked down at the ground disappearing under his feet, and he saw the houses and cars and fields and highways grow smaller. He recognized a farmhouse down there. Was it his boyhood home in Colorado? It all grew dimmer. But there was no sadness in that for him.

No looking back.

Now he was aware that there were others. Flying. An army of human beings rocketing upward. A voice was calling. The voice of a woman. His mother? It was her voice as she led his Sunday school class when he was a boy. What verse from Scripture was that from? The voice was saying ...

Caught up ... Caught up ...

Joshua looked around in utter amazement. A sea of faces. He called out to find one in particular. He had to find her. The woman he loved. He was searching frantically for his wife.

Abby! Abby! Where are you?

But the lights suddenly went out. Darkness. He was falling. Hurtling downward.

Tumbling back to earth.

Mayday! Mayday!

Joshua found himself grabbing frantically for the controls. He realized he was in the cockpit of a jet and it was going down. Warning bells were ringing from the flight deck. He tried to bring the jet out of its death spiral, but it plunged toward earth in a sickening, dizzying spin.

Hit the Eject button. Now.

He fumbled for the control that would blow the canopy open, flinging him into the sky with the line of parachute in a thin trail above him, catching the air and expanding over his head with a billowing curtain of safety.

More frantic grabbing. He couldn't find it.

The earth in all its permanence was racing up to meet him at supersonic speed. *No time . . . the end . . . I'm going to . . .* Silence. And darkness.

Joshua bolted upright.

He tried to clear his head, wondering whether his eyes were open or still shut.

Where am I?

He was in bed, sweat beading on his forehead. The realization now hit him.

A dream. It was only a dream. All of it.

Joshua ran his hand over his face and swung his legs over the side of the bed. He grabbed the clock on the nightstand next to him. Five in the morning. What time zone was this? Then he remembered. He was in a hotel in Asia, and in a few hours he would be speaking to a large church group. *Might as well get up,* he thought.

He made his way to the bathroom, turned on the light, and splashed water on his face. He looked in the mirror. The face still had a square jaw framed against the athletic neck and shoulders. But his dark, short hair was thinning into a widow's peak, with signs of grey at the temple. There were bags under his eyes.

Getting older.

He had the unmistakable feeling that time was running out ... the two-minute warning for the world. The powerful impression left from his dream still hung in the air, like a thin white contrail in the sky. He had always been a rock-solid guy, not one to put much stock in dreams. But this one was different. He felt immersed in the sensation of urgency, as if he had just taken a bath in it and was still dripping wet. But there was something else. An undeniable sense of impending danger.

He tried to shake it all off and threw more cold water on his face. But it was still there, almost palpable. He toweled off and walked back to the hotel bedroom, which was blandly decorated with grass paper and paintings of thin, wispy trees. Joshua picked up the small framed photo from the nightstand. A picture of his wife, Abigail, taken shortly before they were separated by circumstances beyond their control. She was still beautiful, ageless it seemed. Dark hair, dark eyes, and a deep dimple that appeared in her slender face when she smiled.

Abby, are you alright?

The room felt gloomy. The darkness was breaking into dawn outside. A few moments later he could see slivers of sunlight framing the window shades. Joshua dropped to his knees next to the bed with the simplicity of a boy.

Time to talk to God.

ONE

Seoul, South Korea

Early morning in Seoul. The sunlight was starting to flash across the windows of the high-rise towers of the city, causing the panes of glass to look as if they were mirrors of fire.

In his hotel room on the city's outskirts, a few blocks from the huge Junggye Gospel Church, a North Korean national, Han Suk Yong, was getting dressed. Soon he would climb into his rented car and drive to a service at the church. He was breathing faster. His heartbeat had quickened, he could tell. He would have to control it. He had to look and act natural, collected, if he was going to accomplish the single passionate plan that burned within like a flame. By the time the church service ended, he hoped to have fired several bullets into the man he hated.

Han knew his target would be heavily protected. He had cased the church the night before and noticed the security staff setting up metal detectors in the lobby, at each entrance to the ten-thousand-seat sanctuary. The main speaker was controversial, and the church was not taking any chances. But Han anticipated that. During his time with the North Korean military, he had worked with a team that specialized in advanced small-arms weaponry. When he had slipped covertly across the border the week before, he had brought a sample with him.

The newly developed .45-caliber lignostone handgun was perfect for the job. A super-compressed wood product, lignostone was as strong as steel but much lighter. More important, it could pass through metal detectors. Russia and their Arab allies had used the material for many of its weapons in the recent ill-fated invasion against Israel. The lightweight material had avoided radar detection, and the newly designed Russian trucks, Jeeps, and tanks constructed from it would have been effective had it not been for the frightful forces of nature that seemed to revolt against the military assault.

But Han told himself that his plan was different. He was a skilled assassin against a single high-profile target. And no one, he told himself, had a more powerful reason to kill.

After straightening his tie, Han assembled his lignostone gun and inserted the clip full of bullets made of the same material. He put it in his suit-coat pocket, packed his suitcase, and carried it to his car in the parking lot. Before turning the ignition, he sat behind the wheel for a moment. He pulled out a photograph and stared at it. He saluted the North Korean officer in the picture, gave a quick bow, and put it back in his pocket. Then he reached over to the passenger seat where he had a printout of a Seoul online city newspaper. He lifted the front page to his eyes, reviewing the photograph, just under the headline, which showed the man who was scheduled to be the main speaker at the Junggye Gospel Church. The target of his rage. Han studied the smiling face of the man who would soon be dead.

The gunman glanced once more at the headline —

"Joshua Jordan to Speak at Seoul Church."

□□□

Every seat was filled as the thunderous applause echoed through the mammoth sanctuary. On the dais behind the pulpit the church's pastor, Lee Ko-po, was smiling broadly and nodding. Next to him was Jin Ho Kim, one of South Korea's hottest professional pitchers. Earlier that day he had pitched a no-hitter with his blazing fastball and led his Nexen Heroes in a 5-0 victory over the Han Wha Eagles. The baseball player seated behind the podium had his eyes glued on the speaker in front of him.

At the lectern, against the backdrop of a fifty-foot stained-glass cross on the wall behind him, Joshua Jordan was trying to finish his message, but the crowd kept interrupting him with wild applause. This was not just because he was the man whose engineering genius had saved New York City from a North Korean missile attack three years earlier — or because in so doing he handed South Korea's communist enemy to the north its most humiliating defeat to date. It had more to do with the fact that Joshua was connecting powerfully with the audience by articulating a timeless message that went beyond geopolitics or national security or even their most basic hopes about good or their fears about evil.

What Joshua was speaking about was God's master plan and the future of every member of the human race.

When the crowd quieted down, Joshua continued. "Long before I started my defense-contracting business, I had been in the United States Air Force. And I chose that life for a specific reason — because I wanted to protect my country. I was honored to achieve the rank of colonel and to fly some of the most exciting missions a pilot could ever hope for. When I retired from the service, I started my defense company so I could work with the Pentagon and continue that mission — once again to protect America. While it turned out that my anti-missile invention was the right answer to the greatest airborne risks that faced America — it proved to be popular with the wrong kind of people ... Some bad folks wanted their hands on my design, and the next thing I knew they had me in their clutches and I was taken by force to Iran. I was locked in a jail cell as a hostage, and as you know, they did some rough things to me there. But frankly, it made me appreciate the courage of other brave men who have endured much, much worse. On the other hand, there's nothing like being tortured, totally alone, in a totalitarian state, thousands of miles from home to make you feel utterly helpless. Yet all of that taught me something. Yes, I believe in a nation's right to defend itself. But in the final analysis, it is the living God who is our ultimate protection. We can trust in Him. In Psalm 125 we read this:

> *Those who trust in the LORD are like Mount Zion,*
> *which cannot be shaken but endures forever.*

As the mountains surround Jerusalem,
so the LORD surrounds his people
Both now and forevermore.

Joshua closed his Bible, which his wife, Abigail, had given to him two years before, the last time they had actually been together face-to-face. It was during their clandestine reunion on board a ship off the coast of New York, anchored on the very edge of American borders and the beginning point of international waters. Given the legal spider web that had ensnared the couple, and the outrageous and unfounded criminal charges lodged against Joshua, it was the only way they could meet. Now, on the platform of the church in South Korea, he reached out and touched the brown leather cover. Joshua longed to put his arms around the woman who had given it to him. For a moment he felt a tightening in his throat. But he steadied himself. He couldn't afford to think of that right now. So he looked over the sea of faces and moved to his final comment.

"When Israel was attacked two years ago by an advancing wave of Russian and Arab League armies of overwhelming strength, military leaders gave Israel little chance of victory. But the miraculous rescue of that nation was the fulfillment of a promise God had made thousands of years ago. You can read it for yourself in chapters 38 and 39 of the book of Ezekiel. So, what is the message? First, we see over and over in those verses from Ezekiel, God is telling us through His chosen prophet exactly why He could rescue Israel in such a stunning display. He says: 'So that the nations may know me . . .' to prove that He is truly the Lord.

"But there is something else, and we must not miss this . . . the message is that human history will shortly be wrapped up. All signs are pointing to that. The news of the day seems to be shouting it to us. The Son of God is on His way. Christ is coming — to establish His Kingdom, to reign and to rule. Jesus Christ, the King, is returning . . . get ready, ladies and gentlemen, boys and girls. The King is coming . . ."

As Joshua moved away from the podium the crowd leaped to its feet, clapping and cheering in a roar of praise and amens and hallelujahs. Then Pastor Lee, waving his hands to the sky, led the congregation in a hymn, followed by a closing prayer of benediction.

At the other end of the mammoth church, Ethan March, Joshua's tall, muscular young personal assistant, had been watching from a side entrance. Ethan's job, ever-changing it seemed, was to coordinate security that day and keep the media under control. There had been a request for a formal press conference, but at the last minute Ethan had nixed the idea, and Joshua reluctantly deferred to his assistant. But Ethan knew that some in the media would still try to grab a comment or two from Joshua as he exited the church. Ethan scanned the thousands of attendees who were starting to disperse. He eyed the two security guards stationed in each aisle, each with a wireless radio. One by one they delivered their messages to Ethan, and he bent his head slightly to the side and covered his other ear with his finger, so he could listen in his earpiece to their security check.

"All clear." "All clear."

Ethan felt himself unwind. The service was over. No incident. No threats to disarm. He knew Joshua was still the target of several hostile nation-states — some, like North Korea, partly out of a desire for payback against Joshua for engineering their missile failure and the destruction of one of their naval military vessels with all hands on deck. Other nations simply wanted to get inside Joshua's head and learn what he knew about his own RTS weapon design. Any one of them could have slipped their agents into a crowd like this. But now it looked like the risk to Joshua was over.

Being a part-time bodyguard, part-time scheduler, and full-time personal manager for Joshua Jordan was a job that Ethan, a former Air Force pilot like his boss, had never trained for. How could he? His job was just as improbable as the way that their lives had intersected. As Ethan watched the crowd slowly wind its way to the exits he thought about how, having once served under Joshua's command at an air base, they had been brought together again years later. This time through a chance meeting on a plane with Joshua's daughter, Deborah. Sure, there was some heartbreak, the way things ended between Ethan and Deborah. But it did bring Ethan face-to-face again with a man he had admired like few others. Joshua had his own take on that, saying that the two pilots had been brought together "by divine providence."

But that was what made them different too. Ethan just couldn't buy into Joshua's newfound faith. The "God thing" wasn't Ethan's thing. Not that it diminished Joshua in his eyes. After all, any guy who had been strung up from hooks by Iranian tormentors until his shoulders were dislocated, then beaten with rods and electrocuted — an experience like that could radically change anyone who survived. The way that Ethan saw it, religion was simply what got Joshua through the experience.

Ethan now strode up to the dais and shook hands with the pastor. Joshua was chatting with the pitching marvel, Jin Ho Kim, who had just presented him with the winning baseball from the game he had pitched that day.

Joshua spotted Ethan and flagged him over. He introduced him to the pitcher. Motioning to Ethan, Joshua couldn't help mentioning his background to Jin, "This is my assistant, Ethan March, who knows something about pitching, by the way. Before joining the Air Force, he tried his hand on the mound in a triple-A ball club in America."

"Oh, you pitcher?" Jin Ho Kim exclaimed with a bright smile. "Have a good fastball?"

Ethan blushed. "Yeah, well, Mr. Jin, I had a pretty good fastball. Except for one thing —"

Jin jumped in. "Problem with control?"

Ethan laughed loudly. "Exactly! Problem with control." Ethan was the only one who got the joke. His desire for control was the one thing that drove him onward more than anything else. But the reckless abandon that typified much of his life, the risk-taking, the broken rules at one Air Force base after another — didn't that seem to undermine his obsession in trying to control his own future? It was pretty funny that the one thing that dashed his dream for a big-league career was that very thing — a problem with control. On the other hand, maybe it wasn't so funny.

"I know one thing," Joshua said, pointing to Ethan, "he turned into an excellent pilot." Then with a smile Joshua added, "And I ought to know. He was one of my rookies at an airbase in Florida. He set a few flying records."

Ethan silently thanked his lucky stars that Joshua had too much class to mention his several trips to the brig for bar fights with a couple of Marines and his failure to get clearance before taking out a few new test planes.

Joshua looked at the baseball he had received from Jin Ho Kim and tossed it over to Ethan. "Let's see if you still know how to handle one of these."

Ethan caught the baseball with ease.

"Okay," Joshua said, "you'd better show me the way out."

"The side door," Ethan told him quietly. "Less likely to be ambushed by the press." The two men moved toward the exit.

In the rear of the sanctuary, still hanging back as the crowds trailed out, stood two men. One was an Australian newsman. The other was a stone-faced Han Suk Yong, with forged media credentials hanging from his neck. He stared at Joshua and Ethan as they passed through a side door into an adjacent hallway. The Australian reporter was watching him. "You're a newbie, right?"

Han gave him a funny look but kept eyeing the doorway.

"A rookie reporter, I mean."

Han nodded a little nervously. The Aussie grabbed Han's fake press credentials badge hanging around his neck and studied it. "*South Korean Weekly Journal*?"

Han nodded again.

"Never heard of it. Must be small."

Han said, "Very small. Just started."

"Well, you're not exactly competition for me, I guess, so I'll do you a favor. I've got a hunch where we can get up close, get in Joshua

Jordan's face for a quick Q&A. I've scouted out the church. I think I know which route he's taking. Follow me."

Han brightened. "Great idea." He slipped his hand into his coat pocket until he touched the smooth lignostone surface of his handgun. "I would like to get up close. You know ... get right in Joshua Jordan's face."

TWO

Joshua and Ethan walked down a corridor that led to the back parking lot of the church. Ethan walked a step ahead, checking corners and intersecting hallways as they went. He told his mentor, "The back exit's coming up."

From behind a voice called out. A security guard trotted up. "Colonel Jordan, let me escort you."

Ethan turned and cut in. "Not necessary, thanks. I got it covered."

The security guard stopped, still looking at Joshua, who had a cautious look on his face.

Ethan lowered his voice and flashed a grin. "Josh, really, I got this. I know we're in South Korea," he said with the mock cadence of a school teacher, "which is right below North Korea, and I know you've got some nasty history with the North Koreans. But I'm your security guy on this trip. I've checked the route. Let me earn my salary here, okay?"

Joshua studied his assistant for a moment. Then he nodded to the security guard. "Thanks so much for your help. We'll take it from here. God bless."

The security guard smiled, waved, turned, and headed out of sight.

As the two men continued down the hallway, Ethan thought of something. It had been on his mind for a while, but it was touchy. Now seemed like a good time.

"So, Josh, I was going to mention something. I've got this friend back in the States. He knew pretty much everything that had gone on, you know, how I'd been interested in your daughter, and about the fact that Debbie eventually gave me the heave-ho, telling me that she didn't think it would work out between us. Well, when I told him I'd been hired as your personal assistant, he thought I was crazy. He told me this kind of arrangement would never work. He said, 'How can you ever hope to impress your boss, when your boss knows his daughter told you to buzz off?' Which got me thinking ..."

"About what?"

"My working for you. You have to admit we have a pretty unusual working relationship."

Joshua stopped in the hallway and studied Ethan's face. Then he said, "Actually I think you're missing something."

"Oh, yeah?"

"After Debbie told you that it wouldn't work out between the two of you, I wondered why in the world you would still want to work for her dad."

"That's easy," Ethan responded. "Despite everything, you're still one of my heroes. I always wanted to work for the best. You're it."

"You're giving me a big head," Joshua said, giving Ethan a pat on the shoulder. "Let's get moving."

Ethan picked up the pace and trotted ahead. He came to an exit door, pushed down the bar handle, and swung it open. Ethan was now out in a private parking area that was blocked off from the public lot by a toll gate at the other end. He had the plastic pass key to swipe at the gate, and he craned his neck to survey the area, first looking to his left. The parking lot that was empty except for their rental car. Then he turned to the right but jumped a little to see two men standing against the church building, next to the open exit door.

Han Suk Yong was standing off to the side, a little behind the Australian.

"Sorry," Ethan barked, "this area's restricted. You both have to leave."

The Australian journalist lifted up his press badge, which was hanging around his neck. "Aw, now, that's not friendly. I'm a reporter. International press corps. I always thought you Americans believed in freedom of the press."

"In case you didn't notice," Ethan snapped back, "we're not in America. Maybe you ought to find an Outback somewhere and have them grill you some shrimp on the barbie — "

But a voice stopped him. "Ethan," Joshua said as he put his hand on his assistant's shoulder. "It's okay. I'll give them a few minutes. Then we'll be on our way."

"Thanks much, Mr. Jordan," the Aussie said. "You're a true gentleman." Then he snatched his tiny notepad from his pocket. "Just wondering, sir, whether you have any regrets — "

"About what?"

"About designing the Return-to-Sender anti-missile system, which ended up dropping two nuclear warheads onto a North Korean navy vessel and incinerating it, evaporating every sailor on board."

Joshua had heard that one before. Different approach, but with the same sharp point at the end of the stick. He said, "I don't regret the fact that my RTS stopped those nukes from detonating in New York City where they were heading at the time, no. And yes, I know that my RTS system — my missile-defense shield — took the trajectory of those nukes and reversed them, sending them back to the vessel that launched them. I'd always hoped that my RTS laser defense would be a deterrent to war. Saving lives. And protecting nonaggressors, my country in this case, from the hasty actions of despots who fire missiles first and think later."

From where Joshua stood, the Aussie was blocking Han Suk Yong from view. So Joshua could not see the eyes of the North Korean, which were so intense they looked like they had been lit on fire.

"And then," the Australian continued, "there is the matter of the criminal charges pending against you in the American court. Charges of treason. Your group, the so-called Roundtable, was blamed for botching a vigilante attempt to stop some unidentified individuals with a portable nuke. As the leader of that group, of course, you must take some responsibility. So how do you feel knowing that as a result, thousands died in New Jersey when the bomb went off?"

"There isn't a day that goes by that I don't think about that — the loss of life," Joshua replied. "But one clarification. In point of fact, the allegations technically refer to my supposed conspiracy to interfere with the operations of the United States government. False charges, I might add."

"If that's true, rather than avoiding extradition, which you've been doing, why not return to America and fight the case like the hero that some folks think you are?"

Ethan intervened. "Okay. Interview's over ..."

"No, Ethan, I want to answer," Joshua snapped back. Then he stared the reporter down and threw him a cocked eyebrow. "You see, sir, I've been given advice from Abigail Jordan to remain out of the jurisdiction of the U.S. until I can get a fair trial for those wrongful, politically motivated criminal charges brought against me by the current administration in Washington. Now, the thing about Abigail is this — she's not only my lawyer, she's also my wife. So right there," he said, breaking into a grin, "I've given you two good reasons I ought to listen to her. Now, if you'll excuse us, we have to be on our way."

The Australian scratched a few notes on his pad, nodded and then trotted off.

Han Suk Yong approached Joshua.

"Sorry, no more interviews," Ethan said.

"But Colonel Jordan," Han said, "I am great admirer."

"Thanks," Joshua said.

"I am with, uh ... a very small news office." Han lifted his phony press badge. "But I have something very, very personal. Need to ask you. Just take a minute. Please sir, could we just walk to quiet place. Here in parking lot?"

"It's okay," Joshua said to Ethan. "It'll just be a minute."

The two men walked across the parking lot to a point about thirty feet away and stopped.

Han's back was to Ethan, who was at the exit door, studying him and nervously rolling the baseball that he still had in his hand. Ethan glanced down at his watch and muttered to himself, "Come on, Josh, don't do this to me. Let's get out of here."

Han Suk Yong was struggling to keep a tight-lipped smile, as if his face had been fashioned out of metal. "You don't know me, do you?"

Joshua noticed that Han's right hand had now been slipped into his right coat pocket.

"No, I'm afraid I don't," Joshua replied.

"I am the man who will be the hero of my country."

"South Korea?" Joshua asked.

The metallic smile vanished from Han's face. "No, not this nation of dogs." Then he spit on the ground in disgust. "No, I speak of the Democratic People's Republic of Korea. North Korea, Mr. Jordan. The honorable nation whose ship you blasted into a ball of fire with your RTS device."

Joshua glanced down at the man's press badge. It read "Han Suk Yong." As he thought about the name, he flashed back to the Pentagon briefing after the unsuccessful missile attempt by North Korea. Though it was three years ago, he still remembered. How could he forget?

Afterward, he had been given the classified details of the ship that had launched the nukes at New York City. That vessel, *The Daedong*, and its entire crew were vaporized when the guidance systems of the missiles it launched were reversed by Joshua's RTS system and the nukes were looped back to the ship. Joshua recalled the name of the captain of that ill-fated vessel. *Han Suk.*

"You are related to the captain," Joshua began to ask, "who was — "

That is when Han pulled out his handgun and pointed it at Joshua's chest. "You will not speak the name of my father. You are not worthy to have my honorable, departed father's name on your filthy American lips."

From his position at the exit door, thirty feet away, Ethan could see the look on Joshua's face. Ethan could see he was in trouble. Ethan moved quickly to one side to get a better look. He saw something in Han's hand. Joshua tried to shake his head no, warning Ethan not to get closer, but Han caught that. He whispered to Joshua in a guttural voice, "Tell him not to come any closer."

"Stay there," Joshua shouted to Ethan who could now see something shaped like a clip-loaded revolver in Han's hand. His mind was whirling. He had to figure out a plan. In milliseconds. *If I rush this guy, he'll get off a shot, point-blank. Right into Josh.*

Thirty feet away, Han grunted to Joshua, "You're going to die like the coward you are." Han lifted his gun to the left quadrant of Joshua's chest, directly at Joshua's heart.

Ethan muttered a single, desperate hope.

Strike zone.

He gripped the seams of the baseball in his right hand, all one-hundred and eight red, double stitches. Ethan did a pitcher's wind-up, kicked his leg up, and let fly with a ninety-four-mile-per-hour fastball. Han's eyes darted to the side momentarily, as if he had noticed something. But it was too late. Ethan's fastball buried itself with burning speed into the assassin's left shoulder.

Han screamed out in pain, his body went limp, and he began to crumple to the pavement. Joshua grabbed the gun out of Han's hand and moved away from Han, who was now kneeling on the asphalt. In two seconds Ethan sprinted to the scene and jumped on the gunman, pinning him to the ground. He put him in a wrestler's full nelson. "Josh!" he yelled. "Get security and have them call the cops. I'll keep this guy quiet here."

Joshua glanced at the gun in his hand, then began to run back to the church building. As he did, he called back, "Nice pitching. You just earned your salary."

Ethan, still pinning Han down, shouted, "Actually, high and outside. And I was aiming for his right shoulder, not his left."

Joshua slowed down just slightly. "I'm the umpire here ... a solid strike!"

It took the officers from the Seoul Metro Police Agency only six minutes to arrive and take Han into custody. The SMPA investigators took statements from Joshua and Ethan and headed back to the station with the assailant. Back in the church, Joshua said his good-byes to the pastor and his staff, assuring them that he would be safe, and receiving their extended, heartfelt apologies for the attack.

"You must let us make this right," Pastor Lee Ko-po said, bowing with tears in his eyes.

Joshua grabbed the pastor by the shoulders and smiled. "By your kindness to me, you already have." Then Joshua climbed into the rental car with Ethan at the wheel.

When they were within three blocks of the hotel, Joshua checked the Allfone watch on his wrist. He then pointed to a side street that ran alongside a large park. "Ethan, turn off the boulevard right here."

"That's not the route we took from the hotel earlier today."

"I know. Just take it."

Ethan turned off the boulevard and down the quiet tree-lined street. A black limousine was parked along the curb.

"Pull behind the limo," Joshua said.

Ethan followed orders but shook his head as he did. "Josh, what's going on?"

Joshua gave only a cryptic reply. "Now for the second reason we came to South Korea."

Ethan wasn't going to wait for an explanation. "Whatever this is, why didn't you let me in? Why am I always on the outside?" But before he could continue, he noticed a military star on the license plate of the limo in front. He lowered his voice. "Okay. I'm starting to get the drift … sort of."

"You'll find out shortly," Joshua said and nodded toward the South Korean military attaché who had just climbed out of the limo and was coming their way.

Ethan kept talking, and there was anticipation in his voice. "Looks like things are beginning to get interesting."

"And dangerous," Joshua added.

"You mean an attempt to assassinate you doesn't qualify?" Ethan shot back.

Joshua smiled but didn't respond. At the side of the car, the South Korean officer saluted Joshua and then reached through the open passenger window to shake his hand. "Colonel Jordan, it is a great honor to meet you."

"Likewise, Lieutenant Colonel Quan." Then Joshua introduced Ethan to the officer.

"Well, gentlemen," Quan said with a placid expression that belied his next comment. "Are you ready to make history?"

THREE

Ethan glanced around the room, which was occupied by several special-ops professionals. The place was windowless with thick sound-deadening walls, located deep within the tactical operations sector of the South Korean Army headquarters. It was impervious to outside surveillance. The participants around the conference table included a Middle Eastern–looking couple with International Red Cross ID tags hanging from their necks. The man, known as Gavi, was affable and had an easy smile, shaved head, and a muscular neck and torso. His partner, Rivka, was a slender woman with dark, intense eyes, who wore a short-sleeved shirt that revealed tight biceps. Ethan figured out they were more than humanitarian-aid workers.

The head honcho, the implacable Brigadier General Liu, sat at the head of the table and welcomed the attendees, identifying them by name, and called the meeting to order. Next to him was Lieutenant Colonel Quan, who had met them at the car earlier, and to his right was Major Chung, who would lead the briefing. The only other person was a young Asian man in blue jeans named Yung Tao.

Chung began with an intriguing question. "How many people, outside this bunker, even remember Captain Jimmy Louder of the United States Air Force?"

In an instant, the pieces fell into place for Ethan. As a former pilot, he knew the story well. Three years earlier, Louder had been flying a Navy Prowler along the DMZ between South and North Korea. Louder's jet was shot down in a skirmish with a sortie from the North. It rapidly escalated into a military crisis with the United States. No one could have foreseen the cyclone of geopolitical events that followed. A misinterpreted message was bulleted from Pyongyang to a North Korean nuke-armed ship on maneuvers in the Atlantic. That scrambled digital telex to the nuclear destroyer caused it to launch a retaliatory strike against America. The two nukes launched from that ship were aimed at New York City but were diverted when the Pentagon chain-of-command ordered the use of Joshua's brilliantly designed RTS anti-missile system. The warheads turned back like twin boomerangs and returned to the North Korean ship that had launched them, liquidating the ship and its captain, the father of the gun-toting Han Suk Yong.

Ethan had always wondered why President Tulrude had never publicly addressed the outrage of North Korea's keeping Captain Louder hostage — she had seemingly forgotten about his plight — but clearly the South Koreans hadn't. Nor had Joshua. Ethan had even heard rumors from his flier buddies that the Department of Defense was, under the radar of course, supporting some kind of effort to get Louder out. It now looked like it was coming together.

Chung continued, "Those of us in the South Korean military remember Captain Louder, who provided courageous service by monitoring the border with our enemies to the north. We do not forget his bravery. And neither do you, Colonel Jordan. Thank you for playing your part."

Joshua nodded and said, "Captain Louder's a good man. I'm glad we're going to get him a 'furlough' from that North Korean prison."

A glimmer of a smile broke over the face of Brigadier General Liu.

Ethan's heart rate jumped. *Whatever this is, I want in*, he thought.

"We have a double agent inside the North Korean prison," Chung continued, "and he has processed the request by the International Red Cross to inspect the conditions of Captain Louder's confinement. And at the same time our source in the prison slipped a message to Louder, suggesting that he ask for a personal visit from Colonel Jordan. It was thought that the North Koreans would jump at the chance to get Joshua Jordan, their public enemy number one, within their reach and would do anything to accomplish that, including allowing the

International Red Cross to gain access to their prison. And of course, we were right. But our intelligence also indicates that they won't arrest Colonel Jordan until he has made face-to-face contact with Captain Louder. The North Koreans plan to have guards posted in the meeting room at first, but then a short time later they will be called out of the room. The North Koreans have bugged the room and are hoping that Colonel Jordan or Captain Louder might get sloppy when they think they're alone and reveal some useful information before Jordan is taken into custody. But our plan should short-circuit all of that. Literally. It will happen quickly, within just a few minutes of Colonel Jordan and our 'Red Cross' workers entering the room."

Everything was clear to Ethan now. The mission needed an entry to the communist north and then into the prison where Louder was being held — and Joshua was their ticket in. It didn't take much imagination for Ethan to guess what the North Koreans had planned for Joshua once they had him within their borders. He began to raise his finger to ask a couple of pointed questions about Joshua's safety, but Joshua gave him a disapproving shake of the head. Ethan didn't like it, but he knew how to take orders — mostly. And Joshua was the boss. So Ethan complied and put his hand back down as Chung explained the plan.

"Gavi and Rivka will play the part of International Red Cross workers and will escort Colonel Jordan to the security facility where they are holding Captain Louder. There, the prisoner meeting will take place. Afterward, the three of them — Gavi, Rivka, and Colonel Jordan — will exit the building."

Ethan wasn't going to stay quiet. He didn't know why Joshua had volunteered for this mission, though knowing his boss the way he did, he wasn't surprised. Ethan whispered his concerns to Joshua. "You're a hated guy up in the north. Case in point — they tried to kill you today at the church. Once you're inside North Korea, they'll never let you go."

Joshua quietly replied, "They won't need to." Then he motioned for Ethan to pay attention to the rest of the briefing. Chung described the operation. He finished by saying, "If the operation is successful, then

Captain Louder will be walking out with our two friends posing as Red Cross workers and Colonel Jordan."

Gavi had a question. "What about the timing of the shut-down of the security grid?"

"Satellite telemetry will direct the overcharging of the system. The timing will be accurate within a tenth of a second — occurring when you are five minutes into the meeting with Captain Louder. We should be able to override their software and shut down their security codes, their door lock-downs, and their information systems, and then insert our own command codes."

"And the backup software?" Rivka asked.

"That's where Yung Tao comes in," Major Chung said and nodded to the young man in blue jeans, who picked up the explanation from there.

"The North Koreans have a secondary software backup, of course, which is engaged instantly when there is a power loss. We will input our data and codes, which I can manipulate at will. I know all their algorithms and the codes for changing the data in that backup program." Yung Tao flashed a grin. "My software company in North Korea installed their systems." Then he added, "Obviously, by this time tomorrow, my company's small staff will have relocated to new offices outside North Korea."

When the briefing was over, Ethan and Joshua were the only ones who remained in the room. Ethan cornered his boss. "I'm not questioning your judgment, but why didn't you bring me into the loop earlier?"

"I wasn't sure this was a definite go until we arrived in Seoul."

"And those two Red Cross workers — are they for real?"

"If you mean, are they really members of the International Red Cross ... the answer is yes. If you mean, does the Red Cross know that Gavi and Rivka are also highly trained agents of an intelligence agency, the answer is no. This time the North is letting them inside — but only because I'm accompanying them."

"Who else do Gavi and Rivka work for?" Ethan asked. Then he answered his own question. "I'm betting the Israeli Mossad." *Yes*, Ethan thought, *that fits.* Israel's commandos handled most of the difficult foreign intelligence and national security work in protecting Israel. Then he wondered out loud to Joshua, "And my role?"

Joshua patted him on the shoulder. "To stay here in Seoul. You need to monitor this from headquarters."

"You just pulled the rug out from under me," Ethan complained. "Come on, I was Air Force too, Josh. Trained in combat. Survival skills. The whole nine yards. I've got a top-secret security clearance with the United States government. I can be useful somehow ..."

"You will be," Joshua said. "Back here in Seoul. This is my deal, my risk. For a long time I've felt a personal connection to Jimmy Louder. He and I were swept into the same tidal wave together — at opposite ends maybe — Louder being shot down over North Korea, the event that sparked the launching of those North Korean nukes in the first place — and my being back in New York as a defense contractor, working with the Pentagon to stop those missiles. As a pilot I came close to crashing behind enemy lines myself. I would have liked to know there were guys out there willing to come after me. Anyway, I made up my mind if I ever got the chance to help Louder, I would do it. Then, several months after he was shot down, I happened to be at an Air Force reception in Washington, and Louder's wife was there. I told her the same thing — to her face, Ethan. I never really thought I'd have the chance to make good on that promise. So there it is."

Then Ethan caught a look on Joshua's face — but not one that expressed bravery or loyalty or even the keeping of a sacred promise. It had to do with something else. After a moment Joshua explained. "And then there's Abigail. She doesn't know about this, and obviously neither do Cal or Deb. To my knowledge no one back in the U.S. is aware of the plan, except for a few people in the Pentagon. If things go down bad, you have to be the one — "

"The one?"

"To explain it to Abby. You're the only one who could. She's the love of my life. I've always felt she got the short end of the stick when she married me. The least I can do is to make sure she's told the truth. And considering my history with the current president, you can bet that Jessica Tulrude and those in her administration wouldn't care if Abigail ever found out. After all, this whole mission is off the Pentagon's official ledger. The Defense Department's support is strictly backdoor. It's a matter of principle with the Pentagon that we get one of their fliers out of a North Korean prison camp."

"Let me make sure I understand," Ethan said bitterly. "I'm staying here in case I have to be one of those messengers that no wife wants to meet ... knocking on her front door one day. So I can tell her how you died ... and why? That's why I'm staying behind?"

"Not a happy thought. But yes, that's the tough duty you have. And I wouldn't trust it to anyone else." Joshua broke into a grin that reflected an air of confidence, but still with a weighty look in his eyes. "On the other hand, I'm trusting God in this, Ethan. Let's leave the outcome to Him."

There it was again — the familiar angle that Ethan couldn't argue with. Ethan had chosen a different path from his mentor when it came to religion, and he was okay with that. Still, Ethan had to admit to himself privately that he was curious about the change in Joshua. When Ethan fell quickly for Deborah, Joshua's daughter — too quickly, as it turned out — he soon learned that the "God-stuff" was huge in her life as well. And the same with her mother and her brother. Of the whole family, Joshua had been the last holdout — until the hostage situation in Iran nearly cost him his life. Since then he seemed preoccupied with idea of the second coming of Christ, even more, it seemed, than with his anti-missile defense system.

As Ethan broke out of his thoughts, he eyed Joshua and noticed that his boss had tapped his wrist Allfone and pulled up a small image of Abigail on the screen. After gazing at it, he waved his finger over the screen and the image disappeared.

Ethan was struck by two thoughts, both of which hit him like a punch to the chest. He knew, once again, how Joshua was willfully exposing himself to high-stakes danger for the sake of another person. But there was something else. When Ethan saw Joshua looking at the image of his wife, that impressed him even more — how much Joshua was about to lose, what he would be leaving behind — if the mission failed.

FOUR

Manhattan

Abigail Jordan strolled into the den of the high-rise penthouse. Several of her bar-association certificates hung on the wall, including her admission to practice before the Supreme Court and her black-framed law degree. She walked up to Cal, her twenty-year-old son, seated at the desk with his laptop, and she looked over his shoulder. He was tapping furiously on the keyboard. Then he stopped. And waited.

Abigail knew Cal had been trying to contact Joshua.

"Okay," Cal said with his fingers still on the keyboard. "It'll take a couple more minutes to finish the encryption to get an email contact with Dad."

Using the complicated security-enabled email procedure to communicate with Joshua while he was exiled overseas had become a regular routine for the Jordan household. Ever since Joshua had found himself facing trumped-up charges brought by the Department of Justice, Abigail had been counseling her husband to take advantage of the asylum that had been provided to him by Israel — at least until Abigail could prove his innocence and guarantee him a fair trial. But given the energy put into the case by the administration of President Tulrude, and the political corruption that Abigail believed was at the bottom of it all, she knew that would be a Herculean task.

The charges accused Joshua of treason, painting him as a domestic terrorist who had used his own defense-contracting firm and the

34

Roundtable group to infiltrate the Department of Defense and manipulate America's national-security apparatus so it would conform to his own political agenda. Abigail considered the allegations an absurd insult. Her husband was a decorated hero — yet the Tulrude administration and its attorney general had concocted a wild theory that through Josh's leadership of the Roundtable, he was attempting to create his own "shadow government," using his influence and connections to subvert American domestic and foreign policy. There was no greater patriot than her husband. Painting him as a revolutionary willing to use violence to oppose the White House policies was an atrocity. It was the lowest kind of "dirty tricks" that the Tulrude administration and Attorney General Cory Hamburg could have used. Abigail believed that the criminal case against Joshua was the only way to shut him up, to stop his work in exposing the dangerous direction that President Tulrude had taken the country.

For the last two years, the case had been hanging in limbo in the U.S. District Court for the District of Columbia while Joshua remained in Israel, beyond the court's jurisdiction. Meanwhile, Abigail and her husband's lawyers reviewed the evidence that the Department of Justice had been ordered to disclose during discovery. It all boiled down to one witness: the government's case hinged on the testimony of a lawyer by the name of Allen Fulsin. The attorney had told the federal authorities that he had been interviewed by a member of the Roundtable, Fort Rice, a retired judge, about joining the Roundtable. That much was true, as far as it went.

But it didn't end there. Fulsin, who was later rejected for entrance to the group, went on to tell the DOJ that according to Rice, Joshua had repeatedly declared his Roundtable group existed for the purpose of "revolution." That also was true, though only technically. Fulsin had cleverly parsed Joshua's actual words, which in the full context were much different: Joshua had stated to the members of the Roundtable that they were in the "business of revolution — a moral and political revolution in America — from the top down, starting with the federal government and the White House." Clearly, Joshua had been talking about lawful means to turn around the wretched direction that Washington had taken over the years.

But Fulsin's other statements to the feds were pure fantasy. He recited a raft of supposed quotes from Joshua, calling for an armed militia to take down the government, allegedly declaring that the Pentagon and the national security apparatus needed to be "interdicted." When Abigail read Fulsin's bogus story the first time, she screamed — right in the middle of the conference room at the Department of Justice — "This is a pack of lies straight from the pit of hell!"

But Fulsin's story, and the DOJ's willingness to use it, wasn't the only problem. While Josh's attorneys were convinced of Joshua's innocence, they had repeatedly voiced doubts about their chances of proving it at trial. Sensing a near-certain verdict of guilt based on Fulsin's sworn statements, they had badgered Abigail to pressure her husband into accepting a plea bargain, pleading guilty to a lesser charge in return for a recommended sentence of two years in prison. In response, Abigail fired them all and took over her husband's case herself. It was time to brush the cobwebs off her former career as a trial lawyer. Still, she knew she was on thin ice. She herself would almost certainly be called as a witness if the case ever came to trial, and ethics rules made it difficult, if not impossible, for her to wear both hats at once.

But then, she never planned to allow Joshua's case to get to trial anyway. The optimal strategy was to expose Fulsin's lies and get the case dismissed. Until she could do that, she pleaded with Joshua to stay in Israel, his temporary home, where the government had given him asylum and refused the U.S. government's extradition requests. It tortured her to be separated from him. Her lawyer's brain told her that if Joshua were to rush into a courtroom now, it would be disastrous — the machinery of the entire government would be mounted against him, and he would end up spending the rest of his life in prison for a crime that didn't exist.

Because of the legal restrictions placed on her by a court order naming her as a "material witness" in her husband's case, and prohibiting her from leaving the United States, she and Joshua had to live at opposite ends of the world. Their lengthy separation, limited to chatting by videofone or email, was killing her. She was tired of it, right down to her soul. And so was Josh. He would always say that he missed her like crazy and kept threatening to ignore her professional advice and return to America and, in his words, just fly right into the flak. But she would talk sense to him and urge him to give her a little more time to figure things out.

This had been the hardest separation Abigail had ever had from Joshua. They had endured separation before. Many times. But there was always the promise of an ending point. Missions had beginnings and endings. Assignments would last for a finite amount of time. But not this one. She ached for him and prayed endlessly for their reunion. In the end, however, she was convinced that with God's help the only solution to their dilemma rested in her own hands. She had to find a way to crack open the phony case against her husband.

Suddenly she noticed Cal looking up from the computer screen.

"Okay," he said, "earlier I sent a message to Dad and asked him to update us. Now something just came through from him. But it looks like he embargoed it — sent it earlier but timed it for release now for some reason. I'm going through the ChangeCipherSpec sequence for encryption."

Cal held the palm of his hand close to the screen for five seconds.

Then the screen read — "Palmprint Authentication Complete."

Abigail grinned. "I can't wait to hear about his trip to South Korea. He must be back in Israel by now."

A few moments later Cal announced, "Here it comes."

Cal read it aloud: "'I will call you on the encrypted Allfone whenever I can. But currently caught up in paperwork. Love you all more than I can say. Buried in red tape. Be strong, Abby, and know I love you more than life itself. Love to you, Cal, and Debbie too. God is in control. Josh.'"

Abigail stood up straight, a stunned look on her face.

"Mom, what's up?"

"That business about 'buried in red tape' ..."

"What about it?"

"That's code."

"For what?"

"It's our private message. His way of letting me know he's on a dangerous assignment — again. He started using the phrase years ago, when he flew those missions."

"You sure?"

His mother threw him a look that left no doubt. She shook her head. "He hadn't hinted at anything to me. Just going to Seoul to speak at a church, then to return to Israel. His temporary home — the man without a country." Then she asked into the air, "So, what in the world is Josh involved in?"

"You know Dad," Cal said. "He takes risks, sure. But not foolish ones. I'm sure there's a good explanation."

Then a stern look swept over Cal's face, as if he were going to do a tricky U-turn in the conversation. "You know, Mom, I deliberately avoided talking about the deadline today ..."

Abigail's face tightened. She knew where he was going. "Cal, you know I've made my decision. I have to follow the leading of the Lord in this. Not that it's wrong for you and Deb. You had to make the decision yourselves. But for me ... I feel compelled to protest, knowing in my heart and from the prophecies in the Word of God where this BIDTag process is ultimately going to lead. I know what it says in Revelation ... how it all comes together in the end. And so do you, Cal. Total control. A mark that enables you to buy and sell, to function financially. No, I can't believe the BIDTag is the mark of the Antichrist ... but it's the first step, okay? Everything in my spirit tells me to fight this thing, to take a stand."

"You're going to catch heat by not getting tagged."

"Those are my reasons."

"So why did you let Deborah and me get them? Why didn't you tell us you were going to hold out?"

"Because Deborah would lose her job at the Pentagon ..."

"You mean that great assignment where all she does is file papers and sit on her hands? Every time I talk to her she complains."

"She ought to be glad she's there at all. You and your sister happen to be connected to one of the most controversial families in America. Sorry, but that's a fact. I'm shocked that some of our enemies on Capitol Hill didn't block her Pentagon assignment. As far as you're concerned, Cal, you needed to get tagged to get accepted to law school. A law degree is going to come in handy. You've told us you want to continue the work your Dad and I have started, right?"

"But they'll target you, Mom. You're already in their sights. With that material-witness order keeping you from leaving the United States while Dad's case is pending. And now if you refuse to comply with the BIDTag law, the government will come down on you like a ton of bricks."

Abigail had resolve in her eyes, but her voice was soft, confident, settled. "These are extraordinary days. We're called to take extraordinary risks."

Cal narrowed his eyes as he studied the back of his right hand, the site of the invisible laser "tag" that he had received like most Americans. "Well, anyway, I've been reading some stuff. There are some theories out there about possibly reversing the laser tag imprint by erasing the QR code imprinted in the tissues. Or possibly other ways to avoid complying with this tagging law."

Abigail turned to look out the big windows with a wistful expression, taking in the New York skyline. She and Joshua had felt that events in the United States and around the world were racing like a bullet train toward God's prophetic closure. How she and Joshua were going to face all of that as it unfolded — and the example they would set for their children — that was the challenge now.

"You know, Mom," Cal added, still not letting it go, "they will come after you. The White House. The president and her buddies. They won't rest. Just like they went after Dad when he stood up to them and exposed the rotten stuff that has been going on in this administration. They'll hunt you down, Mom. You know they will."

She smiled, but in her face was a faint shadow of fatigue, the signs of an embattled life. As usual, Abigail mustered an optimistic response. "I'm a good runner, remember?"

Iowa City, Iowa

A long line of people wrapped around the government office building and wound down the street. Some were nervous, bouncing on their toes. Others looked around aimlessly, wrinkled their brows, or fidgeted.

A farmer and his wife stood with forty people still ahead of them in the line that stretched up to the glass door with black lettering on the glass: SECURITY AND IDENTIFICATION AGENCY — SIA.

In line immediately in front of them was a man in a suit with shoulder-length hair, who carried a briefcase. Behind them a truck driver was getting impatient.

The trucker patted his pockets for his cell phone, then realized that he had left it in his rig. "Who's got the time?" he called out.

"Almost noon," the farmer's wife replied.

"Oh, great," he groaned, "I've got a load to drop off in Traverse City, Michigan. No way I'm going to make it. This is crazy. Why am I here? Can somebody tell me that?"

"I'll tell you why," the guy in the suit said, whipping around. "Five years in jail and a maximum fine of $50,000 if you don't, that's why."

"You a lawyer?"

"Yeah. And don't blame me. I supported the legal groups that have been fighting this."

"Why didn't the courts stop it?"

"We tried. A few cases were won at the trial level, but even more lost. Then every single legal challenge got shot down on appeal. Very scary."

The farmer wasn't convinced. "I heard they caught some child molester at a theme park yesterday using this tagging program."

His wife chimed in, "Because he had the tag marking on his hand, that's how they got him ... with this laser tattoo ..."

"Fine," the lawyer said, "so this one guy has a BIDTag — his Biological Identification Tag — and the police pick him up. So what? Meanwhile the rest of us law-abiding citizens have the last vestiges of our right to privacy completely stripped away."

"But it doesn't hurt, they say. You can't even see it on your skin," the farmer's wife added.

"Which is beside the point," the lawyer countered. "It's the idea that creeps me out. Inside that glass door, you're going to have to stick your hand into a machine. Right? They put that invisible imprint on you. Bang, right there, keyed into that little digital imprint are all your medical records, court records, tax returns, every public record that ever had your name on it. And all that stuff, every bit of it is accessible because of that laser configuration ..."

"Yeah, I wondered how that works," the truck driver said.

"Look," the lawyer said, "you know those little UPC boxes with those lines inside that look like a maze — you've seen them in the corner of ads? They're called Quick Response, or QR, codes. For years we've been using them. Brilliant actually. Just scan the code box with your Allfone, and bingo, your cell is connected to some part of the Internet where the product is listed. You push a button, and just like that you've ordered something off the web, and in two days it shows up at your front door."

"I just ordered a part for my air brakes using that," the trucker said.

The lawyer bobbed his head. "There you go. Only one problem. The invisible QR code has all your personal data in it. Every time you enter a park, a shopping center, a post office, an airport, a restaurant, the federal scanning screens will be able to pick you up. So some civil-service creep in a government office somewhere can not only check out where you are at that very moment, he'll also know everything about you. With one stroke on a keypad. And they update your data constantly. Anytime you get a traffic ticket, go to court over something, or have a medical procedure, they update your QR code automatically. So now they've got your entire personal data file — everything — instantly accessible on the back of your hand, and at the same time they know where you are at any time. Time was that the government would need a warrant before they could get most of that information — but not anymore."

"All I know," the farmer said, "is that before we started this tag program, we had terrorist attacks all over this country. But not a single one since. I remember telling Mary here when the first one hit — when that ferry full of people got blown up — I said, look out, here it comes. Sure enough, after that we had the bombing at the Mall of America ..."

His wife added, "My sister-in-law knew someone on the plane that got shot down leaving O'Hare. I kept asking myself, how do these people get their hands on those little missile things ..."

"Shoulder-mounted missiles," the lawyer added.

The trucker leaned in closer. "I got a better one than that. So, those scumbag terrorists set off that portable nuke in New Jersey, and that was on a Tuesday. Well, I was scheduled to pick up a load. Guess where? About twenty miles from that exact spot, the very next morning. Can you believe that?"

"Well, actually," the lawyer said, "you're right, the nuke was set off by terrorists. And I know they were supposedly on their way to New York City, and that was their real target. But I think that the feds would have stopped them if that defense contractor, that Jordan guy and his right-wing Roundtable group of billionaire hyper-patriots, hadn't tried to use their private army to stop them."

The truck driver had a comeback. "Well, I thought that the feds, the FBI, and Homeland Security had messed up on that deal and weren't doing anything to stop it ... or that the White House blocked them or something ... so at the last minute that Jordan guy and his Roundtable had a bunch of former special-ops men try to stop them, and then the terrorists ended up pulling the trigger right then. I mean ... I don't want to sound like a jerk, but a few thousand dead in New Jersey's a lot better than a million dead in New York!"

The lawyer shook his head violently. "No way, no. We can't have a bunch of private Rambos trying to stop nukes, can we? They should've stayed out of it altogether. I'm glad they're prosecuting him. I hope he rots in jail."

"It's a crazy world," the farmer's wife said. "My brother keeps saying this is the beginning of the end — "

Her husband elbowed her and whispered, "Let's leave Bobbie out of this; the guy's got problems ..."

His wife shrugged but kept on talking. "I'm just saying that with what happened over in Israel, the way that war ended there, with earthquakes and volcanic eruptions — anyhow, Bobbie said that's what finally convinced him. Ever since then he's been going to church regular, talking about Jesus and the Bible all the time. And if you knew my brother before, my gosh, you'd never believe it was the same guy."

"Hey, look," the truck driver said pointing. "Finally. The line's moving."

The Security and Identification Agency, Washington, D.C.

Jeremy, the data clerk, stared at the list of names on his computer screen. As his supervisor, Mr. Porter, walked by, Jeremy flagged him over. "Mr. Porter, I have a question."

Porter carried his cup of coffee over to his clerk's desk. "What's the problem?"

"No problem. It's just I'm not sure of the directive."

"Which one?"

"The ETD — Enhanced Tracking Directive."

"You know the drill."

"Yeah, I understand the ETD. I've already synced everything onto the BIDTag tracking matrix, with the list of names with outstanding arrest warrants, the terror watch list, the dangerous deportees list, all criminal defendants … I've got all that already loaded into the system."

"Then what's the issue?"

"This list, sir." He pointed to the screen. "Just got this today. It looks like the names of people who have failed to submit to the BID-Tag program, the ones who haven't been tagged. I assumed, based on your memo, they needed to be in-putted too."

"Right. The nontaggers. You need to put them into the same ETD system."

"Okay, I've been doing that. For some time. I'm up to the Js now. But two questions. First, if they haven't been tagged, how are we going to track them under the ETD system?"

"You forgot," Porter said, pointing to the computer screen, "to do this." He touched a small icon that read — FRS. When he did, a small box on the screen lit up with the words *FACIAL RECOGNITION SYSTEM*.

"You have to make sure you also load the nontaggers into the FRS program. So we can pick them up using facial-recognition coordinates off their drivers licenses rather than the BIDTag, which, of course, they won't have. Then we can pick them up through the video scanners and follow them wherever they are, just like the others on the list."

"Gotcha," the clerk said with a nod. "Second question. This is a list of people who never got their BIDTag. But today's the deadline. Some of them may have waited until the last minute to get their laser tag."

"No problem," Porter said. "We can simply purge their names from the list if they end up getting tagged today."

The supervisor gave a nod, indicating the end of the discussion, and he toted his coffee back to his office. The clerk returned to the list of names. He touched the screen to feed the next nontagger's name on the list into the tracking system.

The screen read: "JORDAN, ABIGAIL."

FIVE

The prisoner, Captain Jimmy Louder, was in his green jumpsuit, his face gaunt and eyes sunken. He was thinner now than in the pictures Joshua had seen in Seoul.

In the North Korean facility in Pyongyang, Louder was sitting at a metal table in a stark white conference room. Two military guards in drab olive uniforms and square caps were a few feet behind him, standing at attention, ramrod straight. Each held an automatic weapon.

Across the table, Gavi and Rivka, with their Red Cross ID badges hanging from their necks, sat on either side of Joshua. Gavi had a clipboard and was reading from it — a banal series of questions, inconsequential but perfunctory sounding. He asked about Louder's physical condition, sleeping habits, medical attention ...

Joshua stole a glance at his Allfone watch. They had been there three minutes. Two to go. Then it would begin. He felt the sweat trickling down his back, and his heart pounded. For an instant he wondered if the thumping in his chest was loud enough for the guards to hear. An impossibility, he knew, but he felt vulnerable. He was feeling his age. He could no longer run ten miles without getting winded or breeze through survival exercises. The years were catching up with him. He was not the special-ops pilot he used to be, but just a civilian defense contractor, currently barred from returning to his own country. And now he was in North Korea, trying to help a fellow pilot. As Joshua sat in the metal chair he wished he could encourage Louder somehow about the rescue that was about to take place, but he knew he couldn't. He had one simple hope, and he put it into a silent prayer. *God, I don't want to let this poor guy down. Help me.* And he added another unspoken request. *And let me see Abigail again.*

"Your eating habits," Gavi said to Louder without a flicker of tension, with an almost bored expression. "Are you eating regularly?"

Louder nodded. His eyes showed that he might be expecting something, but what, Joshua couldn't decipher. Did he know about the mission?

"Yes," Louder replied, "I'm eating."

Joshua had one job now, as he sat across from Louder. He simply had to keep his cool. That was it. But it was crucial. The plan to use these two Israeli Mossad agents, posing as Red Cross workers, to launch a rescue had been in the works for over a year. In the White House, President Tulrude had balked, undoubtedly because of her stated goal of melding the United States with the growing international movement toward a single global government. Then there was the pressure from Tulrude's close confidant — the secretary-general of the United Nations, Alexander Coliquin. He had urged the president against taking any unilateral action, even against tyrannical nations like North Korea, and presumably including even the rescue of a downed American pilot, for fear of another retaliatory nuclear strike. That concern had struck Joshua as far-fetched as long as the United States still had Joshua's RTS anti-missile-system technology. On the other hand, Joshua also knew how the Pentagon had decided to rescue one of its own, quietly, under the radar, encouraging and assisting the mission to get Louder out.

The only problem had been the North Koreans' repeated refusal to allow Red Cross inspections, until, that is, an idea was hatched: they would use Joshua as bait. When the idea was slipped to Louder through the inside double-agent, encouraging him to make a request for a visit by Joshua, and when he then voiced that demand to his captors, the North Korean military command reversed their decision. They said that the Red Cross could come — but only on the condition that Joshua Jordan joined them.

Ethan was right, of course, about one thing. And Joshua knew it.

By the end of the briefing, Major Chung made it clear that the North Koreans would have no intention of releasing Joshua once they had him. His knowledge of his own RTS system, and the revenge the North wanted for the nuking of its ship, were reasons enough. There was only one chance for a happy ending — not just for Louder's rescue — but also for Joshua to escape arrest by the North Koreans who wanted to subject him to a quick show-trial followed by torture and a painful execution: the mission would have to be executed flawlessly.

"And your diet, Captain Louder," Gavi continued, "the Red Cross would like to know about your meals. What kind of food have you been eating?"

Louder paused for a second.

One of the armed guards shifted slightly in place, narrowing his eyes and then staring directly at Joshua.

Joshua stared back. When he did, he gave a half-smile to the North Korean guard.

"Your diet, Captain?" Gavi asked nonchalantly.

But there would be no answer. In an instant the room was plunged into darkness. An alarm sounded, and a red light began flashing in the hallway, which cast a sliver of red light under the door.

At first, Joshua could only hear the attack, grunting and muffled groans, but then in the dim, red flashing light coming from under the door, he could see, in broken frames of light, like an old-fashioned movie, Gavi's arm striking out like the arm of a pitching machine. He was sending a series of blows to the throat of one of the guards. Rivka kicked the other guard in the groin, and then a high-wheeling kick to his face. His machine gun clattered to the ground as he collapsed.

Joshua tapped the "illumin" feature on his Allfone. A thin beam of light shot out like a miniature high-beam flashlight. He trained the light on the two disabled guards. They were out. Gavi and Rivka dragged the bodies behind the desk.

In the room lit only by his Allfone, Joshua made his way around the table to Louder, who had a startled look on his face, but he was already on his feet, instinctively ready for whatever was next. Grabbing Louder by the arm, Joshua said, "We're here to bring you home, son."

Louder gave a garbled gasp. He was fighting back tears. Then, just as suddenly as the lights had gone out, they blinked once and came back on. Everyone squinted in the stark illumination. Then a knock on the door. Gavi calmly went over to the door and opened it.

A tough-looking North Korean guard with sergeant's stripes stood in the doorway with an electronic com-pad in his hand. This next step was critical. Joshua knew that. He found himself holding his breath. It had to work perfectly. No room for error.

This sergeant, who was the inside source for this prison mission, spoke in fairly good English. "The guards?"

"Behind the desk," Gavi replied.

"Then follow me," the sergeant said. "And stay close."

SIX

The sergeant strode down the hallway with Louder in handcuffs, followed by Gavi and Rivka. Joshua, a step behind, brought up the rear. He was already wondering whether Louder, in his yellow prison garb, could get past the sentries who would be posted at each door. He knew the plan — from his distant location, Yung Tao, the IT genius, would hack into the prison's computer system and insert a new directive ordering the transfer of Captain Louder, under the custody of the sergeant, and to another facility for questioning. Once out of the prison, a local agent, posing as a police officer, would pick them up and take them to a rendezvous point by the river.

As the group walked, a few North Korean officers passed them in the hall. The sergeant held his electronic clipboard in his hand. He tapped it, swooped his hand over the screen, then touched the corner. "Got to check the daily orders for this facility." But as he did, his head bobbed down just a fraction to read what it said, and when he did, his jaw clenched. He slowed his pace and turned to look at the foursome behind him. Joshua could see the tight lips and the stress on his face. Something was wrong.

The hallway was momentarily clear. The sergeant touched his right ear where the tiny combination earbud/AllFone was located; then he tapped the External Line icon on the screen in his hand. He began to speak softly in Korean. "This is the sergeant."

Yung Tao, located somewhere in the North Korean capital, responded.

The sergeant got right to the point. "Got a problem."

The group could see the sergeant listening through his earbud to Yung, but the sergeant wasn't satisfied with the response. He shot back a hoarse whisper to his colleagues as they walked. "The MIS — master information system — hasn't been updated with our implanted information — doesn't say anything yet about allowing Captain Louder to be transferred out of the building ..."

The sergeant was at the point where the hall intersected with another corridor. Before turning right, he stopped. Louder followed his lead. Gavi, Rivka, and Joshua caught up to them from behind. The sergeant muttered something in Korean. To Joshua, it didn't sound pleasant.

The sergeant waited another few seconds, checked his digital clipboard again, but shook his head in disgust. Then, in English he addressed his group. "We can't wait any longer." Then another message in his earbud. The sergeant bent his head to listen, then said, "Yung Tao says he is rebooting, refreshing the system, says the new orders should appear on all the digital clipboards in a few minutes." Then he added. "He'd better be right — or we're all dead."

The sergeant motioned for the group to follow as he turned the corner into the intersecting hall. Now they could see a security desk with armed guards a hundred feet away. As he walked, the sergeant glanced down at his e-clipboard and gave a half shake of his head with a grimace. His jaw was still clenched. As he walked, the sergeant dropped his left hand to his side, close to his side-arm. Yung Tao's hacking job might not happen in time.

Four guards stood at the table ahead. Two of them, standing behind the desk, had patrol rifles, which to Joshua looked like the Chinese version of the AK-15. Though they were slower firing than a full automatic, they could still fire a full thirty-shot magazine with blazing speed. More than enough to take down their whole group.

The other two guards had clip-loaded pistols. One of the guards was already standing, while the other, even more mean-looking, remained seated at the desk in front of a laptop. Soon he too started to rise.

The sergeant slowed as he approached the security desk, still glancing down at his digital clipboard, still frowning.

Joshua had a single thought. *Oh man, this is getting close.*

The guard who had just stood up shouted something in Korean and gave a quick wave for them to hurry up.

As the sergeant stood at the table, he and the guard in charge began to talk. Another guard threw him a questioning look and a scowl. Then he motioned for the sergeant's digital clipboard. Then he snatched it up and stared at it. The angry guard bent down to his own laptop, tapped on the screen, and began comparing his data with the sergeant's e-clipboard. Then he straightened up. His face relaxed slightly as he picked up the sergeant's electronic clipboard, took out his digital pen, and quickly signed off on the bottom.

The sergeant bowed and then roughly pushed Louder ahead of him, playing the part of a military jailer, followed by the other three, as they all moved past the guards. Joshua could see the end of the corridor about thirty yards ahead. There was a doorway to the right. It looked like some kind of utility area. It had a red sign on it. To the left was another hallway. Now Joshua's group was about ten yards from the turn. The electronic pad was now flashing some kind of red warning message. The sergeant half-turned, picking up his pace as he did, and spoke in a tone that cut like razor wire. "We have been detected. MIS now reports our computer hacking. All orders suspended."

Behind them, an angry guard was shouting. The group was at the end of the hallway, and the hallway to the left led to one more security desk with armed guards, and beyond that, Joshua could see the streets of Pyongyang.

The sergeant turned to the utility door with the sign to his right. He pulled out an electronic card and swiped the card-box next to it. The heavy metal door clicked open. Once he swung the door open he reached around and swiped another card into the slot to jam the electronics. The door began buzzing and an alarm sounded. The group ran through the open entrance, and the sergeant slammed the door behind them with another loud click. They could hear the muffled sound of gunshots and the metallic ping as the bullets struck the other side of the heavy door.

They raced along a metal catwalk. "Hurry, hurry," the sergeant yelled. They sprinted along the walkway, down several flights of stairs, taking several steps at a time. When they got to the ground floor the sergeant led them to yet another heavy metal door that had large red and yellow warning signs. He swiped the door again with his card, and he swung it open.

Daylight and a blue sky above. A pathway led through a grassy yard outside, between two tall, windowless buildings with a concrete wall at the end, just a short distance away, perhaps forty feet. Inset in the wall was a single door. They could hear the car horns and street sounds of the capital just beyond the wall. It all looked too easy.

The sergeant unlocked Louder's handcuffs and swung around quickly to face the rest of them. But his face was now telling a frightful story. "This yard is a minefield," he said. "You must follow me — exactly."

He carefully inched out into the grassy pathway. The rest of them were close behind in a tight, snaking line, with Joshua at the end. The sergeant moved slowly to the right until he was three feet from the adjoining building and he reached out his arm until he could barely touch its bricks, as if to measure some invisible point. Then he stopped and half-turned his head but kept his torso and legs perfectly still.

"This way. Follow exactly."

Gavi, Louder, Rivka, and then Joshua followed the leader, walking with deliberate speed, with bodies hunched and tensed, careful not to let a foot stray to the side. When they were fifteen feet from the door in the wall, they heard it. A little snap, like a tiny twig breaking.

"Oh" was all that the sergeant said. He froze and looked down at his right foot, which was immobile on the spot where he had just depressed the trigger on a high-explosive land mine. There was silence for a second or two as the line halted behind him. The sergeant slowly waved them to pass him on his left.

Gavi led the way, stepping one foot in front of another, until he was even with the sergeant, who cautiously removed his handgun, which dangled gingerly from his fingers. "Take it," he said to Gavi.

"Go, straight-line now, to the door. Use gun to blow lock on the wall."
Then he added, "Save the bullets. Use them if you get caught. Better
that way ..."

When all of them had arrived at the locked door, Joshua turned to
survey the sergeant's desperate situation. He was still frozen in place,
halfway down the grassy path. Joshua said to Gavi, "We can't leave
him."

"We have to, Colonel Jordan," Gavi snapped. "No choice. Besides,
he's got a plan." Gavi then peeled off his shirt and pants, revealing
another outfit underneath, and he gave the clothes to Captain Louder
to cover up his prison garb.

Gavi fired a shot at the key lock, blowing it open, and stuffed the
handgun in his pocket. After swinging the door open, they quick-
stepped out onto the sidewalk along the busy boulevard. Gavi turned
to the group. "We're looking for a police car."

They didn't have to wait long. A North Korean squad car, driven by
a man dressed in a police uniform, stopped at the curb. Gavi jumped
in the front, the rest in the back. As they pulled away, Joshua leaned
over the front seat and said to Gavi with a voice full of pathos, "What
kind of plan could he have had?" But before Gavi could answer, everyone in the squad car flinched as the sound of an explosion reverberated from the grassy yard on the other side of the wall.

For a long time they drove through the city traffic of Pyongyang
without saying a word. Joshua was the first to speak. His voice broke.

"What was the sergeant's name?"

SEVEN

Gavi explained they were heading to the industrial harbor of the Tae-dong River, past the Nampho Cargo Terminal and the dry-dock shipping yard. The driver pulled up to an old loading dock on the river, and the group piled out. Gavi led them to a pier that stretched about thirty feet over the water. A half mile down the harbor, Joshua could see a few trucks unloading cargo from a ship. Other than that, the area was clear.

"Taedong's deep," Gavi said, leading them to the end of the pier. "Hopefully deep enough ..."

Joshua asked, "For what?"

"You'll see." He motioned for them to follow him down a flight of rusty stairs to a wooden landing below, slimy with green algae, at the surface of the water. Gavi glanced at his watch. "A few minutes to spare."

Now they would wait. Joshua turned to Jimmy Louder, who had been quiet during the rescue mission.

"You okay, pilot?"

"Roger," Louder said with a struggling smile, and added, "Thank you, Colonel Jordan. For everything. Man alive, I can't believe you're really here ... and I'm out of that hell-hole ..." His voice started to quiver. His eyes filled with tears.

"We still have a few miles to go," Joshua said, patting his shoulder. "But things are looking good. God willing, we'll get you back to your family."

Louder smiled. "Oh, I can't wait to see Ginny ... my wife. And my two daughters. I've wondered what's been going on out there in the world. I've been so cut off. Haven't heard any news. What's happening in America? Who won the World Series? What are gas prices at? Let's see ... I guess Virgil Corland is still president ..."

"Not anymore," Joshua replied, his face tightening.

Jimmy Louder studied him. "What happened? Something bad?"

"President Corland had some serious health problems. Had to resign. His vice president, Jessica Tulrude, is in the White House now."

Louder looked down at the ground, like he was thinking back, searching his memory. "Oh," he groaned, "Tulrude. You're kidding?"

Joshua shook his head. "But that's just the beginning. So much has changed. A single, unified international power is growing. Spreading. Infiltrating like a cancer. God's clock seems to be speeding up. The light beginning to fade. Darkness coming. World events rushing up to the final climax. The return of Christ. Jimmy, I really believe we're getting close."

With a shake of the head, Jimmy Louder said, "Josh, I never took you to be a guy who's into that stuff."

"I wasn't. Not always," Joshua replied, "but one day God had me surrounded. He got my attention."

"You sound just like my grandfather, Eddie March," Louder said with a smile. "He was a pretty good guy. Backwoods sort of fella from West Virginia, who played guitar and sang in this little church. Always full of jokes. But serious about God. He used to talk to us about the Bible all the time when we were kids."

Gavi had stepped over to them and interrupted. "Excuse me, Captain Louder, but for this next phase, I'll have to calculate your weight."

Leaving Louder to be prepped by Gavi, Joshua walked over to Rivka. He asked, "How long till something happens?"

"Just a few minutes."

Looking out to the opposite bank of the river, Joshua noticed something. A line of willow trees gracefully swayed in the breeze. Suddenly he was somewhere else — recalling the willow tree in the backyard of his family home when he was a boy. Funny, he thought, how that house, a simple ranch-style with shutters painted an ugly neon green, had slipped out of memory for so long, tucked underneath everything else in his mental attic, long forgotten until a few days ago — when he had that powerful dream the night before delivering his message to the Junggye Gospel Church.

He was still studying the willows when Rivka stepped closer. "Why'd you do it ... the mission? You didn't know him, did you?" Rivka motioned toward Louder, who was talking with Gavi.

"Oh, I knew him," Joshua said. "Air Force pilots tend to be a pretty close-knit group. But there's something else too. A personal commitment that I made to somebody once." Rivka studied Joshua as he went on. "You see," he said, "I've been rescued myself. Once that happens, it's natural to try and rescue others ... because you know the feeling. Going from imprisonment to freedom."

"You mean the Iranian incident? The jailbreak?"

Joshua took a moment to reflect, then said, "Yeah, I was saved from an Iranian torture cell by some brave Americans, and your partners in the Mossad helped. But there's another part too, another kind of rescue I'm talking about. The kind that only God can orchestrate."

Rivka hesitated for a second. Joshua noticed that. It was as if her next question had a certain risk, a calculated danger to it — ironic for an iron-willed, take-no-prisoners member of Israel's famed spy service. But Joshua understood the look in Rivka's eyes. He had been there himself. Finally, Rivka asked, "So, what's the other part you're talking about, Colonel Jordan?"

Joshua thought back to that turning point in an ugly blood-stained cell in Iran. "I met a Christian pastor in that jail in Tehran who told me something I'll never forget ... he said there are different kinds of prisons, and they don't all have walls you can touch. At that point in my life, I was locked inside two kinds of prisons, but only one had bars on the door ..."

At that moment Joshua heard something — the sound of rippling water, like the rush of a wave hitting the pilings under the pier. He scanned the surface about ten yards away. The water seemed to be parting. The plan became clear. He now knew how they would escape the greater Pyongyang area — and North Korea.

Gavi strode up beside him. "Good thing the Taedong River is as deep ... deep enough for a mini-sub to get in and exit to the Yellow Sea."

"What about North Korean sonar?" Joshua asked, but the answer visualized in front of him. As the mini-submarine surfaced quietly, Joshua recognized the gilt of metallic plates — almost like fish-scales — lining its exterior.

Gavi smiled at him. "You remember J-Tech 100, the anti-sonar, anti-wake program for submarines?"

Joshua smiled back. "Of course. The wave-cloaking sub skin ..."

"Well your Pentagon was kind enough to lend us the prototype for this mission. It was designed jointly by a couple of defense companies, but the real genius behind it was a New York – based defense shop called Jordan Technologies ... just one more nifty military design by your outfit, Colonel Jordan. Too bad the project was cancelled after the initial prototypes were built, like the one in front of you ... on loan from the United States DOD."

Joshua nodded and gave a sly grin. "Let's hope my guys did their homework on this one."

Gavi addressed the group as the streamlined mini-sub continued to surface and a hatch opened on top. "Listen up, these will be tight quarters. I hope none of you are claustrophobic. I'll go in last and secure the hatch. No talking, no noise, the minute you enter the sub. I'll be communicating with our captain through my digital memo pad. Remember, absolute silence."

As Joshua followed Louder onto the metal topside of the sub, he passed Rivka. She looked as if she had something to say. Joshua wondered whether she was still thinking about his last comment to her and whether she was feeling caught in a prison of her own, the kind without bars.

After Gavi had watched everyone else disappear down the small round hatch, he slipped into the opening himself. No sooner had he pulled the heavy metal hatch over himself and spun the locking wheel than the slender sub submerged into the Taedong River and disappeared from sight, leaving no more of a wake behind than a fish might as it trolls under the surface.

Seoul, South Korea

Ethan March fixed his bleary eyes on the large, wall-sized screen in the headquarters of South Korea's National Intelligence Service, the NIS, in Seoul. On it was an illuminated map of North Korea, with the Taedong River snaking through it and leading out to the sea.

A U.S. Army major with a red-dragon arm patch on his shoulder was in the room with the rest of the rescue detail. He sauntered over to Ethan. "You've been up for forty hours, Ethan. Why don't you crash in the next room?"

Ethan shook his head. "No, thanks. I'm staying right here. I need to see that blip on the screen with my own eyes."

Major Chung joined them. "If they've managed to slip by the patrol boats and get through the waterway locks — that's the tricky part — then they should have passed by Ori-Som Island by now," and with that, he directed his laser pointer to a tiny misshapen circle in the Taedong River. Ethan caught something in Chung's explanation. "What's tricky about the locks?"

"The mini-sub had to tag a ride directly behind one of the big commercial vessels to clear the locks to avoid detection. Otherwise, the security system at the locks will close the water gate, and they'd be trapped."

"Tell me again," Ethan said, surveying the big screen, "where you think the blip for their mini-sub will first show up?"

Chung sent his red laser pointer to a point on the map beyond where the mouth of the Taedong River flowed into the Yellow Sea, directly under another small island. "Right here," Chung said. "Assuming everything goes well, they are supposed to leave the river estuary and enter the sea. As they pass by Sangchwira-do on their starboard side — " Chung pointed to another circle, this one in the open water — "the mini-sub captain will engage his Sat-locator, and we'll pick him up on our screen. Then we can get our aircraft to escort them out of there."

Ethan nodded as he eyed the area on the map where that lighted blip needed to appear. He stretched his shoulders and rotated his neck a little, trying to loosen up the stress. He turned to the major. "I get the impression that the Pentagon couldn't join this thing officially."

"Just like I'm not here now," the major said with a smile, "officially."

"Man alive, I can't figure that out," Ethan muttered.

"Politics and poker, Ethan. That's what we're dealing with. My unit — the 501st Military Intelligence Brigade — would have loved to have manned this rescue mission from top to bottom. A U.S. Air Force pilot captured by the North Koreans? We're stationed right here along the DMZ. We would have been the perfect group to spearhead this — would have been proud to do it. But the madam in the big White House on Pennsylvania Avenue wouldn't commit. That's what I heard from some of the Army brass."

A grin broke over the major's face. "On the other hand, we're glad to have lent our South Korean friends our mini-sub, our satellite service, our Defense Intelligence Agency data, and our clandestine service contacts inside Pyongyang — and outside too."

Ethan laughed. "Oh, is that all?" Then he realized that the Pentagon was pitching in some double agents inside the North Korean capital and had possibly helped to enlist the two Israeli Mossad agents as well. Things grew somber again as Ethan and the major stared at the screen. They looked at the spot where they hoped to see the lighted blip.

Just outside North Korea proper was a little circle, a tiny island in the field of blue on the illuminated map, and beyond the island, the open sea — and safety. Ethan looked at it, trying not to blink, but his eyes were heavy. He felt himself swaying where he stood. He caught himself. His eyes closed. Just for an instant. When he opened them, he blinked once. Then involuntarily closed them from fatigue. When he opened them again, he saw it. The blinking light. Right under the island of Sangchwira-do. In the open sea. And freedom.

Ethan leaped up, swung his fist in the air, almost striking the major, and yelled out, "Josh, you did it, man! You did it!"

EIGHT

Washington, D.C., the White House

Standing behind the podium with the seal of the United States of America on it in the press briefing room of the West Wing, President Jessica Tulrude was trying to put an end to the press conference, but one reporter's question seemed to go on forever. "Going back to the reason for this press conference in the first place," the reporter said, "and the successful rescue of Captain Louder in North Korea, there are reports the Pentagon backed this mission but that you vehemently opposed it ..."

"False rumors," Tulrude snapped. "I will never rest as long as I know one of our brave members of the military are in an enemy prison camp." Then, as she blinked a few times and nervously adjusted the collar on her suit jacket, she added, "I supported the rescue effort plain and simple."

"And as for Colonel Joshua Jordan, a highly decorated former Air Force pilot who is the subject of a criminal prosecution by your attorney general, is it correct that Colonel Jordan actually helped in this rescue effort?"

"What media group are you with?" Tulrude shot back.

"AmeriNews," she said.

The president snatched her prepared statement off the podium and smiled generously to the room full of press. She wasn't going to take any questions from AmeriNews, that newly formed media group spearheaded by Joshua Jordan, which seemed to relish every chance they got to expose what was going on in her administration, challenging her policies of bringing the United States under the blanket of international treaties. She knew what was good for America. She understood how a global society, a world system of government, was the future. Reactionaries like Joshua Jordan, his Roundtable extremists, and their AmeriNews project were practically ice-age creatures. She would be happy to help speed them into extinction.

"Thank you, all," the president announced without answering the last question. As she turned to exit out the side door, a reporter in the third row shouted out, "Any update on the condition of former president Corland?"

Tulrude whirled around and tossed out the answer, halting momentarily. "Still convalescing and permanently disabled — " she clasped her hands over her chest as if officiating at a funeral — "but while he can no longer serve America, I am sure you will remember him and reflect on what he meant to our great nation and place him in your warmest thoughts." She was about to turn toward the exit, but she stopped and added, "And your prayers, of course."

President Tulrude strode out the press room and walked down the private access corridor through the West Wing. Her chief of staff, Natali Traup, was waiting for her. "Well done, Madam President," she said brightly, though she had to jog to keep up with Tulrude who had just blown past her.

"Did you hear that?" Tulrude snapped.

"I caught it all on the monitor — "

"I want that AmeriNews reporter barred from all future White House press conferences. In fact, no one from AmeriNews is allowed within a hundred yards of me." Then she slowed down to issue the next directive to Natali. "And make sure AmeriNews doesn't get an invitation to the holiday media party ..."

"You mean the White House press Christmas party?"

Tulrude shook her head at her COS's miscue. "*Holiday* party, exactly as I said." As she swaggered down the hall the president added,

"This is an election year. I won't stand by while those AmeriNews morons launch torpedoes at me."

United Nations Headquarters, New York City

At the weekly policy meeting, two men sat in the secretary-general's office. They were the only two in his inner circle that he trusted. These two high-ranking United Nations staffers sat patiently in the overstuffed chairs as they waited for Secretary-General Alexander Coliquin to finish reviewing his agenda notes in his velvet wing-backed chair.

Bishop Dibold Kora, the balding special envoy on climate change and global wellness, had a placid smile on his face, hands folded gently in his lap.

The other executive, Ho Zhu, the deputy secretary-general, who managed Coliquin's administration, was customarily expressionless, but as the minutes ticked by he occasionally glanced over at the engraved black-walnut grandfather's clock in the corner to check the time.

Finally Coliquin looked up. "The Israeli situation," he said, "where are we on that?"

Ho Zhu said, "Our special reporter is broaching the subject with Israel. We thought it best to approach it as a human-rights issue, moving it up the ladder in Jerusalem."

"Meaning?"

"We believe Prime Minister Sol Bensky already knows we want to talk. We're waiting for a response."

"*Waiting*, you said?" Coliquin snapped. His rhetorical question was designed to show the self-evident stupidity of Ho Zhu's point. Coliquin, the handsome Romanian polymath, had little patience with his underlings — brilliant though they were — when they failed to keep up with his genius, particularly when it concerned his obsession with Israel. Of course, he was able to see things that they missed, but at least they should understand his priorities.

"I want no foot-dragging on this," Coliquin said, waving his hand in circles. "Timing is everything. Can you see that? Israel is in a unique position. On one hand, emboldened by the natural disasters that blocked the Russian-Arab incursion, yes, of course. Attributing their rescue to an act of God—and so, they have been basking in the sun ever since, like an overfed lizard. But at the same time, the people of Israel, deep down, fear further conflict. I know this to be true. They wish to avoid that kind of heart-wrenching drama again. There is a dread among the people at the prospect of further war. So very tired of conflict. Year after year, having to defend their homeland, yearning for some kind of permanent solution, which is exactly what I have for them—if they will only negotiate."

Coliquin raised a finger just then, as if he were playing the part of a history professor giving a lecture. "Never underestimate the effectiveness of human fatigue ... and national weariness. Remember Joseph Stalin's speech to the Politburo in 1939, outlining how Russia could advance into Germany and take it over after the defeat of the Third Reich. Stalin was counting on, even hoping for, a long and protracted war—so that England and France and the other allies—in his words—would grow *weary*, thus allowing the Soviet Union to seize Germany for herself. And in part it worked. It would ultimately become East Germany." He repeated, "Never discount the weariness of your opponent. It's a major strategic advantage."

Abruptly changing the subject, Coliquin asked Ho Zhu, "And the political situation in the United States, where are we on that? President Tulrude has been a strong supporter of our vision. We need her."

Deputy Ho bobbed his head, as if calculating the odds. "Our American sources tell us that President Tulrude is the favorite right now. She has the benefit of being the incumbent."

Bishop Kora chimed in, "But not elected—constitutional succession from her position as vice president when President Corland became disabled."

"Yes," Coliquin said, "that may reduce the benefit of her incumbency. Look what happened in a slightly different setting to Gerald Ford when Nixon was forced to resign." The secretary-general wasn't happy thinking about that. "How strong is her opponent?"

"Senator Hewbright is running an extremely aggressive campaign.

TIM LaHAYE AND CRAIG PARSHALL

He'll get his party's nomination. The race will be close, by a very small margin."

Coliquin then asked a question that wasn't really a question. It had all the resonance of a mandate.

"Things could happen to change that margin?"

NINE

Arlington, Virginia, Pentagon

The little communications-center TV set hanging over the desk of Lieutenant Deborah Jordan was set to C-SPAN. Deborah's eyes were trained on the screen. President Tulrude had just hung the Medal of Honor around Captain Jimmy Louder's neck. Next to Louder, his wife, Ginny, a petite brunette, was beaming and dabbing her eyes with a handkerchief. Louder's head was held high, his back straight, and his face now fuller than it was since the first pictures on the web newspapers that broke the story of his rescue from North Korea.

Deborah made a private bet with herself as she watched. She knew that Medal of Honor winners were usually permitted to say a few words. *But not this time,* she mused. And she knew why. There was no way Tulrude was going to give Jimmy Louder the chance to publicly acknowledge Deborah's father's role in the rescue.

And she was right.

After President Tulrude shook Captain Louder's hand, she stepped back to the podium and talked about Captain Louder. "This humble, likeable guy, Captain Jimmy Louder, patrolled the dangerous DMZ to keep that region safe and was shot down by hostile forces. He exemplified the most extraordinary strength, resolve, and bravery during his captivity — some of the finest conduct America's military has ever seen."

Tulrude motioned to Captain Louder and applauded him,

wrangling the applause of the attendees in the Rose Garden like a maestro. Then she quickly escorted Jimmy Louder and his wife into a private White House reception, away from the reporters who were calling out questions.

Deborah shook her head silently, then turned the volume down on the TV. She returned to her work. Her office was located right next to the Press Operations Center in the titanic, five-sided fortress of the Department of Defense. The location of her desk was an anomaly because she hadn't been assigned to the press center. As it turned out, nothing, including her desk assignment, had matched her expectations since her graduation with honors from West Point.

As she resumed her review of a raft of bids for the new DOD computer software installations, she noticed someone standing, cap in hand, by her desk. He was a young red-headed fellow, a second lieutenant like herself. There was something familiar about him. Then Deborah pieced it together. She had seen him linger at her cubicle before as he had passed by.

Deborah gave him a glance.

"Lieutenant Jordan," the young man began, "just wantin' to congratulate you on your father's successful mission in North Korea. The folks around here all know about it and salute your father ... even if the politicians don't ... if you get my drift."

"Thanks, Lieutenant." She tossed him a half smile and eyed him more closely.

"And I'd say — *hooah*, Colonel Joshua Jordan, if I may."

Her smile got bigger. "Yes, you may." She glanced at his name tag — Lt. Birdow. "Soldier, you have a first name?"

"Yes, ma'am.' Tom."

"I'm Deborah."

"Pleased to meet you."

Birdow cocked an eyebrow at her. "If I may ask, are you with the DOD press center?"

"No. People just think that because my desk is here."

"Then you're in the Defense Information Systems Agency unit like me?"

"Right. Except ..."

He filled it in, "You didn't get assigned to Fort Mead in Maryland where the rest of us in DISA are stationed."

"Nope." She didn't elaborate.

Tom Birdow looked like he was going to follow up but decided against it.

Deborah was enjoying the company — and the break from the tedium. "So what brings you to HQ?"

"Just dropped off some papers at the E Ring."

She wanted to ask him why he had just couriered something to the inner ring of the Pentagon where the senior Army officials had their offices, but she didn't pry. She didn't have to. He explained, "This information coordination between DOD and Homeland Security for BIDTagging citizens is one big complicated system."

Tom's last comment hit a sour note with Deborah, for intensely personal reasons. "I bet," she said, dropping her smile. Now she was thinking about her mother's defiance of the new government mandate and the risks she was taking. Her voice took on a formal tone. "Well, Lieutenant," she said, "back to business."

"I'll stop in again, next time I'm in the neighborhood."

"Please do."

After he left, Deborah felt the urge to call her mom. *Later,* she thought. *I'll call from my apartment.*

She looked around her cubicle and thought about Tom Birdow's unasked question, which she herself had asked repeatedly. Why *hadn't* she been transferred to Fort Mead with the rest of the DISA staff? Instead, she was tucked away in this obscure corner of the Pentagon. Deborah, of course, had her suspicions. And it had to do with the controversial nature of the "Jordan" legacy.

I'm being isolated because of my last name.

Colorado, Hawk's Nest Ranch

Abigail was on the video phone with Joshua, who was back in Israel. He had just finished briefing her on all of the details of the mission to rescue Captain Louder — the ones the White House would never admit and the American people would never learn — unless, of course, it was laid out in AmeriNews, the only remaining news source not controlled in some way by the current administration.

Abigail needed to know, so she asked once again, "So, you're really safe now? Really?"

"Yes."

She sighed. A shiver went down her back as she visualized the dangers and thought about what might have been. Then she collected herself. "Josh … oh, Josh, you know I'm so terribly proud of you …"

"That means the world to — "

But Abigail didn't let Joshua finish. "Please, listen. I'm also devastated by the risks you just took — once again — "

"Honey, let me explain — "

"And honestly, I'm a little angry — "

"I need to tell you something — "

"No," Abigail said. "Strike the record. Let me rephrase the question to the witness. Would it surprise you, Colonel Jordan, that I am not just a *little* angry. I am *very* angry — "

"I couldn't tell you about the mission."

"Top secret?"

"Absolutely."

"Clandestine?"

"You've got it, Abby."

"There's one thing you forget. I've been through all this before. Standing by you when you accepted every assignment during your Air Force days, the test-pilot days, the secret recon missions over deadly territories. When you took on every mission, I supported you and waited, praying and hoping you'd come back alive but always wondering if I'd hear the doorbell and see your commanding officer standing at the door with that painful look in his eyes. But you're out of the service now. You're a private citizen! If you'd at least told me something I could have prayed for you. But you shut me out!"

"Yes, I'm civilian now, but that doesn't change everything. It doesn't change my obligation to do the right thing."

"Let me suggest something, my darling husband."

Joshua was quiet. She could see on the screen that he was listening. Really listening. She continued, "Your obligations start with God — I'm with you on that. Your moral obligations to your country, your friends, your own conscience, you know how much I believe in that ..."

"I know you do."

"But somehow — " She could feel her chin starting to tremble and her voice quivering. She had to keep it together. "The next time you're up there in the wild blue yonder of what's right, noble, and courageous, remember your wife back here, down on the ground." Now her voice was breaking up. "And one of these days, let me know where I fit in as I sit here at Hawk's Nest waiting for you, not knowing when I'll ever feel your arms around me, looking you in the eyes, really seeing you when we talk. Not just having to settle for a video call. Don't you realize how difficult this has been? Josh, you're the love of my life, and I have no idea when we'll ever be back together again ..."

It all came pouring out — all the powerful feelings she had been holding in her heart for the last two years, during their forced separation. She had been trying to be brave about it all, managing Joshua's defense while the two of them were separated by an ocean, being the glue that kept the family together, and trying to be both parents to Deborah and Cal who were fully adults, of course, but still needed support and guidance. She felt guilty putting any of this on Joshua, but something had just snapped, and she had to let it out.

She could see Joshua nodding on the Allfone screen. There was that strong, square-jawed face she loved, which over the months seemed to look a little older, but his eyes, always keen and brilliant, now seemed to be watering.

"Abby, dear," he said, "oh, Abby, I'm sorry. I should have given you a hint — some kind of idea what was going on. I didn't mean to shut you out, baby ..."

Abigail fought to keep it together. She didn't want to make this harder on Joshua. "I miss you, darling."

After a moment of silence Joshua smiled and changed the subject. "You're at Hawk's Nest? I thought you were in New York."

"I was."

"Why'd you fly to Colorado?"

"So I could sit here in our big mountain lodge and feel sorry for myself." Abigail laughed at herself, and Joshua joined in.

Abigail looked at her husband's wide, handsome grin on the screen, as he gazed back at her. "You're still gorgeous, darling …"

She waved off the suggestion. "You can't trust these Allfone video images," she said, wiping a tear from her eye.

He laughed louder and tilted his head. "Wait a minute. I know why you're at Hawk's Nest. A Roundtable meeting's scheduled. I'm sure you've got more on the agenda than you can handle — as usual. "

She cocked an eyebrow. There was a twinkle in her eye. "I wondered how long it would take you to remember. Yes, the regular meeting. But I'm feeling like we're the Continental Congress meeting to fend off the Redcoats — except the enemy is our own government, a corrupt president who's acting like a queen, and who's trading our national sovereignty for a false promise of international peace and tranquility. And then there's my husband! Josh, you're John Adams and Thomas Jefferson all rolled into one. And, darling, you're absence is sorely missed."

"You're sweet, but *way* overexaggerating," Joshua shot back. "So, who's showing up?"

"John Gallagher's here. I think he comes for the home cooking!"

Joshua chuckled. The iconoclastic former FBI anti-terror agent, who had put on a lot of weight since leaving the Bureau, kept assuring everyone he was "thirty days from being in peak physical condition." That was something all of them were waiting to see.

Abigail ticked off the list of other members: "Our self-made billionaire-entrepreneur, Beverly Rose Cortez," she said. "I just love that gal. Tender but tough. She's coming in tomorrow morning. Along with Phil Rankowitz. The rest by videofone."

"About Phil," Joshua said, "I hope our resident media guru will address the issue of using AmeriNews to run the article about the U.N.'s new secretary-general, Alexander Coliquin."

"Already have it on the agenda. Didn't you get the email?"

"Sorry — I must have missed it." Then he added with a smirk, "I was busy sightseeing in North Korea ..."

Abigail tossed him a friendly barb. "See what you miss when you pull one of your super-hero-saves-the-day stunts?"

"Sure, but it goes to show you — ever since I've been a man without a country — you've been running the Roundtable just fine without me." Then Joshua dropped the grin. "Hey, I've been thinking."

"Uh oh, that's dangerous ..." Abigail gave a sly smile.

"How about I come home now? Face the legal music. Fly — "

"Right into the flak? Right. Heard all that before. Josh, I thought we had an agreement."

"We did. But I'm dying here without you."

"You know I feel the same. But we've filed our appeal. Maybe the court will decide that it's crazy to use that trial order to keep me from leaving the United States while your case is pending."

"You're the lawyer, Abby, but to me that seems like a one-in-a-million shot. Besides, it'll take another year for a ruling. I can't wait that long."

She thought for a moment. "I've got one more trick up my sleeve," she said. "I've got a lead into the federal prosecutor's office. I've been talking to some former law partners, and I heard that one of the assistant attorney generals in the AG's office, a guy who was on the team prosecuting you, just quit under strange circumstances. Very sudden. This lawyer — Harley Collingwood — had a reputation for being pretty tough on defendants, but also very ethical and eminently fair. So, you have to ask yourself, why did he up and leave the attorney general's office?"

"More money in the private sector?"

"Could be. But some rumors indicate otherwise. So, honey, I'm asking you to wait a little longer. I want to see if this Harley Collingwood thing might have something to do with your case. Who knows? What if he quit the DOJ because he discovered their case against you has an ugly, illegal underbelly? Until I get your defense set up, they've got a case against you based on seemingly invincible testimony. You and I both know the prosecution's case is built on a lie, but I have to find the proof of that lie first, to show that their chief witness is perjuring himself. I just need a little more time."

"Time? That's exactly what we don't have, Abby. I need to be with you if … or more likely, when …" There was silence on both ends of the line now. Abigail knew what he meant. He didn't have to lay it out for her. They were both keen observers of recent events, and they knew what the Bible said about the signs of His coming. It was too clear now for either of them to deny. They were convinced that the beginning of the end was rushing in like a bullet train. If there ever was a time for them to meet it together, in person, it was now.

"Just a little more time, Josh."

"Okay, just a little." Then he added, "I can't tell you how much I love you and miss you, Abby. And how I need to be near you."

Abigail couldn't dispute any of that. So she said the only thing she could: how passionately she ached for him and needed to be with him too. Before hanging up, Joshua returned to a final bit of business. He said that he would call in to the Roundtable meeting the next day via Allfone video. The discussion was too important for him to miss. Before ending the encrypted conversation, they prayed together. Then his final words to Abigail were, "Please find the loose thread in the government's case, will you, dear?"

Abigail sat down on the cowhide couch and began to weep quietly— until she had no more tears. She knew the kind of man Joshua was when she married him and was glad for it. He would risk his life to rescue a fellow pilot. And she wondered: had she been the wife of Captain Louder, wouldn't she want Josh to do everything and anything to save her husband? But it wasn't just about that. It was about this separation with no end in sight that was beginning to take a toll on her. She picked herself up from the couch and wandered into the kitchen to make herself some tea.

With her cup and saucer in her hand, Abigail moved into the study and sat down at the desk. Just above her on the wall were photos of Josh with members of the joint chiefs of staff and other photos of him shaking hands with presidents. Next to the photos were framed articles on some high-profile legal cases that she had won during her law career.

Abigail flipped open the file on her husband's case and once more dug into the thick paperwork. From all appearances, the prosecution's inflated case was huge and impressive and unreachable — like the Goodyear Blimp. What she needed was a needle to deflate it. Unfortunately, it was buried in a haystack somewhere — and she wasn't even sure which haystack.

But she did have an idea. As she flipped through the papers, she looked for something in particular — the news articles she had collected about the intriguing former federal prosecutor, Harley Collingwood, who had been assigned to prosecute Joshua's case. She was now trying to figure out why he abruptly left the Department of Justice and whether it had something to do with the high-level corruption that she knew lay at the bottom of the case against her husband.

TEN

Jerusalem, Israel

"Caught up."

"Say again?"

Pastor Peter Campbell seemed oblivious to the television cameras in the Middle East studios of the Global News Network. He leaned forward in his chair, looked his GNN interviewer in the eye, and repeated the phrase. "Caught up. That's the translation of the Greek term used in the original New Testament writings. The word *rapture* is also commonly used among Christians for this event. That word was taken from the later Latin translations. What we are talking about here is the supernatural event that happens right before the beginning of the most catastrophic period in human history."

Bart Kingston, the career newsman conducting the interview, struggled to produce a half-baked smile. He had read up on this New York City preacher who headed up the Eternity Church in Manhattan. Kingston knew all about Campbell making news with his band of "Bible prophecy" experts and their doomsday predictions. He always did his homework, even though this was not his kind of story. He considered himself a hard news guy. But Kingston happened to be in Jerusalem covering some political twists in the administration of Prime Minister Sol Bensky, so he was available; the religion reporter who should have handled the interview was already on assignment at a new United Nations center in Iraq, covering something called "One Planet — One Cause — One God" — the One Movement for short, a religious conclave fighting global warming through a collaboration of various religions around the world. Kingston, not a particularly religious man himself, thought the idea of a world unification of religions probably had some merit. Or at least the global conference promoting it could be a decent news story.

"You mentioned the Latin," Kingston said, "could you expand on that a little?"

"I'm talking about one of the epistles — New Testament letters — written by the apostle Paul to the early churches in the first century. In that particular letter he was talking about the fact that Jesus Christ will be coming again, back to earth — "

"The so-called second coming of Christ?"

"Exactly, but not the way most folks think."

"How so?"

"The New Testament lays out the order of events. The Lord Jesus will first be coming for his church, whisking Christians off the planet … literally. Followed by a seven-year period, with the last half devolving into a time of incredible suffering on the earth. Then Christ appears on earth to establish His kingdom. That first part, though — the rapture — is just for Christ's 'church universal'; in other words, those who belong to Him, regardless of denomination, church attendance, or any other external factor — "

"Sounds exclusionary. Not very inclusive."

"Maybe it strikes you that way, but the standard has to be not what you or I think about it, but what God has said in His Word. And the Bible is clear that the true believers in Christ will be 'caught up,' literally snatched up to Christ. They are the ones who have trusted in Christ and in the sacrifice He made on the Cross right here in Jerusalem, a sacrifice for sins. That sacrifice, by the way, wasn't just for my sins; it was for yours as well."

Kingston tried not to react. He changed the subject. "Of course, right now, this week, religious leaders from around the world are attending a convention in Iraq to unify behind a plan to save the planet from a global-warming disaster — brilliant men and women, committed to their various religions. Yet many of them have denounced what you and your group are saying, calling it crackpot theology. And using words like *dangerously divisive* and *nonsensical*. How do you respond?"

Campbell took only a split second to reflect on Kingston's curveball. "During Jesus' earthly ministry He met with a member of the ruling religious group, a fellow named Nicodemus. Jesus explained to him that to know God and inherit eternal life, he would need to receive Christ and be born again. That came as a shock to this man, who was probably a brilliant teacher educated in the Old Testament Scriptures, the Tanakh, and who was undoubtedly a wealthy, influential man — a mover and shaker of his day. The point is this — I consider the opinions of the religious leaders of our day to be a moot issue — unless they're ready to follow the one path that God has laid out through His Son Jesus Christ and described in His Word, the Bible."

There was an edge to Kingston's voice as he dug in. "So then, all these other religions, all except Christianity, you condemn them?"

"I condemn no one. Judging the hearts of others is way above my pay grade."

Kingston offered a half smile as Campbell continued. "I'm just a sinner saved by grace. All I'm saying is that God calls us to an inner spiritual transformation, to be born again, the Bible says. That transformation must come from a personal faith in Christ, not from some outward show of religion. If we do that, then one day — very soon, I believe — we will be caught up with Him, in the blink of an eye. Those who don't, well, they will unfortunately face that short but horrifying phase called 'the tribulation' — unparalleled terror on the earth."

Kingston was more than a little dubious but remained objective; after all, he had a job to do. "How do you respond to your critics who say you're going way too far with this? You talk about the return of Christ as if it's practically on the doorstep of history, as if Christ was galloping down the lane right now, ready to start knocking on the door of Planet Earth. Your critics have called you Pastor Apocalypse … They suggest your brand of extremism whips people into fanatical, even violent, reactions. I've heard the Sol Bensky administration here in Jerusalem is concerned about what people might do as a result of your Armageddon religion — "

"The folks who have actually experienced the spiritual transformation that comes with knowing Christ won't be the ones doing the crazy things. They'll be the ones with the inner peace to know that their Redeemer is getting close. And they know that even the terrors of the end times will be used by the God-of-all-compassion to call the human race to Himself, giving them one last chance to receive Christ as Savior. Wouldn't you want God to give you one more chance, Bart?"

The reporter sized up Campbell's face before checking his clipboard, just to make sure he had covered all the bases. He turned to the cameraman. "We'll cut there. I'll do an intro and a wrap later."

As he stood and gave a perfunctory handshake to his guest, Kingston made small talk with Campbell. "So you're currently located in Israel?"

Campbell nodded. "I've set up an office in Jerusalem, just off the Old City."

"Close to the action, eh?"

He smiled. "In a way, yes. This is the only city in the world where geography, theology, and history are rapidly rushing together in one great climax. I'm keeping my eye on the Temple Mount, in particular. For me, that's where the starting gun of this race will go off. Or to use our national American pastime as an example, it's like being at the ballpark and hearing the National Anthem. That's when you know that the action — the human drama — is just about to begin."

That reminded Kingston of another question. He came at it obliquely. "Okay, pastor, you've raised the baseball metaphor ... I'm a Red Sox fan. You hail from New York — so, you're for the Yankees?"

"No, Mets."

"Ah, the underdogs ..."

Campbell chuckled.

Then Kingston made his point. "So these catastrophic events you're talking about, using your baseball analogy, what inning is the world in right now, would you say? Top of the ninth? Bottom of the ninth?"

"Neither," the pastor said. His face was flush with anticipation. "We're in extra innings."

National Headquarters of Hewbright for President Campaign, K Street, Washington, D.C.

In the middle of the crowded main room, Secret Service Agent Owens flagged down Katrena Amid, Senator Hewbright's harried and slightly mussed assistant campaign manager. As he tried to explain something to her, the noise of the dozen volunteers manning phones at desks made it difficult to hear.

"Let's go to my office," Amid said.

They entered and closed the door.

"Say again — something about a threat?" she began.

"Unconfirmed," Agent Owens said. "Nothing specific. We get these routinely during the political season. Just want you and the staff to be on the alert for unusual or suspicious people trying to get access to the senator."

"I'll be sure and pass it on to him. He's doing a press call right now." She motioned to the adjoining office separated by a glass wall where her boss was on the phone, smiling and gesturing as he answered a reporter's questions.

Just then, Zeta Milla, one of Senator Hewbright's junior advisors on foreign policy, swung open the door and stepped into the conversation. Milla sized up the man in the dark suit. "Secret Service?"

"Got it covered, Zeta," Amid snapped.

"And you are ...?" the agent asked the attractive Cuban refugee.

Zeta introduced herself and described her position on the staff. "Is there a problem?" she persisted.

"Just some information for the senator," the agent replied. "General threat, nothing specific. Just want everyone to be on the alert. Be vigilant."

"I told Agent Owens that Senator Hewbright is on a press call right now, but we'll be sure to advise him," Amid noted.

"This is your call, Katrena," Milla bulleted back. "But if it were me, I'd cut the senator's call short and advise him immediately. Safety first."

Katrena Amid threw Milla a withering look. Then she manufactured a smile for the agent, shook his hand, and thanked him as she walked him to the door. When he was gone, Amid confronted Zeta Milla. "From now on, you will remember that security issues are my department, not yours."

"Fine," Milla responded. Her tone was cool and unflustered. Then she added, "Just make sure you take care of our candidate. You're replaceable. He's not."

Inside the adjoining glass office, Hewbright was fielding the reporter's last question.

"As far as the differences in our vision for America," the senator said, "President Tulrude and I couldn't be farther apart. I see the need for America to regain its greatness as a world leader. To lead, not just join. To model true freedom, rather than trying to copy the emasculated version that Europe and the United Nations and the international community has adopted."

"You say emasculated —," the reporter started to say.

"Right. I use the word deliberately. The current administration has signed onto global treaties against hate speech that are now being used to throw people of faith into jail when they quote the Bible or speak their conscience on issues. Am I the only one who thinks that's just plain crazy? Those treaties have to be disavowed. If I become president I will urge the Senate to reverse all that. Tulrude has orchestrated the downfall of the American dollar and brought us into the CReDO. Sharing in that global currency is going to sound the death knell for any chance of a vibrant, independent U.S. economy. She's drawn down our military defenses, stopped defense weapons development necessary for the safety of our nation, and jeopardized our national security by trapping us in a spider web of international agreements that require us to share our weapons information with the rest of the world. Remember the old painting by Norman Rockwell? A Mom and Dad tucking their child into bed? Underneath it says "Freedom from Fear." Jessica Tulrude has given Americans a lot to be frightened about. I want to replace fear with freedom."

After the interview, Hewbright stepped out of the media office and trotted up to Katrena Amid in the big room. "Was that Secret Service?"

"Yes."

"I've got another press call in exactly sixty seconds. Anything important?"

Amid paused before answering. Then she flashed a smile. "No. Not really. Just a routine security reminder."

Hewbright nodded, then dashed back into the glass-walled office to take his next call.

ELEVEN

Jewish Quarter, Near the Western Wall, Jerusalem

The young bearded messenger, with prayer locks dangling along each side of his face, sprinted up the uneven stones of the street just off the Western Wall plaza. It was the section of the Old City where the massive Herodian Temple on the Temple Mount once dominated Jerusalem in ancient times.

But that was two millennia ago. Back then the smoke from the animal sacrifices of the Jewish faithful would rise up from the Temple and spiral into the sky during the days of Roman occupation, when political and religious strife made Jerusalem as tense as the strings on a lyre. Eventually the Temple would be leveled by Rome's legions in A.D. 70, after which, all Temple worship and animal sacrifices came to an abrupt halt. For nearly two thousand years, the Jews were without a Temple on that sacred plateau — with no immediate hope for its restoration.

Until now.

Breathless, the messenger stopped abruptly when he came to a weathered wooden door. He knocked three times. He waited ... and knocked two more times. He waited ... and knocked once.

The door opened.

A man in his thirties welcomed the messenger in. The messenger bowed to the rabbi seated on the couch at the far end of the room, an aged man with a pale, saggy face and a full grey beard. The rabbi's assistant pointed to a chair, and the messenger sat.

"Rabbi," the young man began. "Important news."

"Speak," the rabbi instructed him.

"About Prime Minister Bensky. Certain negotiations. Incredible ..."

"Catch your breath," the assistant chided. "Speak clearly."

"It's just that," the young messenger said, "as I watched our secret work in preparation ... the fashioning of the altar ... the water basins ... the great bronze basin ... all the sacred implements for sacrifice ... making ready for the day when the Temple will be restored to its rightful place on the Mount ..."

"Yes ...," the rabbi said, nodding slowly. The old man twisted his head slightly to look through the lace curtain of his apartment so he could catch a glimpse of the Western Wall's uppermost row of stones and the Temple Mount above, now occupied by Muslim mosques. He turned to the young messenger. "Please, tell us what you know."

"There are discussions within the Sol Bensky coalition government. I don't have the details yet. But hints. More than just rumors."

"What kind of discussions?" the rabbi's assistant asked.

"Between the United Nations envoy and the prime minister's office ..."

"About what?" the assistant demanded.

"Jerusalem. Some kind of international solution to control and supervise the city."

"That's old news," the assistant chided him.

"No, not this part ..."

"What part?"

The young messenger broke into an ecstatic grin.

"The part about the Temple Mount."

Hawk's Nest, Colorado

In the conference room at the Jordans' ranch, the members of the Roundtable were chatting around a long table of polished birch. The curtains had been pulled open, giving everyone a spectacular view of the Rockies. Even though they had all been there more times than they could count, they still found it awe inspiring.

The group had taken a five-minute break before launching into the last order of business. Some of them, including Cal Jordan, were helping themselves to the snacks on the split-log buffet. Cal grabbed a soda and a huge oatmeal cookie and wandered toward Phil Rankowitz, the Roundtable's head of media.

Rankowitz, standing in front of the floor-to-ceiling windows, stared off at the distant mountains. Abigail was next to him. Phil murmured, "I keep trying to remember that psalm ... about the heavens declaring the glory of God ..."

"That's one of my favorites," Abigail said. "How's your reading-through-the-Bible-in-a-year project coming?"

"Try to keep up with it. I miss a few days here and there. Funny though, thinking back to the old days. I was just like all the other TV exec's I worked around back then — reading the Bible, are you kidding?"

Cal laughed. "I remember not long ago when Dad would have had the same reaction. Funny how an encounter with God radically changes everything, doesn't it?"

"The ultimate paradigm shift," Phil replied. Cal took a bite of his cookie, and Phil reached out and patted him on the shoulder. "Cal, have I told you how glad I am to have you sitting with us on the Roundtable?"

Cal gave a smiling nod. "So, you don't think with my dad being the founder, my mom sitting as chair, and now with me here that it looks like the Jordan family show?"

"Naw," Phil replied. "Besides, even if it did — so what? You've got an extraordinary family. The more of you the merrier."

The rest of the group was now slowly migrating back toward the table. Cal got a back-slap from former FBI agent John Gallagher, a favorite of his, as they sauntered back to their chairs. Cal congratulated Gallagher on looking so fit.

"Dropped forty pounds, and now I'm a lean, mean fighting machine," the former special agent remarked. "Problem is, Cal, I still have the urge to be an eating machine. Got to work on that."

Cal looked around at the accomplished array — a dozen leaders in business, the military, the media, and the law. He had recently found himself yearning to be included. He wasn't sure exactly when it happened, but his plans to go to art school had given way to something else: an intense desire to follow the path forged by his parents — fighting to restore the most basic freedoms in the country they loved. It was almost laughable — how he used to shrug off his parents' commitment — he had silently considered it just a "political obsession." Now he had come to realize it wasn't about politics at all. This was a spiritual battle for the soul of a nation at a time in history when the world looked like it was about to head right into its darkest hour. Even some of Cal's Christian friends called him an "end-times freak" now. A few of them attributed his turnaround to the scary encounter he had had with a terrorist in a New York train station.

And, Cal thought, maybe it did have something to do with that.

Whatever the genesis, Cal had a powerful sense of calling to do what the Roundtable was doing. He would have wanted to be part of it even if his parents weren't involved.

For him, the timing seemed perfect. He had graduated early from Liberty University and had plenty of time before starting law school. Until then he would act as a paralegal for the Roundtable, something he had been pursuing like a dog on a bone. His parents had finally relented to his request. Joshua and Abigail told him, after everything he had been through, he had earned a seat at the table, even though they feared there could be political — and even legal — fallout against their son for his involvement. After all, they pointed out, under the Tulrude Administration, the Department of Justice had filed a vindictive criminal case two years before against every member of the Roundtable. True, for tactical reasons the DOJ had dropped the charges against everyone except Joshua, their prime target, but Cal's parents told him this might be the beginning of political retaliation.

Cal didn't care. It wasn't reckless abandon. Instead, it was a rock-solid conviction that this is where God wanted him, at least for the next few months. The Roundtable existed to counteract the ruthless, abject corruption that had been spawned in the corridors of power in Washington, and Cal now felt privileged to be part of the Roundtable, even in a small way, like today, when his primary task was to adjust the video feed on the big screen, as he was doing now.

The screen at the end of the room lit up. Ethan March's face appeared. The image was a little scrambled.

"Cal, is that you?" Ethan asked.

"Sure is," Cal replied and reached for the remote. "The feed's off. Let me reset the telemetry here."

"Fine. I'll sit tight," Ethan said. "I'm standing in for Josh, playing the part of a test dummy."

Cal chuckled. There had been a time, when Ethan first started working with Joshua, that Cal harbored some bad feelings about the arrangement. Envy? Maybe. Though Cal and his father had been through some tough, amazing things that had brought them closer together, still, there were occasional sparks between the two of them. He used to blame his dad for those. But lately Cal wondered whether he wasn't more like his dad than he had ever imagined. And now Cal felt comfortable with Ethan as a kind of adopted part of the family, even if he was on the other side of the globe, so much so that Cal wished Ethan was back in the States so the two of them could pal around. He didn't have a brother. Ethan was the closest thing.

Cal reset the feed, and Ethan's face was crystal clear. "Okay, you're coming in great. So, how are things in Israel?"

"Hot," Ethan said with a grin.

"And you're not just talking about the desert heat?"

Ethan nodded. "You got it. Yeah, there's talk over here about a major shakeup on the Temple Mount. Josh told me this morning there are plans to rebuild the Jewish Temple up there. Josh says, after two thousand years of waiting, there's a lot of excitement in Israel over this. I can't see the big deal, but then, that's just me ..."

"Wow," Cal shot back. "The Temple rebuilt? That's huge! Listen, bro, you got to get into your New Testament. It's all laid out in Matthew 24. Jesus predicted the destruction of the Herodian Temple on the Mount in Jerusalem when He was on earth. And it ended up happening — in AD 70 — just like He said. In that same place in Matthew, Jesus talks about the desecration of the Temple by the Antichrist at the end of days, which implies that the Temple has to be rebuilt first. Man, we're getting close ..."

"Thank you, Reverend Cal," Ethan cracked. "I'd start the hymn singing except I've got a lousy voice."

Cal chuckled and noticed Phil Rankowitz had finished gathering all the members around the big table. "Okay, Ethan, gotta go. Probably good too. I'm not sure how much of your off-key singing I could take." Ethan guffawed. "Can you do me a favor?" Cal asked. "Have my dad join us on the screen. Good talking to you. Stay safe over there, Ethan."

Cal touched the prompt for the multiple-screen option, and the video broke into quadrants, one for each remote participant. Once the meeting started, Phil Rankowitz took the lead. He described an article written by an eccentric investigative journalist named Curtis Belltether, whose research had revealed a seamy, even criminal, side to the brilliant and suave Alexander Coliquin, then a rising international diplomat with a global, rock-star kind of following. Belltether's explosive article had been mailed to AmeriNews on the same day that Belltether was found murdered in a hotel room. Since then Coliquin had been elevated to secretary-general of the United Nations, and the stakes over publishing the article had been raised exponentially.

"Here's the problem folks," Phil explained. "We paid Belltether for the article before his death. We own the rights. That's not the issue. The question is whether we can afford to release the article over our AmeriNews Internet/Allfone service at this time."

Retired Senator Alvin Leander spoke up. "Why not? Isn't that why we launched AmeriNews in the first place?"

Phil explained, "Well, as you know, we started the news service because the feds pushed all the TV and radio news over to the Internet so they could use over-the-air broadcast spectrum for other purposes. They said it was for emergencies. But it never worked out that way. You remember the story. A handful of networks and technology companies, mostly controlled by foreign money, became the gatekeepers for all the news and information on the web. And the White House willingly collaborated with them, allowing them to maintain a vise-grip monopoly over the Internet as long as they sang the administration's tune. Until we introduced AmeriNews, that is, and got it grand-

fathered onto the Internet through a technical loophole in the FCC regulations. The loophole was quickly closed for all other comers, so AmeriNews is the only show in town where Americans are going to get the other side of the story.

"By the way, an update for you. A few years ago we started delivering our news, free of charge at first, to the Allfones of every American who uses that device — about fifty percent of the population. Fifteen percent cancelled when it came time to pay for the service, leaving thirty percent on our news service. But we've added another twenty eight percent who use the cheaper Youfone device. So as of now, we've got fifty-eight percent of America reading some part of our news every day. We expect even more growth next quarter."

From his quadrant on the video screen, Rocky Bridger, a former Pentagon army general, brought the discussion back to the main point. "Phil, what's the problem? Just transmit the article."

"I'm not just a former TV exec," Phil replied, "I also consider myself a journalist. I have no way to corroborate the information in Belltether's article without going back to his sources to fact-check it."

From another quadrant on the screen, Joshua posed a question. "How long will it take to authenticate the information?"

"Weeks, likely. With Belltether dead, running down all his sources is going to take some time. This is pretty explosive stuff. Belltether makes Coliquin look like a sophisticated, brutal mobster back in his homeland before he gained international celebrity status. And let's not forget his close affiliation with President Tulrude. The shrapnel from our information bomb against Coliquin is going to hit the White House — and you know Tulrude's administration will pounce on any factual weaknesses in the article to tar and feather us."

Judge Fortis Rice, from his chair in the conference room, asked, "Is there a rush on getting this article out that I'm not seeing?"

"Here's the urgency, Fort," Joshua replied. "I think Coliquin is dangerous, and the U.N. he heads is no longer an international lame duck, a world-wide debating society with no teeth. We've all seen what he's turned it into: a coalition of nations that pass treaties and enforces them with large international armies in blue helmets. His

global regulations against climate change have industries around the world being monitored by his environmental police. He's united major religions around this initiative, but I find it incredibly suspect. His international regulations on hate speech, for example, have sent ministers and pastors to jail right here in the United States. He's a man to be watched — and exposed. Until we can expose him, he will continue to hurt people ... good people."

Alvin Leander fidgeted in his chair. "Josh, no disrespect, but could this be about your religious beliefs? Ever since you became a born-again Christian you've been looking for bogeymen under the bed."

Beverly Rose Cortez, sitting across from Leander, cast him a teasing grin. "I don't know, Alvin. I've seen Congress in action and visited the White House. Let me tell you, those folks in power, including our president, really *are* bogeymen ..."

After the chuckles died down, John Gallagher raised his hand but didn't wait to be called on. "No disrespect to any of you folks, but there's only two guys in this room who've ever gotten close to a real bogeyman. One is me, when I worked in counterterrorism. The other is my buddy Cal here, who had his own face-to-face with terror. So Alvin, let's watch the trash-talking about Joshua and his family. As for the issue on the table, if Josh thinks this is a time-critical deal, then that's that. Phil, whatever you've got to do, you got to do it quickly."

Abigail put the motion on the floor for a vote. The ayes had it. Phil would use his editorial judgment in making sure that the Belltether story checked out before disseminating it over millions of Allfones and Youfones, but with the caveat that he needed to get the fact-checking done "with blinding speed."

"Speaking of Washington and the White House," Phil Rankowitz added, "at some point we need to consider whether we issue a formal endorsement in the current presidential campaign."

"No brainer," Rocky Bridger shouted from the screen. "Just think back to before President Corland's medical problems arose, when he was starting to come around. An amazing reversal. Just plain courageous, if you ask me. Then that stroke — or whatever that was — and what do we get? Vice President Jessica Tulrude ... Lady Macbeth in

the flesh gets put into the Oval Office, sells out America to the European markets, dumps the dollar, practically gives away American sovereignty to the U.N., strips our national defense — "

"Been down this road before, Rocky," Leander said. "We all know that AmeriNews, if it endorses anybody, is going to support Senator Hewbright. So Phil, I hear you saying that the question is whether we should even make endorsements. Right?"

"That's it," Phil replied. "AmeriNews is a fledgling news organization, but growing fast. There's something to be said for not endorsing anyone this time around."

Ultimately, after much discussion, the issue was tabled. It was agreed the topic would be brought up again at the next meeting.

While Abigail wrapped up the meeting, Cal felt his Allfone buzz. There was an email, with a basic encryption system. He didn't recognize the sender's address, so he tapped the code into the permissions key. Then the message appeared.

Dear Cal — we have never met. I am writing for my husband, who, as you know, is in poor health. He needs to speak to you. Although he has never met you, he knows something about your story and, of course, has met your father. He has good days and bad days, so I am not sure how much he will be able to verbalize when you get here. But please come if you can. The address and telephone number of the convalescent center is at the bottom of this email. Please keep this in strictest confidence.

When Cal read who had sent it, he felt as if someone had sucked the air out of his lungs. But just as quickly he recalled the day his father received the Medal of Freedom in a Rose Garden ceremony, all because of an incident involving him. Cal hadn't attended that White House event. So he wondered why he was being swept into this strange rendezvous.

The email was signed,

Yours truly,
Winnie Corland — on behalf of President Virgil Corland.

TWELVE

Chicago, Illinois

Men with a strange-looking legal warrant were still downstairs in the lobby of D&H Smelting Co. They had just served process papers on Bob Dempsky, the sixty-six-year-old president and CEO of the industrial plant, who was now back in his office with no intentions of cooperating — and was telling his lawyer as much on the telephone.

"Look," his attorney advised him, "this international agency has the authority to seize your company, the plant, and all your assets. You have a right to appeal, of course — "

"But I've done everything the EPA ordered me to do, and we haven't had a single stain on our pollution record for five years — "

"Naw, Bob," the attorney said, "you don't get it. U.S. law is irrelevant here, except when it's time for enforcement; then the World Climate Enforcement Council — WCEC — rounds up federal marshals to make sure you obey the international orders. The United States is part of all of these world climate-change treaties and global-warming protocols. I've told you this before. If your company fails to convert to what they call 'green practices' — "

But Dempsky was in no mood to listen. He was now crumpling the papers that the foreign official with a French accent, flanked by U.S. marshals, had just delivered to him downstairs.

He shook the ball of documents in the air as he yelled into the phone, "These papers say we put smoke and carbon into the air. Of course we do! We're a smelting factory! But we've complied with every

one of the American regulations. But you're telling me that doesn't matter. Okay, so get this ... on this form, under 'miscellaneous violations,' they're telling me we don't use the right kind of light bulbs, we don't use recycled paper towels in our bathrooms — paper towels, for crying out loud!"

"I told you, Bob," the lawyer said, trying to smooth things over, "to contact that firm specializing in international law on LaSalle Street. Did you do that?"

Dempsky just shook his head in disgust. "So where do I appeal this?"

"To the Hague."

"Where?"

"The World Court, in the Hague, the Netherlands."

"This company was founded by my grandfather. This is America. I'm not going all the way to Holland to protect my family's company — "

"You're going to have to — "

"Oh yeah?" Dempsky shouted as he slammed his Allfone down on his desk. Then he buzzed his secretary on the intercom. "Peggy, call security ..."

"Mr. Dempsky, the marshals and that French gentleman are walking outside to chain the gate to the factory shut — "

"Tell my security team to go out there and stop them!"

"I will sir, but what if the marshals and that French gentleman — "

"Tell my security guys they have my authority to start shooting ..." Then he added with some bitter sarcasm, "But only at the Frenchman ..."

"Mr. Dempsky, I know you're not serious — "

"Okay, fine. At least tell them to order them off my property ... tell them they're trespassing. Do something." Then Dempsky strode over to the big picture window on the third floor that overlooked the factory entrance. His security people in the parking lot were approaching the team of federal marshals and a man in a suit with a briefcase down by the main gatehouse. His guards were gesturing to them. Up in his office Bob Dempsky was alone and began shouting to no one in particular.

"What kind of a country is this anyway?"

Brussels, Belgium, Headquarters of the
World Climate Enforcement Council

Faris D'Hoestra, a billionaire industrialist in his midfifties with a shiny bald head and steel-grey euro-glasses, sat in front of five small web-streaming screens. The monitors were keyed to markets around the world.

All but one. At the top of the menu, that one read: "WCEC Seizures — Service of Process Pending."

D'Hoestra had noticed a blue flag that had just appeared on that screen. He tapped on the site. His eyes followed the status list until he came to the most recent one. It read: "D&H Smelting — Chicago, IL — Seizure Complete."

He closed that site on his screen. He pushed his Allfone's video button and a small screen eased up from the surface of the desk. The face of Brian Forship, his executive director of international acquisitions, appeared.

The face spoke. "Good evening, Mr. D'Hoestra. Working late again, I see ..."

"When do I not?"

"Of course."

"I've noticed the Chicago seizure."

"I did too."

"How soon can we put this on the block for sale?"

"I have my American Midwest connections on this. They are making sure that that Mr. Dempsky will miss the deadline for appeal."

"Fine. Then we can put it up for auction. Which of our ghost-companies will you use to buy it?"

"Probably Union Consolidation, Ltd."

"How many other seizure buy-ups do we have in the works?"

"One hundred and seventy-two internationally. Those are the biggest companies — not including this Chicago company, which isn't big enough to make our list of prime acquisitions."

"Get me the timetable and net asset value of those companies on our prime list, will you?"

"Certainly. Two other things. First, we're still hearing some rumblings about your position as head of the WCEC, which, of course, is in the business of confiscating companies in violation of green standards, while you've also maintained control of your Global Industrial Acquisitions, Ltd. A small article appeared in a news service complaining of a conflict of interest."

"Who did the article?"

"An American news service — AmeriNews. It's available on Allfone and Youfone by subscription. It's only a few years old. They even have a picture showing how your United Nations WCEC headquarters is in the building right next to your private company. The photo in the web article is angled to display the WCEC building, and then off in the distance is the sign for GIA, Ltd."

"Don't we own enough stock in all the Internet news platforms to shut them down?"

"Not that easy. Somehow they managed to slip through some kind of grandfather clause in the Federal Communications Commission regulations. They apparently can't be blocked."

"There's no such thing," D'Hoestra shot back. He leaned back in his ostrich-skin executive chair and reflected. "On the other hand, I don't think this will be a problem. I can show that I kept my ownership in GIA in a blind trust during my U.N. tenure. And with my formal resignation from the WCEC this month, I think it will all blow over."

"I would hope so," his director said. "The second thing — did you see the article on you in *World Money* magazine?"

D'Hoestra swiveled in his chair slightly and grabbed the magazine with his face on the cover. "Haven't had a chance to read it yet."

"Excellent coverage, Mr. D'Hoestra."

After his assistant signed off, the financier took a closer look at the cover. Under his headshot it read: "Faris D'Hoestra — Ready to Rule the World?"

Under that, the subtitle read, "Acquisitions King Expands his Empire."

The Next Day, Babylon City, Iraq

On the platform, the speakers' table was draped with the blue and white logo of the United Nations — arched olive branches surrounding a globe. In the background was a banner that read: "The One Movement — One Planet, One Cause, One God." At the podium, Secretary of State Danburg, the American representative from President Tulrude's administration, was wrapping up his introduction.

Behind him on the dais were a few Muslim muftis, the twenty-three-year-old newly installed Dalai Lama from Tibet, several representatives from the Global Conference of Churches, and a Hindu priest. There were also several heads of state, including the crown prince of Saudi Arabia. Looming in the background was a monolithic office complex, the size of a small city, which was being commemorated that day. Palatial in its intricate stone-carved detail over the windows, doors, and facades, and with blooming gardens and flowering desert plants cascading down from the roof lines, the edifice magnificently captured both the architectural features of ancient Mesopotamia and the modern look of a headquarters of international power.

"We have many people to thank for this moment," Secretary Danburg addressed the audience from the microphone, "including, of course, our own President Tulrude, who has been a tireless advocate for global peace. But today we are here to recognize the vision of our celebrated guest of honor, Alexander Coliquin — not only the recently installed secretary-general of the United Nations, but a man of incredible vision and talents. Whether we're talking about his genius in successfully orchestrating the world's currency, the CReDO, to steady the money markets, or his work in bringing peace and stability right here in war-torn Iraq, so that this project would be possible, or his labors in fighting global warming, Alexander Coliquin — who I consider a friend as well as a colleague — is truly a treasure for our planet. Without further ado — I give you Secretary-General Alexander Coliquin."

Coliquin shook hands with Danburg and received the huge ceremonial scissors that he would use shortly to cut the blue ribbon stretched across the arched marble gate that lead to the front portico of the main building. The secretary-general held the scissors in one hand and paused to wave with his other to the crowd that was already on its feet.

"Thank you," he said, closing his eyes momentarily and nodding to their ovation. Then he began speaking. "These scissors will soon cut the tape to inaugurate the opening of the new Global Center for Peace and Prosperity — a personal dream of mine and, I know, of you good people as well. But there is something I would rather cut with these giant scissors — the chains of ignorance, oppression, poverty, and injustice that still plague our world. With the help of the international community and with the blessings of sacred and holy God, we will do exactly that."

As the audience thundered their response, Brian Forship, seated toward the back of the audience, texted a quick message on his Allfone back to Faris D'Hoestra, his boss in Belgium.

Coliquin has just started. Will livestream his comments to you via my Allfone.

A minute later the response came back from Belgium.

I know this man well. Keep your eyes open. Watch for vulnerabilities. Coliquin has them, I assure you. Advise ASAP.

TH1RTEEN

Wichita, Kansas

Special Agent Ben Boling stood in the field, staring at the decomposed body in a shallow ditch. There, on the outskirts of Wichita, the FBI agent took one more look at the grisly scene, then made a puffing noise as he exhaled and stepped back. Not a fun day.

When Agent Boling had received the call from the local police, he drove straight through central Kansas, down I-135 to his destination. It was a dismal drive. With the multiple-year drought, the state had dissipated into drifting dust and sweeping winds. Miles of agriculture had been destroyed. The nation's "breadbasket" had become a near desert of wheat fields, turned a brittle brown by the sun and the unending drought. Their watering systems simply couldn't keep up.

Many farmers had simply walked away from their foreclosed farms. Several of them, in different parts of the state, had swung a rope over the rafters of their barns, tightened a noose, and hanged themselves. Since the banks couldn't sell the land, it lay in ruins. Agent Boling had noticed a lot of drifters on the road with backpacks. These were not college-aged hikers getting close to nature or going on a quest to find themselves. Several of them were middle-aged, with worn, sad faces. Some had their worldly possessions piled high on bicycles as they trudged down the highway.

Boling had two thoughts. The first was really a question — *even in bankruptcy, don't they let you keep one vehicle at least?* But he knew the answer: *Yeah, but you still need money for gas, insurance, repairs . . .*

The second thought was a flashback to the old black-and-white movie he saw as a kid. *This is* The Grapes of Wrath. *Only bigger.*

After Boling had finished examining the corpse, he stepped over to the deputy in charge of the investigation. "You're sure about the ID?"

"Yep. Perry Tedrich. Local guy. Thirty-five. Divorced. The culprit did a nice job of stripping the body of any identification. Even cut the skin out on the back of his hand where he had his BIDTag laser imprint. But they missed one thing ..."

"What's that?"

"For some reason, the victim kept his gym membership card in his shoe."

"You sure about his political connections?"

"Absolutely," the deputy said, "he was the city campaign manager for Wichita's Hewbright for President Campaign."

"Coroner been here yet?"

"She showed up an hour before you got here. Doubted if we're going to get a definitive cause of death, considering the state of the corpse. They're sending someone to collect the remains so she can do an autopsy, though she might be able to get a fix on an approximate DOD, estimating the month of death at least. That's what she said anyway."

Boling flipped his daybook open and scribbled some notes.

"I thought you guys were high-tech and everything," the deputy said with a smirk. Then he pulled out his electronic Police Data Pad and displayed it. "Everybody in our department's using these."

"Sure," Boling shot back, "real neat way for headquarters to keep tabs on your investigation. I have one of those too. Routine issue for every agent at the Bureau. They log your notes as you write them into the master computer back at headquarters. I don't use it."

"How come? They sure work for us."

"That's the point. They work too well."

The deputy screwed up his face for a moment, then shrugged. "Well, we'll keep you informed."

"Better than that. If you really like being all digital, then why not email me a data file of everything you have on Perry Tedrich?"

"Sure — we can do that."

Boling thanked him and trotted back to his car.

As he put his finger to the imprint starter on the steering wheel and the engine started, he flipped his daybook open to what he had just written. He plucked the ballpoint pen from his top pocket and underlined the part that read: "Hewbright for President."

Denver, Colorado

Abigail Jordan watched as Senator Hank Hewbright shook hands with a group of supporters who had come to the Convention Center to hear his speech. He was standing right outside the door to the greenroom suite assigned to his campaign staff.

From her seat inside the suite, Abigail could see Hewbright through the glass door. She had driven down from Hawk's Nest to hear him, with the intention of just slipping in and slipping out. But Bob Tripley, a Colorado lawyer and a Hewbright volunteer, recognized her and urged her to meet the senator personally.

Abigail tried to beg off, but the attorney was insistent. Abigail was afraid she'd be too much of a political lightning rod. If the press started snapping photos of her with Hewbright, wouldn't it be used to smear the candidate?

The senator breezed into the greenroom, followed by Abigail's lawyer friend and the national campaign manager.

"Senator," Attorney Tripley said, "this is someone I want you to meet, one of the sharpest lawyers I know." He opened his arm toward Abigail, who rose to her feet with her visitor tag dangling around her neck. Then he added, "Mrs. Abigail ..."

"No need for introductions," Hewbright said briskly, reaching out his hand. "Mrs. Jordan, it's a pleasure and an honor. We've never met before, but I know about you ... your courageous fight for this nation, the risks you've taken, and the trouble you've been through." The Colorado lawyer slipped away to talk with some of the staff as Hewbright continued, "And I've met your husband, of course. Unfortunately, a pretty formal setting back then. And highly charged. He was testifying on the Hill at our intelligence committee hearing about his RTS system."

"Yes, I remember. Josh told how fair and evenhanded you were."

"Thanks. Though confidentially, it looked like Senator Straworth was trying to slice him and dice him."

"Josh couldn't tell me details because it was a closed hearing, but it sounded rough."

Hewbright tossed her a smile that told her more than he could share in words. "On the other hand, Senator Straworth's bullying backfired. Let me just say that in that hearing Joshua was a tough customer, a tower of strength."

"That's my husband!" Abigail said. Then she shared her concern. "Senator, I'm a great admirer of yours and a strong supporter, but I was reluctant to meet with you. I don't want to hurt your chances. You know, guilt by association. I know this election is going to be vicious."

"We're ready for it," he said with a square-shouldered look that made Abigail smile. It reminded her of Joshua.

Hewbright signaled for her to accompany him to a quieter corner of the greenroom, which was filling up with chattering staffers, volunteers, and high-value campaign donors.

"How is Josh doing?" he asked.

"Holding strong. But we both hate being separated by oceans and continents. So hard ..."

"I've been briefed on this ridiculous case. It's an outrage."

"We still hope to get the whole thing dropped."

"And this rescue effort in North Korea. Really outstanding. I know the president is avoiding any mention of Josh, but my sources in the Pentagon said he was instrumental."

"He was in the thick of it. But he's safe now, thank God."

"When I'm president," Hewbright said. "Josh will be getting another medal for valor — from me this time."

Two women — Abigail assumed they were campaign workers — strode up to Hewbright, Styrofoam cups of coffee in hand. She knew the senator was scheduled to speak that morning at a technology convention in Las Vegas, which probably meant a redeye flight while the staff worked through the night on the plane. They were clearly pushing caffeine to keep up the pace.

The senator turned to introduce the women. "Mrs. Jordan, this is Zeta Milla, one of my foreign-affairs advisors. She may look young, but she's had lots of experience in the State Department," he said with a playful wink. "She recently left the State Department to come on board with my campaign. As a young girl she escaped from Cuba. Unfortunately, her parents didn't make it out alive, but she did — much to the benefit of my campaign. And America. I work closely with her."

The beautiful Cuban woman smiled warmly and grabbed Abigail's hand in both of hers and squeezed. "Like you," Zeta Milla said, "I am a lover of freedom."

Abigail, an admirer of fine jewelry, noticed the unique red sapphire ring in an unusual silver setting on Milla's index finger. "That's a beautiful ring," Abigail said.

Zeta glanced down at the huge diamond cluster on Abigail's own hand and nodded at it with a grin. "Thanks."

Then Hewbright turned to the other woman. "And here is my assistant campaign manager, Katrena Amid, a brilliant strategist and tough as nails."

Katrena gave Abigail a half nod and a tight-lipped smile. The woman seemed to size up Abigail. She looked uneasy. Then she handed a note to Hewbright. "Senator, here's that donor I mentioned to you. If you could give him a quick call, I think it would be beneficial."

"Well," Hewbright said, "duty calls."

He excused himself. With Hewbright out of the room, the donors and supporters started to drift out of the suite. Abigail followed.

As she made her way to her car in the parking ramp, Abigail was overcome by an oppressive feeling of dread. She struggled to describe it to herself. She should have been thinking about her flight to Washington, D.C., the following day with Cal or the new lead she would be pursuing in her husband's case. But she wasn't. Her mind was somewhere else.

Women's intuition? Or maybe spiritual discernment?

Whatever it was, Abigail found it hard to shake. She found herself seized by the fear that Senator Hank Hewbright was in danger. It was palpable. She had an inexplicable feeling of being trapped. As if she had been locked into an airless trunk.

When I get back to Hawk's Nest, she thought, *I need to check into something. Maybe it's nothing . . . but I can't take the risk. I can't ignore this.*

FOURTEEN

Fair Haven Convalescent Center, Bethesda, Maryland

"So, Cal, your mother's doing well?"

Cal Jordan nodded politely. He was still coming to grips with the fact he was sitting across from the former first lady of the United States. A guy who looked like a Secret Service agent was posted just outside the lavish sunroom with its curved wall of glass and its view of the trees and gardens outside. This was all too surreal. Cal had racked his brain to sort out the reason behind this meeting but couldn't get to first base. He asked himself, *Why me?*

He did have one guess. A little more than two years earlier, before the president's health problems, Corland had made a dramatic turn in his policies, much to the chagrin of his vice president, Jessica Tulrude. As part of that reversal, President Corland had decided to honor Joshua at the White House for his bravery in foiling the terrorist-led hostage plot the year before at New York's Grand Central Terminal. Perhaps that was the point of connection—particularly because Cal himself had been the hostage, handpicked by the terrorist in an unsuccessful effort to pressure Joshua into giving up his RTS design plans.

But now that his dad had been exiled from the United States, Cal wondered whether Corland wanted him to be a messenger to his father—or to the Roundtable—or both.

Cal responded to Mrs. Corland. "My mother's in Washington on legal business today. I tagged along. I'm glad I was close so I could stop in to see you and the president."

He thought back to the warning in Mrs. Corland's email that he was to keep their meeting secret. He hadn't even told his mother. Abigail was meeting with a lawyer in downtown D.C. that day. Ordinarily, she would have included him, but since this meeting was particularly sensitive, Abigail had explained that she had to keep Cal out of it. Before they went their separate ways, Cal only told Abigail that he would be "nosing around town, checking the sites." Cal had formulated a lame justification in his mind — meeting with a former president and first lady — they were political monuments of sorts, weren't they?

Rising from her chair, Winnie Corland smoothed her dress. "Well, I will leave you two alone. Virgil is insistent that he speak with you privately."

Cal rose as well. As he shook her hand, she gave him some last words of instruction. "Virgil communicates better some days than others," she said. "But even if he can't tell you everything on his mind ... his heart ... I am sure he appreciates having the company."

She walked out of the brightly lit sunroom. Now it was just Cal and the former president, who was seated in a wheelchair. He was the same man who had once run the country, but he was pale now and thin, his eyes listless.

After a few moments of silence, Cal started the conversation. "I am honored to meet you, Mr. President."

Corland took at least half a minute before it looked like he registered. Then he nodded slowly.

"My father speaks highly of you," Cal added.

Only a blank stare from Virgil Corland.

Cal kept talking. "My dad is Joshua Jordan. He told me about meeting you at the White House, the day that you gave him the Medal of Honor."

Something in what Cal said, or maybe something else, a random memory perhaps, generated a look of urgency, almost desperation, on Corland's face. He spoke, hesitantly, with an athletic kind of effort to each word, "I was president once ..."

"Yes, that's right."

But Corland shook his head, as if trying to move the conversation away from the cordial and superficial. "Vice President …," he strained to say.

"Yes, Mrs. Tulrude was vice president then, before she stepped into your shoes … into the Oval Office … when you had your health problems."

"No, no," he groaned.

Cal feared that he may have upset him.

Then Corland looked up at his young guest. "Never had … a son."

"You didn't?"

Corland shook his head slowly. "Your father. Got the medal. New York …"

"Yes, for saving me in New York. Right. The terrorist who had kid-napped me — "

"But you … too … you too," he said. There was a twisted, labored attempt at a smile on Corland's face. "You … brave too … like your father."

"I was just the victim …," Cal said.

"No. No. I read … the … reports … FBI." Then Corland added, "Brave," and when he said that word, he lifted his right hand and pointed a limp finger right at Cal's chest and gathered up an earnest expression. "Brave," he said again. Then Corland took a deep breath as if he were going to swim underwater. "Tulrude. What happened … no, oh no." But he ran out of breath. His head dropped to one side, as if a string had been cut.

The day nurse from the other side of the room quickly made her way over to Corland. "I think, young man, that the president has had enough for today. He's still quite fragile."

Cal reached over and rested his hand on the wrinkled hand of the former president and said good-bye. As he turned to leave, Cal heard three words, barely audible, from Corland's dry lips.

"Come … back … again."

Clyde's Restaurant, Georgetown, Washington, D.C.

Abigail stirred her Cobb salad with a fork. She wasn't hungry, but she had to go through the motions — the perfunctory professional lunch — to wrangle this meeting with Harley Collingwood, the lawyer now sitting across from her.

Since both had been trial attorneys in D.C., they swapped stories about arguing cases in the District. Collingwood said he knew about her work in Harry Smythe's prestigious law firm and had heard secondhand about her being a top-tier litigator. They exchanged law-school jokes, keeping everything light, amiable.

Eventually Collingwood pushed his plate away and said, "Okay, Abigail, I know you didn't come all the way to D.C. for a nice salad, some chit-chat, and to exchange law-practice war stories with me." She let him continue. "Here's what I think," he said. "I think you found out I just left the Department of Justice and know I was on the prosecution team, going after your husband in his criminal case. So here you are ..."

Abigail kept a pleasant, interested, but nonplused look on her face. She let him go on.

"And," he said, "you'd probably love it if I were to slip you some helpful information about your husband's case."

She was silent for a moment, then asked a simple but disarming question. "Have you found work?"

"Of course," Collingwood shot back.

"Which firm?"

He hesitated. "Consulting for a few different offices. I'm picky."

"In other words," Abigail said with steely calm, "you have not found steady work since you voluntarily left your position at the DOJ, where you were the second highest assistant attorney general in the criminal division. Harley, my point is, you'd been handpicked by Attorney General Cory Hamburg himself, and you left all that — voluntarily — so you could be picky in looking around for other employment?"

Collingwood stiffened. "My law practice is really none of your business."

"True," she said, "but justice is. And so is the truth. If I know anything about you, the truth is your business too. You're regarded as one of the most aggressive prosecutors in Washington — and one of the most ethical. I need your help. My guess is that you discovered something rotten in the prosecution of my husband — so rotten that it led you to report it to DOJ's Office of Professional Responsibility." The former prosecutor was stone-still, listening. Abigail continued, "But knowing what I do about Attorney General Hamburg and his deference to the Tulrude administration, I'm betting he made sure that OPR stuck your ethics complaint in the permanent out basket. Which put you in a real dilemma."

Collingwood still didn't move a muscle.

"Now that you're out of the DOJ, either you can keep what you know to yourself and see an innocent man — my husband — hunted down around the globe for the rest of his life by federal authorities and railroaded with phony criminal charges ... and maybe you could salve your conscience by saying that by your silence you're actually protecting DOJ's privilege of lawyer's confidentiality. Or else, and here's the kicker, you will actually have to *do* something about what you know — tell someone — someone who can take your information and do what ought to be done. For justice and for truth."

Abigail looked Harley Collingwood squarely in the eye. "Have I stated the matter accurately, counselor?"

FIFTEEN

In the Desert of Southern Israel, Near Eilat

Joshua's mind had been fixed like a metal rivet on the test he had just witnessed at the IDF weapons site. His RTS system had failed. Again. Not that it hadn't reversed the test missile and sent it back to its point of launching. The problem was, for some reason, it had not captured the guidance system in the nosecone completely, so that the ground crew could manipulate its flight and send it in new directions. He had already been on the phone with Ted, his senior engineer at the Jordan Technologies headquarters in Manhattan, trying to work out the glitch.

"Don't worry," Ted assured him, "we'll get the kinks out."

"Without three-sixty capture of the guidance systems of incomings," Joshua said, "we'll be slaves to any bad guys who launch from civilian areas, knowing that we wouldn't send missiles back to a spot where they would wipe out innocent people."

Joshua rode away from the test site, jostled in the Jeep driven by Colonel Clinton Kinney, his close buddy from the Israeli Defense Forces.

Soon Kinney took a turn in another direction, away from Jerusalem. After a few minutes he pulled to the side of the road and turned off the engine. Joshua realized why.

Kinney pointed to a stretch of desert across the highway. Joshua nodded without saying a word. He momentarily forgot the failed missile test and everything else. For him, now, it was all coming true. Right in front of him. He was a witness to the unfolding of something incredible.

From the Jeep, Joshua saw hundreds of bearded Orthodox Jews in the distance, in neon green vests, carrying boxes and plastic bags as they wandered the surface of the desert. They were bent over, searching the rough terrain that had recently been made so ruthlessly jagged, filled with volcanic pumice, huge charred boulders, and caverns that had ripped through the ground.

An uninformed visitor might simply have said the land looked ravaged by the recent massive, unprecedented volcanic eruptions and earthquakes — so-called *natural* events. But to the Orthodox who were scouring the land for the human remains of their enemies so that they could arrange the burials — and in fact, for almost every citizen of Israel — it had been a supernatural miracle brought forth by the hand of God.

"What are they called?" Joshua asked, pointing to the men who were collecting the last remains of dead Russian and Turkish soldiers, as well as Sudanese and Libyan.

"They're part of the ZAKA — a group of Orthodox Jews who for years take on the job of cleaning up the bodily remains after disasters and terrorist bombings. To keep the land ceremonially clean. But this is the largest job they've ever had — or will ever have."

As Joshua surveyed the scene, his mind traveled back. He himself had been caught in the thick of that war, on the border of Israel, just on the other side from Syria when it happened. He remembered how the Russian-Islamic coalition had swept down from the north against the tiny nation of Israel like a rolling storm. At the same time they came up from the south through the Sinai Desert, with their hundreds of thousands of troops, tanks and mobile missile launchers, and hundreds of jets launched from the Russian aircraft carriers anchored off the coast in the Mediterranean.

The invasion looked unstoppable. The IDF headquarters was bracing for a fight to the death, and Israel's military commanders were convinced that all was lost.

Then the unimaginable had occurred. The earth itself rocked, cracked open, and exploded with a force greater than multiple megaton nuclear detonations.

Joshua had been there, an eyewitness to the awesome display of divine intervention. How could he not believe that this was the long-promised reckoning?

Colonel Kinney eyed the scorched wilderness. "Now that you're a believer in the prophecies and promises of the Bible," he said, "you have to admit ... this is an incredible sight."

"I know," Joshua said, shaking his head, "I was there. Saw it all. Felt it. And barely survived it. Fire in the sky, tremors in the earth. Everything God predicted in Ezekiel 38 and 39, when He described thousands of years ago how he would vanquish the Russian-Islamic invasion of Israel. And that's exactly what happened. And I lived through it to tell the tale." After a moment, Joshua continued. "And then this," he said, pointing to the ZAKA, "just one more proof ..."

"Ezekiel 39:12," Kinney replied. Then he recited it from memory. " 'For seven months the house of Israel will be burying them in order to cleanse the land.' "

"And by my calendar, we're now in the seventh month, aren't we?" Joshua asked.

Kinney nodded and touched his finger to the ignition pad on the steering wheel. The Jeep's engine fired up. "I'm one of those rare things in the IDF — a Jewish follower of Jesus Christ the Messiah — Yeshua ... though there are more of us since all this happened," he said, pointing to the landscape where volcanic cones rose from the desert floor in the distance. He turned toward highway 90 to head north, first along the Dead Sea and then to Jerusalem. Kinney added, "It's nice to be able to talk about this with someone who understands." Then he asked, "Your young protégé, Ethan March, he'll be waiting for us where we dropped him off ... back at the bottom of Masada?"

"Right. He wanted to hike to the top. Knowing Ethan, he'll do the whole thing at a jog. The guy's a terrific athlete."

Kinney glanced over at Joshua. "Okay, so, you said you had a high-level political question to ask me. Fire away."

"Prime Minister Benksy ..."

"What about him?"

"How well do you know him?"

"Only casually," McKinney replied. "I'm just a colonel, not a general. I don't sit in on security meetings. Just the operational stuff. On the other hand, this is a small country. Everyone knows something about everyone."

"Gotcha."

Kinney shot another look at Joshua as they picked up speed on highway 90. "Okay, what gives?"

"I've got a theological question, which is also a philosophical one, so I need you to put on your philosopher's hat for a moment."

"That's interesting," Kinney said with a smile. "You're a former test pilot and a spy-plane hero for the U.S. Air Force, with an engineering degree from MIT and a defensive-weapons designer of some of the most advanced hardware and laser gadgets any military could ask for. You're one of the bravest guys I've ever met ... and one of the brightest. But in a mechanical kind of a way. You're a hyperadvanced sort of technical fix-it guy, an action hero, Mr. Wizard with laser shields. But frankly, not exactly the philosopher type."

Joshua smiled. "Take away all the superlatives, and I'd say you had me nailed." Then his face dropped and his eyes fixed on some unseen point on the horizon. "There's a time and a season for everything."

"So, ask your question," Kinney said.

"As followers of Jesus Christ, we believe in the Scriptures. And as one of the few Jewish followers of Jesus in the IDF, you can appreciate that."

"Sure. Psalm 119 reminds us of that. And several verses in the New Testament."

"And that includes the prophecies foretold by God," Joshua added.

Kinney nodded. "Absolutely. First epistle of Peter, chapter one, says the Spirit of Christ moved within the Old Testament prophets and they 'predicted the sufferings of the Messiah and the glories that would follow.' The first chapter of the book of Revelation says, 'Blessed is the one who reads aloud the words of this prophecy, and blessed are those who hear it and take to heart what is written in it, for the time is near.' So, yes, I think followers of Christ need to study the *whole* counsel of God in the Bible, prophecy included."

Joshua chuckled. "Remind me not to play Bible Trivia with you."

Kinney smiled. "Okay, out with it. What's up?"

"What if you know that God has foretold something and told us clearly in Scripture that it's going to occur? You would consider that an expression of His sovereign will, right?"

"Agreed."

"Unchangeable."

"Correct."

"We accept it?"

"You mean as in — don't take any action that opposes it?"

"Right," Joshua bulleted back. "Let's say that something evil, horrendous, is about to happen, and God inspires His prophets to predict that very thing, thousands of years ago in Scripture. And suddenly, you start to see it unfolding — right in front of you. But you have the opportunity, within your sphere of power, to try and stop it, this nightmare. And you are in a situation at the epicenter of converging events to do something about it. So the question is this — do you take that chance?"

Kinney shot back. "You're still hedging. I've never known you not to get to the point, Josh. What's going on in your head right now?"

"You've seen the news, about the United Nations negotiations with the Bensky administration?"

"Sure, more peace proposals."

"Well, along those lines, Joel Harmon contacted me recently."

"The fighter pilot from the Knesset?"

"Right."

"Contacted you about what?"

"He's a member of a coalition party, the Hamonah. You know, I've heard of the other political parties over here: Likud, Kadima, Shas, Labor. But not that one, until Harmon got hold of me."

"That's because it's new. Just formed after the dust settled from our recent war — the one they're calling the War of Thunder ..."

"Yeah, I heard that."

Kinney nodded. "… After the verse in first Samuel, chapter two. 'Those who oppose the Lord will be broken. The Most High will thunder from heaven.' Anyway, this new political party was named Hamonah based on the verse in Ezekiel about the cleansing of the land. So, Joel Harmon talked to you?"

"We met once. He told me he's leading the effort to stop Bensky from going along with this U.N. initiative being pushed by Secretary-General Alexander Coliquin."

"And he's enlisted you," Kinney remarked with a studied look on his face. "Smart move. You're a national hero to a lot of folks-in-the-know here. Your RTS system averted a nuke attack from Iran. They *ought* to love you. So what's the problem?"

"He wants me to be present when he and his political group meet with Bensky, to convince him to reject the U.N. deal."

Kinney thought for a moment. "Okay, here's another verse for you — Psalm 119:46 — 'I will speak of your statutes before kings and will not be put to shame.'"

"Great verse. Only one problem. For me, it's not a matter of shame."

"Then what?"

"Fear."

"You've got to be kidding. You? Afraid of the prime minister of Israel?"

"No. Something else."

"What?"

"God."

Kinney fell silent.

Joshua explained. "I don't want to do anything that would go against God's sovereign plan. I don't want to get in the way. There's something dark and evil coming. It's almost here. I'm not talking politics or international policy. It's much different. We both know that. Something more monstrous than anything the world has ever witnessed. And for the first time in my life, I feel paralyzed. Conflicted. Undecided which way to turn. I'm afraid of making a colossal mistake — of biblical proportions."

Then he motioned toward the huge boulders on the desert floor on the other side of the highway that were covered with a thick layer of volcanic lava from the recent upheaval of the earth.

"I feel like I'm turning to stone."

SIXTEEN

Tel Aviv, Israel

Prime Minister Solomon "Sol" Benksy was seated at his usual place at the head of the long conference table. The security cabinet was there, along with the chief legal counsel and the head of economic advisors. The meetings were always lively, occasionally combative, but in a cordial kind of way. Today, however, the gloves were off.

Normally the meeting would take place at the NSC headquarters at Ramat Hasharon. But on Thursdays, following long-established custom, the prime minister always conducted his business at the IDF compound in Tel Aviv, in the conference room just down the hall from the big bronze bust of David Ben Gurion.

The secretary raised her voice above the din, trying to quiet the argument that was in full swing.

"Ladies and gentlemen, attention, please. We will now hear, once again, the short executive summary of the proposal — "

But the head of counterterrorism wouldn't quit. "You call that offer from the United Nations a *proposal*? I call it a Trojan horse!"

Prime Minister Bensky stepped in. "Please, everyone, quiet. Bring yourselves to order. Mrs. Kiryas, read it."

The NSC secretary proceeded to read aloud from the government bulletin: " 'Summary of the communiqué from the secretary-general of the United Nations, the most Honorable Alexander Coliquin, to the Honorable Prime Minister Solomon Bensky. Key Points. Number one.

The Temple Mount plateau in Jerusalem shall be divided according to those coordinates on the attached addendum 6, with the Islamic Waqf Trust to continue its current control over the Al Aqsa Mosque and the Dome of the Rock in that portion marked "section A," and with the Nation of Israel to possess the right and title and full control over "section B," on the Temple Mount, including but not limited to the right of Israel to construct sacred buildings, synagogues, or a temple for worship — ' "

The chief of security policy interrupted. "We have concerns about the accuracy of the measurements necessary for any kind of Jewish construction on the Temple Mount. We need to avoid a violent reaction later from the Muslims over that. After all, they've had possession of that plateau for a long time. They're not going to give any of it lightly."

But the head of foreign policy stopped him. "We've been in touch with the IAA, our antiquities experts, as well as geologists, engineers, surveyors — all of them tell us that if you take that one-million-square-foot plateau on the Temple Mount, and you take the U.N.'s measurements, and look at their attached diagram, it certainly looks to all of us that the section they're giving us would be more than ample for the construction — "

A voice boomed from the corner, "*Giving* us?" It was the chief rabbi for the city of Jerusalem. "Did you say the U.N. is *giving us* a section of the Temple Mount? That's blasphemy! The Most High King of the Universe — He is the one who gave it to us. The *whole* of the Temple Mount. It is only because of our cowardice and lack of faith that we have not resolved this issue long ago."

Prime Minister Bensky jumped in. "Gentlemen and ladies, please. Let's not argue over semantics. The point here is that the United Nations, and, I might add, the Palestinian Authority and the entire Arab League of Muslim nations — they have all supported this proposal. And President Tulrude is an enthusiastic advocate for this approach, as well as the entire U.N. security council. This is historic ... the opportunity to take control of a large segment of the Mount. And as our chief of foreign policy was about to describe, the construction ..."

The prime minister paused and lifted his hands up for just a half second, enough for the Rabbi to intervene.

"Construction of our Temple," the rabbi pronounced with the passionate tone of an epiphany, "the central place for holy worship on Mount Moriah, to become the epicenter of all Judaism, after two thousand years of waiting." Then with eyes half closed and hands outstretched he said, "Finally, in my lifetime, it may yet come to pass ..."

"With all deference to our chief rabbi," the security-policy leader added, "there is the reality of the secular, nonreligious segment of the Israeli population. To them, the rebuilding of the Temple on the Mount may have some historical and cultural interest, of course, but it will certainly *not* be a religious priority."

The prime minister's economic advisor tapped his pen on the table. "You are forgetting two things. First, the construction of the Temple would not only be a religious, historical, and cultural event, it would also be an economic benefit of monumental proportions. My staff has already done the calculations. Tourism would double in the first twelve months and increase exponentially each year thereafter. The construction effort alone would be a tremendous asset to our economy in terms of job creation, both primary and secondary employment, and contract labor. We have estimated that international nonprofit groups, many of them religious, would contribute up to sixty percent of the building costs. And then there is the second point: increased internationalization of Jerusalem through this peace plan will actually *lessen* the risk of violence in Jerusalem."

Prime Minister Bensky jumped on that. "This is why I am in support of this proposal." He looked directly at his scowling chief of counterterrorism as he continued, "The Palestinians and the Arab League are calling for the cessation of hostilities against Israel in the future as part of this plan. And look at point number two in the Coliquin proposal—the United Nations becomes a permanent board of mediation on any disputes within Jerusalem. By agreeing with the U.N. plan, we put on the white hats. We are the good guys. We start winning back much of the esteem that we have lost over the last few decades in the international community."

The chief of counterterrorism was not convinced. "I am not as concerned about what color our hats are as I am about the explosive belts and missile launchers that some of our enemies will be carrying. This plan does nothing for my concerns — except to invite the United Nations to exercise control over the nation of Israel."

"And yet," the prime minister's female media advisor added, "the polling data tells us something different. The majority of Israelis want a peace plan. Even with the miraculous victory we just won against the Russian-Islamic invaders, our citizens are tired … tired of war, tired of waiting for their cell phone to ring, wondering if a loved one has just been blown up in a bus attack or in an explosion at a sidewalk café. Fatigue and fear, ladies and gentlemen — those are powerful emotions. And they are powerful political realities."

On the Top of Masada, Near the Dead Sea

"I still can't believe we ran into each other." Ethan smiled at the athletic and attractive Rivka, who was dressed in hiking shorts, with a water bottle dangling from her belt. They were both looking out from a spot near the ancient ruins on top of the sandy plateau down to the desert floor far below. Then he added, "First, that planning meeting in South Korea, and now here, at this spot, with you, actually hiking and taking it easy."

"Why does that surprise you?" she asked. She had a mischievous smile.

"Okay, look, I'm former military myself, so I understand downtime, and furloughs …"

"But you just don't picture people like me taking time off, is that it?"

"Maybe, yes. Military is one thing. But your outfit, Israeli's spy shop — the Mossad — "

"Who told you that's where I work?" she said with a sudden flash of anger. "I work as a clerk in the statistics department of the IDF."

Taken aback, Ethan studied the athletic, pretty Israeli woman. Then he noticed a flicker of another smile. "Okay," he said, "now you're playing with me. So, are you or aren't you? I suppose you can't say anyway, even though you and I were both in that North Korean deal together — or, well, actually you were, I was just sitting back in South Korea with my hands in my pockets. Though I wondered why Israel was involved in that deal in the first place."

She dodged his first question, about which agency signed her paychecks, but she answered the second one. "The last few years, Israel and South Korea have become very close diplomatically. We have more in common than meets the eye."

"Like?"

"They send a high number of tourists to Israel each year, and, like Israel, they have learned to live their lives under the shadow of enemies who are very close. And then there is the matter of our past historic alliances with the United States."

"*Past historic*? You're making a point, I take it?"

"American foreign policy is different now and impacts both Israel and South Korea in similar ways. Your country used to be smart about picking its allies, and even smarter about choosing its friends. Things have changed considerably."

Rivka shrugged off that topic and took a step toward the edge of the high plateau, looking out over the desert. "So, you're here in Israel with Colonel Jordan?"

"Always glued to his side."

"But not right now?"

"Well, almost always. I get some free time."

"I'm glad for that," she said with a smile. She pulled out a water bottle and uncapped it. She raised it to her lips, but instead of drinking from it, she gave it a shake in Ethan's direction and playfully splashed water on his face, and they both laughed loudly. Rivka took an extra T-shirt from her belt, pulled it out, and dabbed the water from his face.

Ethan took a long look at Rivka, all five feet six inches of her, as she grinned back at him. And he thought how things seemed just a little bit bizarre at that moment. It was almost laughable.

Is this woman who's flirting with me really the same Rivka I met in Seoul? The same one Josh said had kicked a North Korean guard into unconsciousness?

Apparently she was.

They started the steep climb down from the high cliffs of Masada, the place where the ancient stone walls and crumbled structures testified to the siege that took place there two thousand years before — the last desperate stand of the Jewish rebels against the legions of the Roman Empire. As Ethan and Rivka began to hike down to the desert floor, Ethan had another thought. *Okay, Rivka, let's see where you and I go from here.*

SEVENTEEN

Baden-Baden, Germany, Emperor Hadrian Hotel, Headquarters of the Order of World Builders

Faris D'Hoestra adjusted his steel-gray glasses with two fingers and maintained his expression of calm satisfaction. The session was progressing well.

He had traveled from Brussels, where the largest of his mansions and office complexes were located, to attend the quarterly meeting of the Order of World Builders — or simply "The Builders," as its members referred to it — and to preside as its permanent chairman.

The fifty members were seated around a mahogany table on the top floor of the hotel — the entire level of which had been reserved for the Builders on a hundred-year lease. Four similar leases stretched back to the eighteenth century, when the hotel was founded, but the history of the Builders went back much farther than that.

D'Hoestra's last motion had been carried unanimously, just like all the others that day.

Now for the last one.

The secretary of the Builders read it aloud — and it was moved and seconded — that "action be taken immediately to circumscribe and limit, by any means necessary, the international authority of the office of secretary-general of the United Nations, while creating an alternative international organization that shall be more receptive to the membership and influence of the Order of World Builders."

A small red light on the polished table, directly in front of one of the attendees, lit up.

D'Hoestra called on the deputy prime minister of India.

"Mr. Chairman," the Indian representative said, "I question the wording of the phrase 'circumscribe and limit.' You want to reign in the power of the office of the secretary-general when in actuality, you want to reign in the charismatic secretary-general himself, Mr. Alexander Coliquin, perhaps even to depose him. Am I correct?"

Several heads were nodding.

"I'll answer that," D'Hoestra said. "Because each of us pledged to keep these proceedings secret, as has been our honored tradition, and each of us understands the consequences that come with any violation of that pledge, I can be candid." D'Hoestra stood up from his executive chair and began to stroll slowly around the circumference of the mammoth table. "Mr. Coliquin has played the game of global chess quite well, squaring nations off against nations, constructing international coalitions behind the scenes to do his bidding. And he possesses what no prior secretary-general has ever had before — a lock-grip over the U.N. Security Council, including having Madam President Tulrude at his beck and call. A singular, titular head of global power like this — resting in the person of one man — is simply not good for the future world order. It is certainly not good for us. It is ruinous for the Builders. Our heritage stretches back through the annals of time. Yes, Coliquin must be dealt with. Quickly and decisively."

Another red bulb lit up. Lord Raxtony, an English Lord from the Royal Society, was leaning forward to speak. D'Hoestra recognized him. "Yes, well, if I may, this raises, rather well, I think, the problem I see with the other phrasing in your motion. You say we will limit Mr. Coliquin 'by any means necessary.' There is an implication there, clearly, that we will limit him without regard for any moral or legal limits. It has, Mr. Chairman, been a rather long time since this body has been asked to authorize the use of extreme sanctions."

D'Hoestra motioned to Deter Von Gunter, the controlling head of the large industrial and military armaments company the Von Gunter Group. He clearly wanted to address Lord Raxtony's comment.

"You accurately point out," Von Gunter said, his voice as smooth as warm honey, "that it has been a long time since extreme sanctions were authorized by this body. Those sanctions are called 'extreme' because they are exceptional and to be used sparingly." He paused. Then his voice suddenly jumped up a pitch, as he slapped his hands on the varnished table top. "But *extreme*, exceptional sanctions must sometimes be used! Is this not true? Otherwise we should call them *unusable* sanctions. Or *unimaginable* sanctions. Personally, I have tired of Mr. Coliquin and his antics. His international treaties entangle the world and have made life difficult for our companies — mine in particular. He is a wasp in our house. Let's get some bug spray and rid our houses of this bothersome pest."

D'Hoestra was surprised by Von Gunter, not by the outburst itself — which was typical of him — but by the degree of his passion. Then again, some intrigues obviously existed within Von Gunter's world that D'Hoestra could not possibly know about.

The chairman permitted the discussion to continue for another hour. He was in no rush. He could see the dynamics of the meeting slowly bending to his will.

In the end, although two members abstained, the rest of the World Builders voted in favor of the motion.

With his motion passed, Faris D'Hoestra adjourned the meeting. After a few pleasantries with the members, he had his driver take him to his palatial thirty-thousand-square-foot villa on the edge of the Black Forest, outside Baden-Baden. There he would be attended to by his staff of seventy. First, a soaking bath while music from a live baroque quartet in the drawing room would be piped down to his steam room. Then a massage, facial, and manicure from a bevy of female attendants. After that, a sumptuous banquet at which he would entertain six Hollywood celebrities, the president of a small island nation, a Nobel Prize winner, and a news anchor and his wife from the American Internet News Channel.

Finally, at the end of the evening, he would slip into his silk sheets. There, before drifting off to sleep to the scent of rose petals, he would contemplate his expanding empire. And Faris D'Hoestra would wonder at his place among the powerful Roman emperors like Hadrian, who had once trod those very same woods outside his villa.

EIGHTEEN

Manhattan

She shouldn't have been so stunned. After all, Abigail had reviewed the reporter's file once before. Yet there was that one little detail in those materials that she must have tucked away somewhere in her memory. Then it came back to her when she was in Denver, attending the Hewbright-for-President campaign event. Now that she was back in New York and had the big manila envelope in hand with all the documents, she checked it again — just to be sure. She had to be absolutely certain.

Now she was. It was right there in the photo — that unusual ring on Coliquin's finger. Her head was reeling. Abigail was seated on the wraparound couch in the living room of her Manhattan penthouse with her feet up on the coffee table. She normally would have taken time to gaze through the big windows and enjoy the sunset over New York. But not today. Not with what she had just seen in the file photo. She had been leafing through the unpublished article on Alexander Coliquin by the late Curtis Belltether, the eccentric online journalist, and his other materials. It was the same piece that had been mailed to AmeriNews and the Jordans by Belltether, apparently right before he was shot to death in his hotel room two years before. With a landslide of ever-breaking news to cover, the AmeriNews staff sat on the article. But then, when Coliquin was elected secretary-general of the United Nations, his nasty background suddenly became newsworthy.

Now, as Abigail poured over her copy of the dead journalist's notes and his draft article, and the photo, it all came back to her. She realized that the contents of the reporter's file had become important in ways she could not have imagined.

Just then, Deborah, who was in New York for the weekend, swung open the front door of the penthouse and announced herself. She strode into the room with Cal. She was slurping a huge plastic cup of soda.

"Well, howdy," Abigail called out, perking up a little. "How was the movie?"

"Pretty good," Cal said.

"Average," Deborah said, then added, "I'm jumping into the shower. I feel grubby."

Cal dumped himself down on the couch and looked at his mother hunched over the Belltether file.

"Homework?"

"Always."

"Dad's case?"

"In a way."

"That's a shocker!" Cal said sarcastically and gave a bright smile.

Abigail chuckled and set the file on the coffee table. "This might be tangentially related. It's the investigative report by Curtis Belltether."

Cal thought for a moment. "The reporter we talked about at the Roundtable meeting ... the one who was murdered?"

"Yep." Abigail nodded.

Cal studied his mother's face. She wasn't doing a good job of hiding her feelings. "Okay, Mom, what's up?" he asked.

She motioned to the file. "When I met with Senator Hewbright in Denver, something triggered a suspicion. So I did some digging on my computer when I got back to Hawk's Nest that night. Then I had even more suspicions. And then this. For me it was confirmation." She turned on the couch so she could look straight at Cal. "Every once in awhile in life you stumble across something, and once you see it, you can't get it out of your head. Something bad. Evil perhaps. And you know that once you see it, you can't just sit by like a passive observer, as if you're in a theater watching a movie. You have to do something. You have to take action."

"You've completely lost me ..."

"Senator Hewbright," Abigail said. "He's a good man. This country needs him as president. We discussed all this during the Roundtable."

"Right."

She chose her words cautiously. "I think he's in deep trouble."

"As in ..."

"Personal danger."

Cal thought for a few seconds. Then something registered on his face, and he quickly pulled out his Allfone. "Don't know if this has anything to do with it, but saw this blurb on AmeriNews."

"I confess," Abigail said, "I've been so busy I haven't had time to read it recently."

"I got you covered, Mom." Cal tabbed through the recent news releases until he found the article. He handed the device to his mother. "Here it is. Story out of Wichita. The head of Hewbright's campaign for that city was found dead. It's pretty clear it was murder."

"What is going on here? Two politically related murders. Things are definitely not right." Abigail read the article. When she was done, she turned to her son. "Cal, we need to get hold of John Gallagher. Immediately."

NINETEEN

Casper, Wyoming

John Gallagher was seated in a small roadside diner, reading the plastic menu. He knew what he really wanted to eat — blueberry pancakes slathered with real butter and real maple syrup, a large side of hash browns, a side of sausage links and bacon, and a breakfast steak, cowboy style.

But alas, that was pure fantasy. He was watching his weight. The waitress finished waiting on several fellows in jeans and cowboy hats, then sauntered over to Gallagher. "What's yer desire, darlin' — breakfast or early lunch?"

"My desire, darlin'," Gallagher cracked, "is a breakfast big enough to choke a horse. And this looks like the kind of place that could accommodate me. But instead, I'll take coffee, black, no sugar, and an English muffin, no butter, and sugar-free strawberry jam."

She jotted it down and threw him a smile. "Live long and prosper, city slicker."

Gallagher leaned toward the plate-glass window and took in the view of the North Platte River and the mountains in the distance. A moment later, the person he was scheduled to meet was standing next to the table.

FBI Agent Ben Boling reached down and shook Gallagher's hand.

"Sit down. I'll buy you some coffee and breakfast," Gallagher said.

Boling sat but shook his head. "Thanks, but I'm all caffeined up and had something to eat already."

"Not surprising. You strike me as an early riser, Boling."

"And you strike me as a nonriser."

Gallagher guffawed. "Gee, didn't think you knew me that well."

"Your reputation precedes you. So, how have you been since leaving the Bureau?"

"Well, how do you think I look?" he said, stretching his arms out to exhibit his slimmer torso.

"Honestly, Gallagher, I can't remember how you used to look. Remember, I didn't work counterterrorism with you guys in New York. I've always done the mundane stuff—kidnapping over state lines, murder, mayhem. A little fraud on the side."

"Well," Gallagher said, "I wouldn't call that mundane. Your investigation into the death of Perry Tedrich, Senator Hewbright's Wichita campaign manager, sounds an itsy-bitsy bit exciting."

"So, that's what this meeting is about?"

"Bingo. I'm doing some checking, a favor for some friends, people who care about Hewbright's health and personal safety."

"Like the FBI doesn't?"

"I didn't say that."

"So, let me guess. You're here at the behest of that bunch of gun-twirling vigilantes known as the Roundtable?"

"Ben, they're good people who've been given a bad rap."

"All I know is what I read in the Bureau's 302 reports."

"And you believe those?"

"Gallagher, I know you had a reputation as a maverick, bucking the system, pushing the boundaries. But don't expect me to trash the Bureau."

"'Course not. You got a kid in college and another in grad school. Rocking the boat doesn't make sense for you. You see, I've done my homework too."

"I'd be very careful. I could stand up and walk out of this place."

"I know you could, but I don't think you will."

"Why not?"

"Because as special agents go nowadays, you're one of the good ones. Staying on even though you're hamstrung by Tulrude's insane rules and restrictions. And even with Attorney General Hamburg turning the Bureau into a politically correct day camp, you've managed to stick it out and still do your job well — which makes us different."

"Oh?"

"Yeah. Because I was never smart enough to figure out how to do that. So I just left. But then again, for me it was time."

The waitress came with Gallagher's English muffin. When she left, Boling gestured to Gallagher's skimpy breakfast. "Pretty Spartan."

"My doc says I need to change my nutritional habits if I want to stay around for a while, which I definitely do. I've got some unfinished business."

"Like?"

"Helping you catch the person who's stalking Senator Hewbright right now ... and planning his death."

"You talk like that, and it makes my heart go all pitta-pat, makes me want to whip out my little pocket pad and start taking notes. After Miranda-izing you first, of course, seeing as you just inferred a threat against a candidate for the presidency of the United States."

"But you're not going to."

Ben Boling leaned back in the booth. "No, I'm not. Instead, I'm going to ask you what you know, and where you got the information."

"What I know is that there may be a risk to Hewbright from within his own campaign. And I got the tip from Abigail Jordan."

"Ohhh ...," Boling said, rolling his eyes. Then he added, sarcastically, "At least you've got a source that isn't controversial."

"She's top notch. Controversy doesn't mean she doesn't have credibility. I can't tell you details yet, but she has some strong suspicions, and I think she may be right on target. So the question is — do you want to save the senator?" Gallagher raised a toasted English muffin, shook his head with a sorrowful look as he examined it, and took a large bite.

Boling leaned forward and folded his hands on the table. "Okay. I need to trust you here. Which is probably my first mistake."

Instead of giving another smart-aleck zinger, Gallagher just listened as Boling continued.

"You probably figured out why I'm up here in Casper, Gallagher. Hewbright's Senate seat is from Wyoming. His local office is here in Casper. So I'm doing the obvious."

Gallagher offered his take on that. "Obvious as in, scrounging for leads among the locals from Hewbright's stomping ground. And as in, questioning Hewbright's local office for details on the campaign worker killed in Wichita?"

Boling smiled.

"Any leads?" Gallagher asked.

"Not yet. And if I had any, I couldn't tell you the gritty details. You're a civilian now, Gallagher. Sorry."

"And of course," Gallagher said nonchalantly, "you checked the records for the visitors to the Wichita campaign office where the victim worked. To see who, from Hewbright's circle of confidants, may have visited there shortly before Tedrich's disappearance?"

"Did you even consider the fact," Boling shot back, "that the murder may have been purely random — with no political connection to Hewbright's campaign at all?"

"Could be," Gallagher replied, "but I'd still check it out, people in — people out."

"Don't worry. The local police are already doing the spadework."

"I'd check it yourself. Real close. Find out who from Hewbright's national staff may have visited Tedrich unofficially right before he vanished."

Boling squinted. "I just might do that." Then he added, "So, Gallagher, I just have one question."

"Yeah?"

"What's Abigail Jordan's interest in all this?"

"Seems clear enough to me," Gallagher said with a shrug as he popped the rest of the English muffin into his mouth. When he was done and his mouth was empty, he wiped it with a napkin and then finished his thought.

"She wants to save America."

TWENTY

As she sat with her mother in the family's New York penthouse, Deborah Jordan felt particularly low. She had just realized that she was like her father in one way — she too could bury her hurt and pretend it wasn't there. But only for a while. Eventually it would come bubbling out. Like now.

Deborah had to admit her mother was right. "Okay. Sure. At the time, yes, I was devastated."

"I know you were, dear," Abigail said, "but what about now? How do you feel about Ethan?"

"I know it was the right thing to do," Deborah said. She was pensive but sure she was right. Outside, the night had fallen and the lights of the New York City skyline outlined the skyscrapers, as if they were studded with tiny blinking jewels.

Deborah rested her foot on her overnight bag, which was already packed on the floor in front of her. "I like Ethan," she said. "He's a good man ... just not the one for me. Since we broke up I've been absolutely convinced of that. But I owe him some contact. I want to find out how he's doing."

There was a flicker of a smile in the corner of Abigail's mouth. "Oh, he's probably been dragged into a world of trouble, considering that your father's his boss now ..."

Both of them burst into laughter.

Deborah reached out and rubbed her mother's hand. "You really miss Dad, don't you?"

"Honey, I ache for Josh. I know the Lord is allowing this for some reason. But it does hurt being away from him."

"I miss him too," Deborah said. "My constant prayer is that all of us — you, Dad, Cal, and I — can have a grand reunion sometime. Very soon, I hope."

"I feel in my heart it's going to happen. You may be too young to think this way — but I also feel this wonderful peace — about all of us being together with the Lord. Heaven is going to be the ultimate reunion."

"Lately you and Dad seem to be talking end-times stuff constantly. It's pretty clear you think things are rushing toward the last days, don't you?"

"I know some of the media coverage makes us look like we're running around crying that the sky is falling. But when God lays it out in the Bible, and you see the pattern of world events converging — lining up the way that Scripture describes — I think it would be wrong to keep quiet about it."

Deborah tapped the back of her mother's hand with her finger. "This," Deborah said, "is going to be a problem for you, Mom. I'm hearing all kinds of stuff at the Pentagon about how the feds are going after nontaggers. That's what they are calling you people who didn't get the BIDTag. On the other hand, there's something else ... maybe good news."

"What's that?"

"There's this guy, Tom Birdow, he works at DISA, the defense information agency. He's always stopping by my desk — "

"My daughter, the man magnet!"

Deborah tried not to smile but found it impossible. "Oh, you are such a mom ..."

"Alright, so this Tom guy ..."

"Yeah, he's always dropping tidbits of information about what's happening with the Security Identification Agency and Homeland Security regarding the BIDTag. Right before I came up here, he mentioned a possible amnesty program for nontaggers. President Tulrude shot it down, but Tom heard it may come up again."

Abigail smiled and looked out at the black sky and the twinkling lights of the city. "Don't worry about that, darling," she said to her daughter. "I won't be getting a BIDTag. That's all there is to it."

Deborah's eyes flashed like she wanted to pursue it, but instead, she switched to something else. "What were you and Cal talking about earlier — after we got home from the movie?"

"About some concerns of mine, about Senator Hewbright's campaign and the senator himself."

"Concerns ... like what?"

Abigail leaned over and pulled her daughter close. "My dear, have I told you lately how proud I am of your position at the Pentagon?"

Deborah rolled her eyes and smiled. "Nice dodge, Mom."

"No, not dodging. The fact is that you work in the Department of Defense. Given that, I have to be careful about the things I can share with you."

"Come on ..."

"I'm serious. I don't want to put you in a compromising position because of information you learn from me. You know, about the Roundtable. Things like that."

"So — you're shutting me out?"

"No. I'm protecting you."

"I still think that's a lame excuse, pardon my bluntness."

"Once in a while you remind me so much of your dad. Blunt is okay. Sometimes."

Abigail looked down at Deborah's overnight bag on the floor. "I'm sorry to see you leave, but you'd better get going so you can catch your cab to the station. The zip train isn't going to wait."

As Deborah stood up and gave her mother a long hug, Abigail whispered in her ear, "Who knows, dear, how God might use your position at the Pentagon."

Los Angeles, California

The banquet hall was filled with fourteen hundred campaign contributors, who had all given at least $20,000 apiece. In the soft glow of the crystal chandeliers that hung from the ceiling, President Tulrude was wrapping up her address to her party faithful.

The waitstaff hurried the plates from the table, careful not to intrude on the president's address. In the back of the room, one of the smiling waiters had his Allfone turned on video function and was holding it discreetly under a towel with the lens pointing at the president.

"And no one can deny," she said, "my impressive record on national security. Since my succession to the White House and the implementation of my BIDTag program, not a single act of terrorism has been perpetrated against this great nation. When I took over, we had domestic airplanes being shot at and a nuclear nightmare in New Jersey. Today we are safer than we have ever been. Terrorists like Anwar al-Madrassa and his ilk are on the run, hiding in their caves. We have them stymied because they cannot sneak their operatives across our borders. They can't have their thugs show up at airports, malls, public buildings, sports stadiums, or train stations — because if they do, our BIDTag scanners will pick them up. If they have been tagged, then we have access to their data. And if they haven't been tagged, our nation-wide scanners in every public place will alert us — so either way, in a heartbeat, we've got them!"

That provoked a standing ovation. It lasted a full minute. When the crowd finally returned to their seats, Tulrude continued, "We have answered the pundits who said my program wouldn't work. We have responded to the civil-liberties advocates — I know many of them personally and respect them — and the courts have upheld the constitutionality of my identification program. As for the fanatics who wail and moan about my bringing about the end of the world, wondering whether I have a 666 on my forehead ..." The room erupted in raucous laughter. "As for them," she continued, "if they say I'm the devil, well, then I say to hell with them!"

Gleefully, the audience rose again to their feet, laughing, shouting, and applauding wildly.

Islamabad, Pakistan

In a sparsely furnished apartment off Ibn-e Sina Road, the reigning terror king, Anwar al-Madrassa, was holding court. His three deputies sat on the floor in front of him. Madrassa was lounging on a worn couch next to a tea table, on which stood a tarnished brass hookah. The screen on Madrassa's personal laptop was illuminated. They had just finished watching a video on YouTube.

Madrassa smiled beneficently. "So, you all paid close attention to President Tulrude's remarks?"

The deputies on the floor nodded in unison.

"And what did you notice?"

One lieutenant offered a thought. "She is arrogant."

"Of course, of course," Madrassa said, brushing it off. "She is an American infidel."

Smiles and chuckles from the men on the floor.

Another deputy shouted out. "She is very proud of her BIDTag program."

"Ah, yes," Madrassa said, nodding, "boasting that there have been no attacks on her homeland since it began. What she does not know is that we take our time. And now, my beloved friends, that time has come."

He reached down to his laptop and tapped a corner of the screen, then waved his finger over the menu until two photographs appeared. Under each was a name in Arabic.

Madrassa explained, "I have been in touch with certain intermediaries. They, in turn, have been in contact with the highest political powers. You see? From this humble little apartment, Allah be praised, our influence has now reached all the way up to the meeting places of world leaders. By using their blind assistance, we will begin to mount our most dramatic campaign of all. The first stage is ready to begin. Would you like to see for yourselves who will be the first targets of our fiery retribution?"

The eyes of the men on the floor flashed.

Anwar al-Madrassa turned the screen so they could examine the faces. "Two infidel enemies of our most holy jihad have set themselves against us ... but not for long."

On the screen was a photo of a man and of a woman. Under the pictures were names.

Joshua Jordan. Abigail Jordan.

TWENTY-ONE

Haifa, Israel

From his position high on the exterior metal safety walkway of Israel's new energy facility, Joshua had a spectacular view of Haifa Bay and the azure waters of the Mediterranean. He could see flames shooting up from Israel's oil and gas platforms off the coast and the large blades of wind turbines that had been constructed along the shoreline.

His guide, Joel Harmon, one of Israel's rising political stars, had connected with Joshua a few days earlier. He had invited Joshua to join him on a tour of the Haifa energy reprocessing plant today. It was under tight security, but Harmon, with his credentials, was able to whisk his guest through the double gates guarded by armed security and onto the grounds of the facility without a problem.

Harmon nodded to the display of energy infrastructure that stretched out along the coast. "Israel has been blessed with energy resources and the advanced technology to develop them. But what I am about to show you now is the most startling resource of all. No one saw this one coming. Of course, when we were able to turn back that incoming nuke from Iran with your RTS system and it dropped on the Golan Heights for lack of fuel, we all had the same thought — to retrieve the thing before our enemies got their hands on it. Which we did. But then there was a second thought — get the nuclear material, the uranium and plutonium, out of the warhead. As you know, under Prime Minister Bensky we've been tied into treaties that prohibit us from developing defensive nuclear weapons. So, forget the military uses of the material."

"So you're using it for nuclear energy."

"Exactly," Harmon replied. He was pumped now, and Joshua saw it in his face. "As the newest member of the energy committee for the Knesset, I was all over that one. But this," Harmon said, pointing to the metal door next to them on the fourth-story entrance to the massive building, "this was the crème de la crème." He swung open the heavy door.

Inside, Joshua found himself on a metal catwalk several stories above the energy-processing operation. Below he could see a truck dumping a load onto a platform, with another right behind it in line.

Harmon explained, "When the invaders came at us two years ago, led by the Russian army, they were all using the hardware developed by Moscow. Very ingenious. Israel's military radar is usually very effective, but the Russians built troop carriers and missile launchers, even tanks, not out of metal — but with lignostone."

"Right," Joshua added, "super-compressed wood. I've followed the research for years. In fact, I personally saw a handgun made out of it back in Seoul ... at an uncomfortably close range. Impressive stuff."

"You bet. Hard as steel but easy to cloak from radar because the material absorbs the radar pulse rather than reflecting it back like metal does. That gave our enemies a considerable advantage when they placed their troops near our borders. The couple extra hours of antiradar cloaking gave them a huge head start." Harmon pointed to the truck down below. "After the war, when the dust cleared, we discovered we had our hands on massive amounts of lignostone. Tons and tons of it. The bright guys at the Technion Institute and several energy companies got to thinking — why not convert all this lignostone to combustible fuel?"

They walked along the catwalk, watching a load of scrap material being fed onto a conveyor belt that was moving it toward several grinding stations and then on to series of low-temperature furnaces. Joshua was already thinking about the remarkable fulfillment of a centuries-old biblical prophecy.

"The key here," Harmon said, "was to create a usable material that can fuel Israel's energy needs. So, how long do you think all of these lignostone armaments will provide energy for Israel?"

Joshua laughed. "Let me guess — seven years' worth of burnable energy, precisely. Exactly as predicted in the book of Ezekiel ..."

"Chapter 39, verses 9 and 10," Harmon added with a grin. "So, as I was saying, we've been burning this material for the last two years at this new facility and processing it into reusable energy cells. According to the Old Testament, we've got another five years of home heating left for Israel. Josh, you are a Christian, and I am a Jew. We have that between us. But we are joined by something important. We both revere the Bible as the Word of God."

"Yes, and something else."

"Oh?"

"We both believe in the Messiah and know that He's coming," Joshua said. "I know His name to be Yeshua — Jesus, the Christ. You, on the other hand, still have to figure out whether your Messiah's coming to this world will be His first time or His second."

Harmon chuckled and waved an index finger at Joshua. "A discussion to be continued later."

They walked down the metal stairs to the third level, where Joel Harmon led them to an elevator to the ground floor.

"The helicopter is waiting on the helipad," Harmon said as they walked outside. "Since you're an MIT grad and a world-class engineer, I figured you'd appreciate a tour of our facility here. Also, you're getting a peek at some good news about Israel's future."

Joshua thanked him as they rounded the corner of the massive building.

Harmon suddenly became somber. "Now for the tough part about our future. When you arrive in Jerusalem and meet with Prime Minister Benksy, you will find him surrounded by vipers."

"That's a pretty harsh assessment."

"I'm being frank. Bensky's a good man, but he's living under a geopolitical delusion, as if he's been bewitched by advisors who have sold him on this crazy plan of the U.N.'s secretary-general."

"I already have strong feelings about Coliquin."

"Sure," Harmon said shrugging, "I read the quote in the *Jerusalem Herald* where you called Coliquin 'an impressive voice full of reason, hope, and peace, but with an agenda straight from hell.' And you call *me* harsh!" Joel Harmon capped it off with a snicker.

Joshua gave him a befuddled look. "Joel, that's why I questioned your decision to have me join you and the members of your Hamonah party when you meet with Bensky this afternoon. I'm nothing but a lightning rod."

"So maybe we need a lightning strike." After a moment, Harmon added, "Look, Josh, whether you like it or not, when your RTS system saved Israel from that Iranian nuke attack the year before last, you became a hero to a lot of Israelis."

Joshua shook his head. "Not all Israelis ..."

"Okay, true," Harmon shot back, grinning, "but you've read the Old Testament ... our wandering in the desert under Moses ... arguing, squabbling. Since when have Israelis ever been able to agree on much of anything?"

Joshua chuckled. "Seriously, Joel. I think you need someone else to plead your position to Bensky. Not me. This is when I wish I could substitute my wife, a brilliant lawyer with terrific negotiation skills. But not me. I've never been strong on diplomacy. If I open my mouth, I'll be a bull in a china shop."

Harmon halted and lifted his index finger into the air. "We need a real hero like you, who loves Israel, who has already helped to defend her." Then, after pausing and lowering his hand, he added, "And a man who has connections ..."

"What kind?"

"Let's be honest, if Tulrude wins your presidential election, Israel will be in serious trouble. Tulrude has abandoned all support for our nation. On the other hand, if Hewbright wins, our future looks a lot brighter. When Hewbright was in the United States Senate he consistently backed Israel on security and terrorism issues. And we happen to know, Josh, that you, your wife, and your entire Roundtable group are backing Senator Hewbright. And we also know that the senator admires you."

"And here I thought I knew something about clandestine surveillance," Joshua remarked. "You Israelis always impress me with the accuracy of your covert intelligence."

By now the helicopter was in view. As the two men approached it, Joshua still didn't feel any differently about the upcoming meeting with the prime minister.

He said a silent prayer.

God, help me keep my feet on the ground during this meeting ... and my foot out of my mouth.

Office of the Prime Minister of Israel, Jerusalem

The meeting lasted over an hour. Some heated words were exchanged, but Harmon and the three other members of the Hamonah Party kept the rancor to a minimum. Prime Minister Bensky listened throughout but talked little. He left that up to his two advisors, Chad Zadok, his chief of staff, and Dimi Eliud, his press secretary.

Near the end of the meeting Zadok looked up from his digital clipboard and said, "The prime minister appreciates your thoughts on the U.N. peace proposal. Thanks for dialoguing with us. However, the prime minister has another meeting."

Joel Harmon leaned forward in his chair, his hands open, as if he was going to grab someone by the shoulders. "Please, Mr. Prime Minister, can you at least share with us that you are open to our concerns, that you are willing to delay this dangerous deal with Mr. Coliquin and his envoy?"

"Why?" Zadok shot back, "so you and your fledgling little Hamonah Party can have more time to muster coalition strength behind your weak position?"

"This treaty with Coliquin and the U.N. is bad for Israel. Some truths are self-evident," Harmon said, shooting a quick glance at Joshua.

Now Dimi Eliud jumped into the fray. "Quoting from America's Declaration of Independence isn't the right answer for an Israeli problem." Then she directed her attention to Joshua, who had been silent. "Or does Colonel Jordan think differently?"

Joshua smiled but didn't bite.

Chad Zadok joined in. "Yes, why don't you share your thoughts with us, Colonel Jordan?"

Joshua's smile quickly evaporated. Instead of answering, he looked at Prime Minister Sol Bensky, who gestured for him to speak.

"I would rather not," he said, hedging.

"And I would rather you did," Bensky said in a soft voice. "I have heard many things about you, Colonel Jordan. Some good and some not so nice. So please speak freely. What do you think about this peace proposal? About Secretary-General Coliquin?"

"I tremble," Joshua began.

Chad Zadok latched onto that. "You what?"

"I said I tremble."

"You? The great Colonel Joshua Jordan, trembling with fear?" There was derision in Zadok's voice.

"I tremble," Joshua continued, "because of what I have read."

"About what?" Bensky asked.

"I have studied the Bible for the last two years," Joshua replied. "I am no scholar, but I tremble at what it says in 1 Kings 11:1."

Benksy's face looked as if he were searching his memory, but coming up blank.

Joshua quoted the verse from the Old Testament. "'Solomon, however, loved many foreign women —'"

"How dare you!" Zadok cried out.

"Mr. Prime Minister," Joshua said, disregarding the chief of staff, "adultery can come in many different forms, don't you agree? I know you must see that God has warned Israel throughout Scripture about entering into political treaties and intrigues with foreign powers — political adultery — when it can cause the nation to depart from God's purposes."

Dimi Eliud jumped to her feet. "Gentlemen, this meeting is *over*."

Sol Bensky said nothing. He sat motionless in his high-backed chair, glumly staring straight ahead, as Joshua, Joel Harmon, and his small entourage tentatively rose to leave. Then the group was briskly escorted from the room. Zadok and Eliud closed the door and quickly returned to their chairs across from the prime minister.

Zadok led off. "Now you see, sir, exactly what we are dealing with.

Joshua Jordan is the foreign enemy here. He is the agitator. And our young, impressionable member of the Knesset, Joel Harmon, has been taken with Jordan's radical views."

"You still have a strong coalition in the Knesset behind you," Dimi Eliud added, "for a while. We don't know how long that will hold. The treaty with the U.N. must be signed immediately."

"And," Zadok added, "Colonel Jordan must also be neutralized before he wins any more converts to his anti-Coliquin views. Sadly, he does have a certain influence among some Israelis."

"But he is a defender of Israel," Bensky said limply, "and I for one appreciate the RTS technology he designed ... and for his zeal for our nation. This is so difficult." Bensky put a hand to his forehead and rubbed it slowly.

"Of course, Mr. Prime Minister," Zadok said in a voice that was soothing, almost musical, like chimes in the wind, "we understand. That is why you must allow us — Ms. Eliud and myself — to take care of this Colonel Jordan business. You needn't worry about it anymore."

"Yes," Dimi Eliud added, "Joshua Jordan can be taken out of the equation. And very quickly."

Eliud and Zadok locked glances. Without a word, all three knew what had to be done.

TWENTY-TWO

Washington, D.C.

When Abigail received the text message, it was a jolt. It was from former Department of Justice Prosecutor Harley Collingwood. His text simply said "Meet me at Jefferson Memorial" and gave the time.

So once again Abigail chartered the family's private jet from the hangar at JFK and flew down to Washington. And once again, Cal went along for the ride. Abigail had been so absorbed in trying to dig up further information on the potential threat against Senator Hewbright that she had been able, for a few hours at least, to put her husband's excruciating legal dilemma out of her mind. But not entirely. She couldn't forget that Collingwood's inside information about the activities of the prosecutors in Attorney General Hamburg's Department of Justice office might be her only hope. Collingwood might know how they had managed to get Attorney Alan Fulsin to spin his false story about Joshua's alleged plan to create a takeover of the defense and security apparatus of the U.S. government.

Abigail and Cal had just landed at the private hangar at Reagan International, and she was about to step into the limo when she said to Cal, "So, you'll be all right?"

He nodded with a smile. "Mom, I'm old enough to take care of myself. Don't worry."

"What are you going to do?"

He shrugged. "I'll fill you in later. I'll be okay. Really."

She hesitated. "Something's going on. Anything you want to share?"

"Mom, get to your meeting. You're going to be late."

Ignoring her maternal instincts, Abigail ducked into the backseat. The driver closed the door and hopped behind the wheel.

After ten minutes of heavy traffic along the Potomac, Abigail's All-fone lit up. It was John Gallagher. When she answered, he gave her the update on his Hewbright investigation. "Okay, Abby. Here's the dope. I've been in contact with the FBI agent, as you know."

"Right. Agent Boling."

"We've been talking. I got him to open up. No small miracle, by the way. It turns out that shortly before the disappearance of this Hew-bright campaign worker, this Perry Tedrich guy, he had a visit from someone on Hewbright's national campaign staff."

"And?"

"Hewbright's assistant campaign manager. Woman by the name of—"

"Katrena Amid."

"Abby, you take all the fun out. Right. That's her. You know her?"

"Just met her once. In Denver, after one of the Senator's speeches." Abigail didn't yet elaborate about the sixth sense she had around Ka-trena. After reflecting a moment, Abigail followed up. "But you're sure it was her—Katrena Amid—who visited Perry Tedrich right before he disappeared?"

"Sure I'm sure. Why?"

Abigail didn't respond.

Gallagher went on. "You know, Abby, you never told me why you thought that Hewbright might have some kind of mole or dirty opera-tive within his staff. Wanna share that with your good buddy John Gallagher?"

"Not yet, John."

"Any reason?"

"I don't want my ideas to color your investigation."

"Wow. Now you're sounding like my old supervisor at the Bureau. Always went by the book."

"It's just that I have such a high regard for your ability, John. I need your untainted impressions. All of this could be just a wild-eyed theory. Maybe I've got you chasing a fantasy."

"On the other hand, one thing is not fiction."

"What's that?"

"Hewbright's Wichita election guy was murdered and dumped in a shallow grave. Nothing make-believe about that."

Bethesda Convalescent Center

On his second visit, Cal could see a remarkable change. Former President Corland was sitting up straight, his eyes bright and clear, and his speech — while still slow — was intelligible and coherent. When Cal arrived, Corland's wife had told Cal that her husband was having "one of his better days." Then she headed down to the cafeteria, leaving Cal and Corland alone with a nurse nearby.

Corland asked Cal, in a series of strained words, about his plans for the future.

"Law school," Cal said.

Corland smiled and nodded. "Following your mother ..."

"Sort of. Though she never pressured me. I was going into art at first. Actually had some of my paintings shown in a gallery up in Boston. But things changed, and I decided to go in another direction."

"Happens sometimes," Corland said and then nodded to the nurse to leave them alone. She smiled and dutifully left that area of the day room.

He noticed that Corland followed her with his eyes too. Now the only person in sight was a Secret Service agent seated on a chair just outside the room, out of earshot.

Corland immediately opened up. "I wanted you here ... to tell you ..."

"What?"

"Secrets."

Cal didn't know how to respond.

"Can I trust you?" Corland said.

"Yes. Absolutely. But why me?"

"I trusted your dad. And he was right about what he told me in the

White House. About threatened attack. But my people wouldn't listen. They undercut me. Nuclear attack ... New Jersey ... never would have happened ... if they had believed your father. I'm glad his Roundtable ... tried to help. At least New York was saved. I wish your Dad was here for me to tell this to ..." Corland stopped. Then after thinking something through, he continued. "But he's not."

"No," Cal said with emotion in his voice that had suddenly arisen and surprised even him. He struggled to say it. "I wish he was here too."

"So," Corland said with a smile, "I have to trust someone. I'll tell you then. Trust you. Maybe you ... are like your dad?"

Cal smiled. It was an accolade he didn't think he had earned, but he nodded and leaned back in the soft chair in the sunroom to listen.

Corland proceeded to explain about his White House physician having health problems himself, and how his personal doctor had to resign. President Corland had been treated for his condition of transient ischemic attack, a syndrome that threatened his ability to continue in his duties if not kept under control. The public had not been told about it up to then. When Corland's own White House physician left, Jessica Tulrude insisted that until a new White House doctor was appointed, Corland ought to use the vice president's personal physician — Dr. Jack Puttner. Up to that point, Corland pointed out to Cal, his own doctor had prescribed only blood thinners to decrease the risk of blackouts.

"But Puttner gave me something else," Corland said, "and right after that ... after a speech in Virginia, I had that terrible attack in the limo. Almost died."

"What kind of medicine?"

"Not sure," Corland said. Then his face took on an intense, twisted grimace. "But I think ... Dr. Puttner and Tulrude ... tried to kill me."

TWENTY-THREE

"The idea was easy to understand. Elegant in its simplicity. Joshua Jordan was a domestic terrorist."

Former federal prosecutor Harley Collingwood spoke matter-of-factly as he stood on the bottom steps of the Jefferson Memorial. The crowd was sparse that day. Even so, he kept his voice low.

He continued, "I looked over all the evidence we had to support that theory of the case against your husband. I was given the file by the DOJ lawyer supervising the whole case — not just the charges against Joshua, but those against you and all the members of the Roundtable. That attorney was Assistant Attorney General Dillon Gowers. So I read it all through. Several times. The theory was that when your Roundtable group hired those ex-special-ops guys to stop the portable nuke from entering New York City, that was a powerful piece of evidence we could use to convince a jury that you were running a private vigilante force, bent on usurping the United States Government. Sure, you intercepted the truck and kept it out of New York. But your special-ops volunteers paid a dear price when the terrorists detonated it along the New Jersey shore. And so did the thousands of people in the nearby town who died in the blast. It was just blind luck that the heavy winds blew the radioactive cloud out to sea and more people didn't die."

Abigail interjected, "Harley, we tried to warn the federal authorities through multiple avenues about the nuke. Our private intelligence sources told us the bomb was bound for New York, and we told the government that. But they did nothing."

"Sure, we knew you'd probably assert a Good Samaritan defense. On the other hand, as I viewed the case, I felt we could overcome that defense, but it required one important piece that was still missing."

Abigail put her finger on it. "Attorney Allen Fulsin."

"Right. Of course, we had Fulsin in our corner already, but the stuff he gave us in the FBI 302 reports — that Joshua was talking about revolution and all that — could all be explained away logically. It was clear Joshua was talking politics and social change, not armed uprising. So I told Assistant Attorney General Gowers — I said, 'Look, you need something stronger from Fulsin, if that's possible, or you'd better contemplate ditching this case.' A week later, he sent me an email. In the attachment was a second statement from Fulsin, and what Fulsin alleged in this new witness statement was incredibly powerful. He claimed Joshua had said it was time for an armed militia to arm-wrestle our national defense out of the hands of the Defense Department — by force if necessary — and that he was creating his own private army. But as I looked at Fulsin's second statement I noticed it was not an FBI 302. It was a supplemental statement from Fulsin, which had been transcribed directly by Gowers himself during his own interrogation — with no other witnesses present. That's when I got suspicious."

A couple of joggers appeared on the walkway along the Potomac, heading their way. Collingwood stepped further up the stairs toward the Jefferson Memorial, and Abigail followed.

"So I started digging around," he continued. "I found out that in the intervening week when the second interrogation took place and his second statement was obtained by Gowers, Fulsin had been threatened with a phony criminal charge of 'human trafficking' by Gowers. Apparently, Fulsin had a girlfriend from Canada living with him who had entered the United States illegally. So Gowers railroaded Fulsin with this ridiculous criminal charge, alleging that Fulsin was running a business of bringing prostitutes into the country. Fulsin got scared. That did the trick."

Abigail scampered up a few more stairs ahead of him, until she was standing over Collingwood and stopped him in his tracks. "So Fulsin was coerced into making up false testimony against Joshua by being threatened with a phony criminal charge himself?"

Collingwood looked visibly uncomfortable. "Look, Fulsin's no saint. He just wanted to get close to the Roundtable so he could spill the beans to Tulrude's staff in hopes of currying favor. They took the information and gave it to Hamburg so it could be used in a prosecution, but Fulsin ended up getting nothing out of the deal."

Abigail shook her head, astonished. "I knew Tulrude's people were corrupt, but I had no idea how corrupt. And Assistant Attorney General Gowers — he was part of this?"

"He as much as admitted to me that after Tulrude became president the gloves were off — no limits — Joshua Jordan was to be destroyed. Your Roundtable and your media outlet, AmeriNews, has made life a nightmare for Tulrude, with all of your investigative reports, starting with her longstanding objections to your husband's RTS system when she was vice president. Then, when President Corland had one of his blackouts and the North Korean ship launched the nukes at New York and the Pentagon utilized the RTS anyway and saved the entire city, Tulrude came out and said that yes, of course she authorized it and tried to take the credit. She even repeated that lie to Congress in the aftermath. AmeriNews was the only source that ran with that story about Tulrude's false statement, and the exposé AmeriNews ran about Tulrude violating the law by directing A.G. Hamburg to launch politically motivated criminal prosecutions. Your husband's, as an example.

"Anyway, Gowers distinctly told me that word had come down from the White House through A.G. Hamburg, starting from day one, that a case had to be made against your husband — at all costs. And then, when you were able to get the case against you and all the other members of the Roundtable dismissed, all except Joshua of course, Tulrude went completely crazy and called Hamburg. She screamed at him to chase Jordan 'to the ends of the earth if necessary — to apprehend and convict him.' That's a direct quote by the way. This has become very personal for President Tulrude."

The Jefferson Memorial was now empty of visitors, so Abigail and Collingwood strode up the steps and into the circular rotunda. Abigail had visited it a few times when she practiced law in Washington many years before. She gazed up at the huge marble panels inside, covered with quotes from Thomas Jefferson, chiseled in stone.

"Harley, you're an experienced prosecutor. You understand what's going to happen now. I will take this information and present it to the U.S. District Court here in Washington, where Josh's case is pending. This is the most shocking example of government misconduct in a criminal case that I've ever heard. This is what I've suspected but couldn't prove — waiting for and praying for — and now it's here at my feet. This could result in Josh's case being dismissed. But I have to ask — what made you come here today to tell me all this?"

Harley Collingwood tilted his head and nodded toward the inscriptions on the wall in front of him. "I was just hired by a great criminal-defense firm here in town, Draeger, Proxy, and Lugot. When they told me two days ago they wanted me not just as an associate, but as a partner, I came over here to the memorial to spend some time mulling it over."

Collingwood pointed to a familiar text inscribed in marble and read it aloud, word-for-word, " 'God who gave us life gave us liberty. Can the liberties of a nation be secure when we have removed a conviction that these liberties are the gift of God? Indeed I tremble for my country when I reflect that God is just, that his justice cannot sleep forever.' " He turned to Abigail. "My conscience wouldn't let me sleep. And these words of my hero, Jefferson, kept haunting me."

"So, because of that," she replied, "you decided to disclose this to me?"

"That," Collingwood said with a half grin, "and also the fact that my new law partners can't stand Jessica Tulrude, and they told me that I had their blessing to blow the lid off of this."

TWENTY-FOUR

Jaffa Street, Jerusalem

Chad Zadok and Dimi Eliud, Prime Minister Bensky's top staffers, arrived at the address in Jerusalem. It was a small, nondescript office with a sign outside that read, in Hebrew, TRAFFIC SAFETY OFFICE. When they entered, they identified themselves to a secretary who then showed them to the back office. Seated at a desk, a solid-looking bald man in a black T-shirt and a tan suit instructed them to close the door and sit down.

Zadok and Eliud were now sitting across from an operations member of Shin Bet — Israel's domestic security service. He called himself Ram, though he never gave his last name.

Ram asked them to confirm the reason for the meeting.

Zadok did the talking. "As I explained on the phone, Prime Minister Bensky wants this. The official at your agency told me to come here."

"If you don't mind my saying, on internal security matters like this, especially where it originates from the PM's office, it usually comes to us from someone in the IDF or in the cabinet — not a chief of staff like yourself."

Zadok wasn't flustered. "No offense taken. This is highly sensitive."

Ram raised an eyebrow, but his face was stone. "Everything I do here is highly sensitive. Tell me something I don't know."

Zadok straightened his legs and crossed them casually. "The prime minister wants this action taken immediately. I have already made the necessary contacts with the requesting nation. This transfer can be made very quickly."

Ram had a thin file on his desk. He opened it just long enough to give it a quick glance. "You have anything personal in all this?"

"No. This is strictly a matter of national security and public safety. At the prime minister's request."

After flipping through a few more pages of the file, Ram looked up. "You realize that the authorization for this — the legal hook — is that you say this guy is suspected of anarchist connections. You understand that?" Zadok smiled easy and nodded. "You swear that the information you gave the intake officer is true and correct, under penalties of law?" Again Zadok nodded, a little more eagerly. "How about you, Ms. Eliud. You agree with all this information?"

She nodded yes, but less enthusiastically.

"Do you have a problem with my executing this order, Ms. Eliud?"

She shook her head no and directed her gaze toward Ram's neck.

"Look at me when I ask you a question, please," Ram said.

"No," Dimi Eliud said, looking him in the face. "No problem."

"Very well," Ram said.

Chad Zadok began to stand up.

"Not so fast," Ram instructed him. "One more thing."

"Oh?"

"I want you two to approach my desk."

They followed his directive.

He twirled the file on his desk around so it was open and facing the two of them. There was a photograph in the file.

"Is this the anarchist you are referring to?"

They examined the photo of Joshua Jordan. They nodded. "Yes, absolutely," Zadok said.

Ram pulled the file back and closed it.

Zadok asked, "How long before Jordan is captured and turned over to the FBI for extradition back to America for trial?"

"When it comes to this office," Ram said, "there are no back burners."

□□□

In the City of David section of the Old City of Jerusalem, Joshua made his way through the buckets and shovels on the ground and ducked under metal scaffolding. He turned to Pastor Peter Campbell, walking next to him. "So, I get the feeling you've brought me here for a reason. And it obviously doesn't involve our favorite sporting rivalry on the links."

Campbell chuckled. "When I left my church in Manhattan to set up shop here in Jerusalem, it was serious business. You know the story, Josh. I'm convinced the return of Christ is imminent. Having been the head of the American Prophecy Council of Pastors, I felt led to relocate to Israel and share the gospel right here at the epicenter of prophetic events. But on the less serious side, yes, I did look for a good golf course in Jerusalem, but there aren't any. Up in Caesarea, yes, but that's a long drive. You and I need to take a day trip up there just to try the course sometime. Maybe I can actually beat you for a change!"

Joshua smiled, tipped his head, and remarked, "You just may do that, my friend. My game hasn't been the same ..."

But he didn't need to finish the sentence. Campbell nodded and said, "Right. Your injuries from Iran."

"On the other hand," Joshua said, "I may have lost my golf handicap, but I sure gained something even better in that hellish jail cell in Tehran."

Campbell patted him on the back. "Josh," he said pointing up ahead, "that's why I think you're really going to appreciate this."

They turned a corner, still underneath the scaffolding, and suddenly Joshua was looking at a set of stone steps that had been uncovered in an archaeological dig. They led straight up to a point where they disappeared into the side of a hill.

"I know the guys involved in this excavation. This is incredible. They tell me that during the time of Christ these very steps led up to a corner of the first century Herodian Temple."

"Okay," Joshua said, "what's the rest of the story?"

"These steps led up to the section of the Temple where the Jews who wanted to make a sacrifice would purchase an animal. That was the area where the trades were made. The place where the tables of the moneychangers were located."

Joshua felt the shiver of recognition run up his spine — a feeling of awe and suspension of time, as if all the world's activity had ceased.

"I get it," Joshua murmured, shaking his head in disbelief. "These are the steps?"

Campbell nodded and pointed to the edges worn down by the feet of countless pilgrims who had made their way to the Temple. "These are the steps that would have been trod by Jesus as He climbed up to the moneychangers' tables, where profit had become king. Up there is where He flipped the tables and declared for all to hear that the house of God should not be turned into a den of thieves."

Even though Joshua knew the gospel account, it took several minutes to sink in. Finally he spoke, "He shook things up, the Lord Jesus, I mean."

"Sometimes dramatically. Sometimes a little more quietly. But one thing about the intersection of Jesus Christ with human history — wherever and whenever He shows up, things are never the same again."

"I can vouch for that," Joshua said, still gazing at the steps. "I've changed. Radically. Supernaturally. I'm not the same man since I received Christ." Then he added with a smile, "Just ask Abby."

Joshua then turned to face Campbell. "I caught your television interview, the one with Bart Kingston, about your ministry here."

"I miss Eternity Church back in New York — but what is going on here is epic. I felt the Lord wanted me here. It's almost too much to comprehend. It is getting so close."

"Peter," Joshua said quietly, "I spoke to you earlier about my meeting with Prime Minister Bensky, about the U.N. proposal, giving Israel a piece of the territory on top of the Temple Mount and the building of a new Jewish temple. You said you'd give me your candid reaction. So ... I'm waiting."

Campbell gazed at the ancient steps once more and explained, "After our Lord comes for His church and raptures us, darkness will fall on the earth. Eventually, the Evil One will be fully revealed. You know the Scripture. It tells us that when that happens, he will enter the temple of the Jews. He will declare himself to be god, and in so doing, will revile and desecrate that place. But all of that requires one thing to happen. Right up there—" Campbell pointed up the stone steps to the high plateau of the Temple Mount—"the rebuilding of the Jewish Temple. And now, from what you've told me, I believe it's about to happen. Oh, how the coming of Jesus Christ for His church must be so very close ..."

TWENTY-FIVE

Chicago, Illinois, McCormick Place Convention Center

A dozen Hewbright campaign staffers were crowded into the green-room adjoining the stage. Their faces revealed a positive tension, a sense of anticipation and excitement. Senator Hewbright was about to deliver a speech on the economy to the convention of small business associations, a speech that would set the tone for his entire campaign. This was his Rubicon moment.

Senator Hewbright was seated in a semicircle of folding chairs, surrounded by his top advisors: national campaign manager, George Caulfield; his assistant, Katrena Amid; his domestic policy advisors, two of whom not only had PhDs in economics but also experience in managing Fortune 500 companies; his foreign policy guru, Winston Garvey; his assistant foreign policy advisor, Zeta Milla, and several others. In the corner was Agent Owens, detailed by the Secret Service to protect the senator.

In another corner, a small portable Internet television was tuned to several news channels in the quadrants of its screen, but the sound had been muted.

"Well, friends," Hewbright led off, looking more relaxed than his staff as he lounged in the folding chair, "any last-minute advice for this old political warhorse before I deliver my five-point plan to save America from financial collapse?"

There were a few nervous chuckles. George Caulfield spoke first. "You'll knock 'em dead, chief."

One of his economic advisors said, "Senator, this plan is wonderfully simple — voters will grasp it immediately — yet keyed to the five most important areas of our failing economy. I think we've got a winner on this." Then he added with a smile, "And not just because I helped draft it ..." A few polite laughs followed.

Caulfield pointed to the door leading to the mammoth convention hall. "We've got media from every news outlet out there. They can't ignore us this time. Your plan to rescue America's financial health is going to be the tipping point. Tulrude's going to have to really scramble after tonight." But as he spoke, the campaign manager pointed to the portable web TV in the corner. "Hey, Tulrude's speech in Omaha is about to begin." He called for someone to turn the sound up. The group turned their chairs around to face the television set.

President Tulrude was mounting the podium to an explosion of applause in the union hall. She made a few comments about her love of Nebraska and cracked a joke about the mayor of Omaha, who was seated on the dais behind her. When the laughter died down she began in earnest.

"I know the press reports indicated that I would be talking about national security tonight, but I have something more important to discuss — the state of our national economy."

George Caulfield whipped around and threw a quick glance to Senator Hewbright, but the candidate looked relaxed, a little amused at the seeming coincidence.

Tulrude continued, "Tonight I am revealing the solution for our national financial tragedy. I inherited this state of affairs when I entered the Oval Office. But no matter — I am here to fix it. I assure you," she said, clasping her hands across her chest as if in prayer, "that my five-point plan to save America's economy will create a new financial renaissance in our nation."

Caulfield thrust an index finger at the television screen and mouthed a word, but nothing came out. Then a look of fury burst over his face.

"Hold on, George," Hewbright said, "give our opponent a chance. We don't know what five points she's talking about."

As Tulrude delivered her version of the first two parts of her plan, it became apparent that they were the same as Hewbright's, as if she had read it verbatim from the confidential Hewbright campaign playbook. Caulfield leaped to his feet, yanked his Allfone out of his pocket, and hit Multiple Quick-dial.

Hewbright was frozen. In an instant, his national campaign-intelligence manager in Detroit and his two assistants in Des Moines were all conferenced in.

Caulfield yelled into his cell. "Tell me how this happened!"

His intel manager in Detroit screamed back. "I'm watching right now. This is outrageous. I have no idea how Tulrude stole our five-point economic speech, but we're going to find out."

After clicking off his Allfone, Caulfield paced the room, waving his arms. "There's a massive security failure in our organization. I'm telling you, there's a strategic leak somewhere. This is criminal."

Hewbright was no longer lounging in his chair. He was straight-backed and leaning forward with his forearms tightly on his thighs, his fists clenched. "No question about it, George."

Katrena Amid was blinking and shrugging her shoulders. "Okay, is this some kind of Watergate break-in? Did someone from Tulrude's outfit break into one of our rooms and get hold of our notes?"

Still stunned, Hewbright could feel the tension mounting.

Zeta Milla laughed coarsely at Amid's comment. "Katrena are you kidding? This is the twenty-first century. Political operatives don't have to do burglary anymore. Wake up —"

"Oh?" Amid shouted back, "then why don't you tell us how they could have done this."

"Everything in politics is driven by new media technology. Even in the so-called Third World countries, geopolitical movements are being formed at the speed of light through Allfone links and insta-news feeds. First in the Middle East and now in South and Central America. By the way, Katrena, that's my area of expertise."

Hewbright's brow was wrinkled. He was riveted to Zeta's every word. "So, what's your theory?"

"If it was up to me," Zeta said softly, "I would have your IT chief check every one of your key media-tech devices, starting with your All-fones. Hank, did you put those five points onto the memo-memory-drive of your Allfone?"

"Yes," Hewbright said, finally breaking his silence, "but it's en-crypted — super secure."

Caulfield hit his Quick-dial again. In a second he had their travel-ing media-tech man on the line. He had been eating a fast-food burger out in the hallway of the convention center. In three minutes he came huffing and puffing into the greenroom, his tie loosened and the re-maining half of his burger in a wrapper in his hand.

In twenty minutes, after working on the senator's Allfone, the IT guy summoned Hewbright and George Caulfield to the corner of the greenroom to talk. Speaking in a terse whisper, he said, "Okay. Sena-tor, I've run through all the programs on your memo-memory-drive, and here's the deal. I'm pretty sure — no, cancel that — I'm absolutely sure that your Allfone's been hacked."

Caulfield looked around the room until he spotted the Secret Ser-vice agent. He said to Hewbright, "Can we bring Agent Owens in on this? I think it's a criminal matter."

Hewbright shook his head. "I don't think so. Secret Service is solely for physical protection. They don't get into criminal investigations of political dirty tricks. That's the FBI's territory."

The IT guy handed Hewbright back his Allfone. The senator looked down at the device. "Well, George," he said to his campaign manager, "we've got an enemy in the camp — and I'm talking very, very close by."

TWENTY-SIX

Mayflower Hotel, Washington, D.C.

Cal had been down in the hotel's fitness room, working out with free weights. Physical conditioning had been one of his regular routines for the last few years. After that he stopped by his hotel room to check his Facebook page on his laptop. A Captain Jimmy Louder was reaching out to him. Cal had to think a minute. Then he remembered. *Oh, yeah, you're the pilot that my dad helped to rescue. You just got the Medal of Honor. Cool. I'm absolutely friending you.*

After Cal finished adding Captain Louder to his Facebook, he ambled over to his mother's room and turned on the Internet TV. After all, of the two televisions in their suite, hers had the bigger screen. Now he was standing in his sweats in front of it. He and Abigail had extended their stay after her meeting with the former federal prosecutor. She asked her former law firm in D.C. if she could use their offices to crank out some quick legal papers on Joshua's case while she was in town, and her former senior partner and sometime personal lawyer, Harry Smythe, was glad to oblige.

Silently, Cal had been struggling with something. After Virgil Corland had shared his suspicions that Tulrude's physician — and probably Tulrude herself — had plotted to sabotage his medical recovery, Cal planned on sharing the information with his mother. But things kept getting in the way. He hadn't told his mother about his meetings with Corland. Up to now Cal didn't think he needed to check

160

in with Abigail before responding to Corland's surprising invitations to meet. But now that a former president was accusing his successor of attempted murder, Cal thought now might be the time to consult with the acting chair of the Roundtable — even if that person was his mother. He also thought he should mention his Facebook contact from Captain Louder.

Just then something jumped off the TV screen. Cal couldn't believe it. "Hey, Mom — look at these pictures. Another earthquake ..."

Abigail glanced over. The camera was panning over downtown Minneapolis. Then it focused on a skyscraper — the fifty-seven-story IDS Tower. The tower swayed and shimmied, and the upper floors began to collapse. The video camera caught the very moment when the windows began to shatter, sending a shower of glass onto the street below.

"Can you believe it?" Cal asked. "Earthquakes in Minnesota!"

Abigail's face looked grim, but she was surprisingly unperturbed. "Yes, I can," Abigail said quietly from the wrap-around couch. Her eyes darted back to her Allfone. "I certainly can believe it. We're going to see more of it, Cal. Add it up. We've had three major earthquakes in the U.S. in the last two months."

She reread the text in the little window of her Allfone. There was a tilt to her head, as if it had grown heavy from some invisible burden. Cal glanced away from the TV long enough to notice that. He asked what she was reading. Abigail explained, "First, I've got a copy of the motion papers filed by the Department of Justice, asking the court of appeals to strike the affidavit I just filed with this new evidence of prosecution misconduct in your dad's case — moving the court to disregard it completely. You know, all that information I received from Harley Collingwood."

"That can't be a surprise."

"No, not really," Abigail said. "They're arguing that the information is blocked by attorney-client privilege between Collingwood and his prior employer — the United States government."

"So, is there more?" Cal asked.

"I also just received an instant-memo from the court, an order for a hearing."

"Is there a date for oral argument?"

"Yes. I filed for an expedited hearing, asked that the date for oral argument be moved up as quickly as possible." But there was a look of desperation on her face. "Now I feel pretty foolish. I filed that request yesterday with the court. At the same time I filed the affidavit from Collingwood about the blatant corruption by the attorney general's office."

Something didn't make sense to Cal. "Wait a minute. What's the problem?"

"I didn't think it would come so soon. I thought I would have some time to figure things out."

"Like what?"

"The security entrance at the U.S. Courthouse in Washington. How am I going to get into the building, get past security, to argue the case? I don't have a BIDTag. They'll stop me at the scanner, and I'll be taken into custody. I'll never get into the courtroom."

Now it was starkly clear to Cal. He had been an informal law clerk for the Roundtable while he was waiting to start law school. So his mother had brought him into the inner workings of her wrangling with the first criminal-defense firm that had represented Joshua. Now he saw the handwriting on the wall. He wondered whether his mother regretted having terminated her husband's last set of lawyers. Yes, they had been begging her to talk to Joshua and to pressure him into accepting a plea deal. When Joshua learned about that, he instructed Abigail to dump all of them. But now Cal realized that those lawyers would at least be able to appear before the hearing that was now only three days away.

Cal thought out loud, "Mom, without a BIDTag, you'd have to be a Houdini to appear at the oral arguments yourself, seventy-two hours from now." Cal grimaced. "Wow."

Abigail hit the Quick-dial function on her Allfone and called her husband's previous lawyers. She asked to speak to the partner in the office who had been handling Joshua's case until Abigail had fired him.

She drummed her fingers while she was on hold. She motioned for Cal to conference-in with his own Allfone. He snatched his cell and clicked into the call. After listening to a few more minutes of Muzak, the lawyer picked up. He asked Abigail why she was calling. She explained about the appeals hearing coming up in seventy-two hours. "Things have changed dramatically. I've filed an affidavit from Harley Collingwood, a former member of the prosecution team. This is what we've been looking for. A confession, proving that the attorney general's office coerced false testimony from a key witness."

"And now you want us back on the case?"

Abigail swallowed hard. "That's why I called. I need you to argue it. Oral argument is scheduled in three days. I realize this is extremely short notice, but you're the only ones — besides me — who know the details of this case."

She didn't have to wait long for the answer. "My partners and I half expected something like this, Abby, a last-minute plea to come back in. I just don't think this is going to work."

"You mean you're not willing to make it work ..."

"Something like that." Then the lawyer halfheartedly added, "Why not ask for an extension?"

"I can't. I'm the one who had asked for this hearing to be expedited. Now that they granted it — beyond anything I could have anticipated — I can't retreat. It would make our case look shaky."

"Sorry, Abby. Wish we could help you. But no one in this firm wants to touch your husband's case with a ten-foot pole anymore. It's too messy."

Abigail said good-bye and clicked off her Allfone. She turned to Cal. "I suppose you're going to say, 'I told you so ...'? You and Deb have questioned my decision to not get tagged."

"I know you think it's a biblical stand," Cal said. "Don't you worry that Deb and I did get tagged?"

"I explained it to you. You need it to get into law school and Deborah for her work."

"So, what are you going to do now?"

She shook her head. "Pray and then show up at the courthouse in

163

three days. If I'm blocked from arguing your dad's case, I'll go to jail, I suppose."

Cal stood up straight. He ran his hands through his hair. A thought occurred to him. An all-important magic act was now starting to formulate in his head. "Mom, listen. I've got an idea. First, my mother's *not* going to jail. Neither is my dad — especially for a crime he didn't commit."

Abigail gave a smile that was half pride, half wonderment.

Cal strode toward the door.

"Where are you going?"

"To get my laptop."

"And?"

"I'll tell you when I find what I'm looking for."

At the door, he stopped as one more thought struck him. "Just answer this — are you willing to go all the way on this?"

"Meaning what?" she asked.

He shot back an answer that made sense only to him. "I mean — are you willing to consort with the *underground*?"

TWENTY-SEVEN

The Pentagon

Deborah Jordan stood silently in her cubicle, staring at the document she had just been given. Corporal Tom Birdow was next to her, rocking on his feet and looking up and down the hallway to see if anyone was coming.

Deborah realized she could spend all day looking at this paper, but it wouldn't change a thing. She had known her mother's name would be put on the list of nontaggers, all those who had refused to be BIDTagged, but that alone didn't mean she would be apprehended as a violator. Another step was necessary. Someone high up needed to authorize a specific warrant for her arrest. Deborah had hoped and prayed that step might be delayed — or even overlooked in the morass of government red tape.

But her hopes had now been dashed. The notice read: "ORDER FOR IMMEDIATE SEIZURE — FAILURE TO COMPLY WITH IDENTIFICATION PROCESS — BIDTAG WARRANT LIST."

Now, it seemed, nothing would be able to remove one special name from that warrant list: "Abigail Jordan."

"You realize," Tom said, snatching the paper back from Deborah, "how much trouble I could get into if my boss at DISA or the people at the Security ID Agency found out that I shared this with you."

"Don't worry. Your secret's safe with me."

"Which means ..."

"I won't tell anyone — except my family."

165

Tom shook his head violently. "That's what I mean."

"Put yourself in my position, Tom. Tell me that *you* wouldn't tell your own mother if she were about to be arrested."

Tom tucked the document back into his DISA folder. "Fine. But just remember — you didn't get this information from me." Then he strode off.

○○○

In their downtown Washington hotel suite, Abigail was looking over Cal's shoulder as he pulled up some data on his laptop.

Her phone rang. She checked the caller ID. It was John Gallagher.

"John," she said, "what's up?"

"Got some news on several fronts. First, I encrypted an email to you yesterday on that digging you wanted me to do in the public records in Miami-Dade. You know, on that refugee situation down there from years ago. I think I found what you were looking for. Not sure what that's all about ..."

"I read it late last night," Abigail shot back. "Thanks. When I get a breather, I'll explain. Life has been a whirlwind wrapped in a tornado around here. But a picture is starting to emerge. I've got a person of interest I'm looking at."

"You know, Abby, you're starting to sound more like my old buddies in clandestine services. Vague, intriguing — and smarter than me. Maybe you missed your calling." Abigail chuckled. Then Gallagher gave her the rest of the story. "On the main investigation, the murder of Perry Tedrich, I'm afraid we're at a dead end. I shadowed Ben Boling, the main FBI agent detailed to the Wichita killing, and dropped your hint that maybe it was an inside job. So Ben interviewed Katrena Amid, the only staffer who seems to have visited the victim. But she's got an air-tight alibi. She met with Perry Tedrich all right, but she had left two days before he went missing. She flew out of Wichita while the guy was still very much alive and well." After a pause, Gallagher cleared his throat. "So, Abby, where are we going with this?"

"Actually, that's not bad news at all."

"Oh?"

"No. I never suspected Katrena Amid."

Another pause on the line. "You didn't?" More silence. "Hey, maybe it's time to spell it out for your pal John Gallagher. You know I'm a slow learner."

She laughed. "Okay, maybe it is time."

Just then, the call-waiting lit up on Abigail's Allfone. At the same moment, Cal pointed to something on his laptop. Abigail trotted over and nodded as she read it too. Then she asked Gallagher to hold while she took the other call.

It was Deborah.

"Mom, Debbie here. I'm on a secure line."

"What's wrong? You sound stressed."

"I am. I just saw your name on a list for immediate apprehension as a nontagger. It's just a matter of time before they track you down."

Abigail took a moment to process that.

"Mom, did you hear what I said?"

"Yes, darling. I did. It's just that there's a lot coming at me right now. The Lord is going to have to give me patience, to keep my feet on the ground in the middle of all of this."

"Well, what I'd like the Lord to do is to give you a pair of wings because you need to get out of sight for a while."

"Can't do that."

"You're kidding. Why not?"

"It's complicated. I've got to argue Dad's case in three days ... in the federal court of appeals here in D.C."

"Oh, that's great!" Deborah exclaimed. "You're going to walk into a federal building that's crawling with U.S. marshals and FBI agents. You'll be toast within five minutes."

"Maybe not."

"How's that?" Deborah asked.

Abigail glanced again at Cal's laptop screen to a posting on a blog called *The Underground*. Abigail's reply was cryptic. "Because I may learn a sleight-of-hand trick."

Cal smiled when she said that.

"I still don't understand," Deborah said.

"I'll explain later. Hang on, Deb ..." Abigail clicked back to John Gallagher.

"Okay, John, one question: did you ever check into that health club like I asked? The one Perry Tedrich belonged to?"

"Yeah. I was able to wrangle a look at his records. He worked out at the fitness center early in the morning on the day he disappeared."

"Anyone else check in with him?"

"Nope."

"Bring any female guest to the gym?"

"Nope. Look, Ben checked all this out too ... the member list ... the whole bit. I shadowed his investigation to make sure he didn't drop the ball."

"How about anyone who might have seen him in the workout area?"

"You shoulda' been an agent, Abby," Gallagher cracked. "That'll be my next assignment. Not that I expect anything to break on this. I can smell a cold case a mile away. This may be one of them. Anyway, I'll check the list to see who else was there at that time. After that, I got to fly out of Wichita and get to Northern California. I've got an uncle getting married — " After a moment, Gallagher added — "for the third time. He ought to know better by now. I met his fiancé. I'll just say that three times is definitely not a charm."

"Do me a favor, John," Abigail said. "The minute you find out anything, call me."

"Will do, Señorita."

Then Abigail clicked back to Deborah. "I need to see you right away. Can you come to my room here in the Mayflower Hotel after you leave the Pentagon?"

"Sure."

"One more question. Do you still have some time off coming?"

"Yeah. Why?"

"Is there any way you could take it right away ... like starting tomorrow?"

"Well — I suppose I could put in for it before I leave. I could say 'family emergency,' that sort of thing."

"Exactly," Abigail said. "I couldn't have said it better myself."

TWENTY-EIGHT

"What am I supposed to be looking at?"

Abigail directed her daughter back to the photo. It was laying on the hotel coffee table next to a file of papers. "Look again."

"All right," Deborah replied, "but all I see is a photograph of a guy sitting in a room with his back to the camera."

"What else?"

Deborah raised an eyebrow and tucked up the corner of her mouth. She stared hard at the picture. "Well ... he's got his hand outstretched to the left, reaching, I guess, for a cup on a saucer on the end table next to his chair. It was shot from the back. Whoever took it was behind him."

"Now, look at the next photo."

Abigail slid another photo out of the file and laid it on the coffee table. After studying it, Deborah said, "Looks like a blow up — magnified several times. It's focused just on the guy's left hand."

"Right," Abigail said, "these were taken by an investigative journalist named Curtis Belltether. He mailed all this to the Roundtable, along with his article, just before he was murdered."

"What are the pictures supposed to prove?"

"The man in the photo is Alexander Coliquin. At that time he was at the end of his tenure as the Romanian ambassador to the United Nations. But he was also the head of a global movement to enforce universal controls over all of the industries of the world."

"The One Movement, right?"

Cal jumped in. "Actually, that's just the religious aspect of it. I've been studying this for the Roundtable." There was audible pride in his voice. Deborah tossed him an older-sister look as he continued, "Coliquin has managed to create an international coalition of major religions to get behind his initiative. That gives him the moral and religious cover for his plan to regulate global business in the name of preventing catastrophic climate change. He was the architect behind the international treaties that created the world climate agency. By the way, the guy that's been running that particular agency — this zil-lionaire from Belgium, Faris D'Hoestra — is one scary dude. They're seizing control of industries that are supposedly out of compliance with their super technical green standards, including companies in the U.S."

"I've missed a lot of that," Deborah remarked, "buried in the Pentagon everyday at my desk. But I haven't seen any of this on the news."

"Apparently you haven't been reading AmeriNews," Abigail said. "That's the only information source on the web that's covering it."

"All thanks to Mom, by the way," Cal said. "She chased that FCC commissioner's limo down I-66 just to get his attention."

Abigail chuckled. "Actually, it was God's doing. A miracle, the way it all transpired. But when Tulrude succeeded Corland, she appointed one of her cronies as the new chairman of that federal agency. Now AmeriNews is the only show in town in terms of alternate communications and news. Until we get another president, of course, which is what we are praying for and working toward."

"Well, as much as I appreciate the political science lesson, I still don't get it. These pictures. Where are you going with this?"

Abigail nodded. "Okay, so you know where Coliquin is now."

"Sure. He's secretary-general of the United Nations."

"And very much supported by President Tulrude," Abigail noted.

Cal had wandered off into the kitchenette to look for a snack in the fridge. He yelled out to them, "They're like kissing cousins."

Abigail nodded. "The point is that Coliquin is dropping obvious endorsements in the press for Tulrude, saying that if Tulrude wins the upcoming election it will not only be good for America, but for international peace, security, unity, and environmental safety around the world. The fact is, Tulrude's victory in November is a political necessity for Coliquin — it will be the glue that holds together the global power base that he's built for his agenda."

Deborah pointed back to the enlarged photo of Coliquin's hand. She waited for the punch-line. "And this picture?"

"Okay," Abigail continued, "look at the ring on Coliquin's left hand. Very unusual. I've checked the design on it in several anthropology texts. It's based on an ancient Egyptian design. Full of occult, pagan symbolism. Belltether must have thought this was highly significant because he obviously snapped the picture when Coliquin wasn't looking. Then he enlarged it. The article he sent us documented the corruption — even allegations of conspiracy and murder — involving Coliquin back in his native Romania. Now that Belltether is dead, the AmeriNews staff is working overtime, double-checking his sources so we can publish it. But Belltether also included a note in the packet. He said he planned on a second exposé against Coliquin, a story he thought would have, in his words, 'even more astounding revelations.' But with his murder, we may never know what he had in mind."

"Okay," Deborah shot back, "maybe Coliquin's a bad actor. So what?"

"Listen carefully to what I'm about to tell you," Abigail said, "and then decide if you can do what I'm going to ask you to do."

She had Deborah's attention. Her daughter had her head forward, eyes glued on her mother.

"Senator Hank Hewbright is in jeopardy. There's evidence that he's threatened, and I mean personally. I'm talking assassination. His chief campaign manager in Wichita was murdered. John Gallagher has heard rumors of Hewbright's Allfone being hacked."

When Abigail paused momentarily, Deborah cut in. "That's all you have? That's pretty sketchy."

"No. There's more. One of Hewbright's closest advisors may be a fraud." Deborah cocked her head and waited. Abigail finished the thought. "The name the traitor goes by is Zeta Milla. She's an attractive foreign-policy expert on Hewbright's campaign," Abigail explained. "Supposedly a refugee from communist Cuba as a child, escaping with her family on a small boat. After I met her in Colorado following one of Hewbright's speeches, I asked Gallagher to do some background investigation into the records down in Miami. There were news reports back then about a family escaping Cuba on a little rowboat with a makeshift sail. The parents died on the trip over, but a young girl survived. Her name was kept out of the article because she was a minor."

"Okay, so it checked out?"

"Not really. John told me he found a death certificate online in the Miami-Dade records for a young girl of Cuban descent, of the same age, who died about a week after the article was published. She was listed as 'Jane Doe.' The cause of death was listed as exposure, but John kept digging and found out that the birth certificate was a double. The original had the name of the girl on it, but someone had it destroyed and replaced it with Jane Doe."

"All right," Deborah shot back, "let's say this Zeta Milla stole the identity of this dead Cuban girl and used the story for her own purposes. Even assuming that's the case, it may prove she's dishonest, but not that she's a threat to Hewbright."

"When I met Zeta Milla in Denver," Abigail said, "I noticed something." Abigail held up the enlarged photo of Coliquin's hand. "She was wearing the same ring that Coliquin is wearing in Belltether's photo. I think these two are part of the same little club."

Deborah took the photo from her mother's hand, a look of shock on her face. "Okay ... I see. Right. What do you want me to do?"

"I need you to contact a friend of mine named Pack McHenry. He runs a private counterintelligence group, the Patriots. You've heard Dad and me speak highly of him. He has super-secret security clearance and has worked with American intelligence services." Deborah nodded slowly. "First, you need him to supply you with a fake ID. Let's call you Deborah Shelly. Use your middle name as your last."

"Mom, what's going on?"

"I need you to get close to someone important."

"But I'm already BIDTagged. A fake ID won't match my bio in the BIDTag system."

"Another reason you need to contact McHenry. While his computer guys haven't been able to duplicate the actual BIDTag laser process — to our knowledge there is only one person in the world who has managed to achieve that — Pack's IT team can do the next best thing — they can substitute personal data information in your government database. Look, Deb, the people you are going to be dealing with can't know you're part of the Jordan family. That's crucial. Now, when you get hold of Pack McHenry, you also have to ask him something else. We need him to access the passport records of this Zeta Milla. See if she has a history of travel to Romania while Coliquin was ambassador."

"And if she did?"

"Deb, I need you to undertake a dangerous assignment, and it can't wait. I would do it myself, but for the next forty-eight hours I'm going to be otherwise occupied."

"Occupied? Doing what?"

Abigail and her son gave each other a knowing nod. Cal filled in the blanks.

"Backpacking in the Northwest. Locating rebels."

TWENTY-NINE

Jerusalem

At the outdoor café Ethan was tilting up the little cup of Turkish espresso to catch the last drop, but in the process he caught a mouth full of grounds. He made a face as he swallowed them, then took a swig from his water bottle. "Josh," he said, "I know there must be a way to drink that stuff without swallowing the grit, but I still haven't learned it."

Joshua pointed to his cup of tea. "I'll have to convert you to this stuff, just like Abigail did for me. I used to be a coffee addict, but Abigail kept after me — even from the other side of the planet — to change my diet, food, drink, everything. I think she wants me to live to a hundred! Frankly, I think I won't make it — because I have the feeling Jesus is coming any day now." He swallowed the rest of his Madagascar tea, set down his cup, and pointed a finger at Ethan. "And when that happens, if you haven't put your faith in Christ, while I'm up there with Him, you're still going to be down here picking up the pieces — living in a shattered world that'll be run by the Devil himself. Something to think about."

Ethan tossed his boss a halfhearted smile. By now he was used to Joshua exaggerating about religious stuff — particularly the "Jesus is about to rapture his church" bit. Since they were both living in a kind of exile now in Israel, at least until Joshua's legal case got straightened out, it was almost a daily occurrence. Something was constantly grabbing Joshua's attention — a news item in the online *Haaretz* or *Jerusa-lem Post* or an archaeological discovery or just the sight of some tourist spot 'where Jesus once walked' — that's all that it would take to launch his mentor into a full-length sermon. When Ethan accepted the offer to work as the personal assistant to Joshua Jordan — world-class spy-plane pilot, engineering genius, and American hero — he never ex-pected to be accompanying a traveling evangelist.

But that wasn't the only thing on Ethan's mind. As Joshua got up and rather stiffly reached his arm around to grab his wallet and pay the bill, Ethan was struggling with something in his own head. *Maybe this gig isn't all it's cracked up to be. I've been in Israel for months. What am I really doing here? My job description changes every day. It's almost like Josh wants me close to him, but why, I don't know. Okay, so maybe he has to stay here because he's got a hairy criminal case hanging over his head. But not me. I'm free to go back — anytime I want to.*

I wonder if it's time to head back to the good old U.S.A. Spruce up my résumé. See if Raytheon is hiring again. I'll think it over. Start breaking it to Josh slowly.

Joshua pulled a piece of paper out of his pocket with the same rigid movement that Ethan knew well — the shoulders seemed to limit his movement. "My grocery list," Joshua said waving the emailed note. "Ab-igail's got me on this Mediterranean diet of vegetables and fruit. Says she thinks maybe it's going to help my headaches and the other stuff."

Yeah, Ethan had witnessed the "other stuff." The injuries Josh had received at the hands of his sadistic Iranian captors two years before were still apparent.

"Let's head over to the Souk," Joshua said, pointing across the street to the Mahame Yehuda Market. "I'll pick up some veggies."

"Just don't invite me over for dinner," Ethan said. "I'm still a meat-and-potatoes guy. And I've developed a taste for Argentinean beef over here."

As they approached the entrance of the open-air market, flanked by trucks that were unloading, Ethan's Allfone vibrated. It was a text. He opened it up, surprised to see that it was from Deborah Jordan.

Hi, Ethan. Deborah here. Been meaning to connect. How's life in Israel? Maybe we can talk sometime. Catch up on your life. Is my dad keeping you in line? Ha. Ha. DJ

"Huh," Ethan muttered under his breath as they walked. Joshua gave him a quick glance but didn't ask about it. Ethan slipped the Allfone back in his pocket. Ten seconds later, it vibrated again. Was this another message from Deborah? *Man, she must really be thinking about me*, Ethan thought.

As the two of them entered the noisy crush of local shoppers meandering through the long single aisle of the outdoor market with food stands on each side, he read the newest text. But it wasn't from Deborah.

Two Shin Bet agents coming to arrest Joshua. Then extradite him to USA. Get out quick.

He tapped the Source function to see who sent it.

Sender not identified.

Ethan pushed the tab on his Allfone for a special application and turned on the function that said, "All Sender Data Fields." But the screen read:

Sender's identity is hyper-blocked.

At the vegetable stand, Joshua had a plastic bag in his hand and was putting an eggplant and a few green peppers in it. Ethan stepped up next to him, his heart pounding and his adrenaline pumping.

"We got to get out of here, Josh," he said quietly.

"What's the problem?"

"Just keep cool. I got a text from an anonymous source, telling me two agents from Shin Bet are coming to arrest you, to extradite you back to the U.S."

"Must be a mistake —"

"I get the feeling it's not. And it's my job to protect you."

"But my relationship with the Israelis has been good here."

"You mean — like the meeting you told me about with Prime Minister Bensky, when you insulted his favorite peace plan right to his face?"

Joshua stepped over to the vendor and paid him a couple of shekels. Ethan scanned the market in all directions. "Let's not take any chances. Okay? Gotta go now. Quickest way is the entrance we came in."

But as they turned, Ethan spotted two broad-shouldered men in sunglasses, one a bald guy wearing a black T-shirt and a tan suit, and the other, a muscular guy in jeans and a tank top. He turned to Joshua. "I think I've spotted them. They don't exactly look like French chefs doing their grocery shopping," Ethan whispered. "We need to get down to the other end — fast."

Joshua tried to look casual as he picked up the speed, but soon he and Ethan were jostling customers as they made their way through the congested market.

"Switch on the afterburners," Ethan grunted, "they're getting closer." Ethan half-glanced to the side and noticed that the men were about twenty yards behind them, coming straight in their direction. "Run!" Ethan yelled. They sprinted down the aisle toward the daylight at the end of the market ahead of them. Ethan could hear the commotion behind him as Ram and his other Shin Bet agent were barreling through customers, knocking them to the ground and tipping over trays of spices and tomatoes as they went.

The two agents were now ten yards away and closing fast. Ethan spotted a truck at the end of the market, just beyond the big metal door that was being rolled down by a food manager. Next to that was a small entrance doorway leading to the outside. A forklift was parked out front.

At the end of the Souk, Ethan shoved Joshua through the open doorway and turned to look behind him. He caught a glimpse of a young female in a green grocer's apron and a scarf wrapped around her head. She looked so familiar he could only ask in that instant — *Could it be?*

The woman was carrying a large tray of fish heads swimming in juice. She tossed the slimy contents onto the ground in front of the two agents. Their feet flew up into the air as they landed on their backsides on the slippery walkway.

Outside, the engine of the produce truck revved up, and Ethan pointed to the empty cargo hold in the back and yelled to Joshua, "Jump in!"

While Joshua climbed stiffly into the back of the truck, Ethan hopped onto the forklift, hit the start button, shifted it into gear, and rammed it into the door opening, blocking it completely. Then he sprinted after the truck as it started to rumble down the street. Joshua was holding on to the metal tie-off loop on the side of the truck with one hand while leaning out of the back of the truck with his other hand outstretched.

He was yelling to Ethan. "Faster!"

Ethan was pumping his legs like a machine, until he reached out and felt Joshua's hand. Joshua yanked hard. Ethan pulled himself up into the truck while Joshua bit the side of his lip and gave a wincing grimace of pain. They pulled the two canvas tarps down over the back of the truck and peeked out through the space between them.

Ram and the other Shin Bet agent had rolled up the big metal door by then. They were now standing in the middle of the alley staring at the truck as it picked up speed and headed out onto Jaffa Street, in the direction of Allenby Square.

On a folding chair on the driveway, on the other side of the door leading into the market where the two angry agents had now disappeared, a food vendor was taking a break. On a table he had his tiny wireless Internet TV tuned to the news. A reporter was standing outside of the Knesset building in Jerusalem. The man turned up the volume. "It was just announced today," the reporter said, "that in a show of political brinksmanship, Prime Minister Sol Bensky has mustered his coalition behind the multifaceted United Nations peace plan for Israel, the Palestinians, and the Arab states. The treaty will be signed tonight in an historic ceremony in the prime minister's residence ..."

The reporter glanced down at his notes, raised his face to the camera again, and concluded. "United Nations Secretary-General Alexander Coliquin has said that the signing of his treaty proposal by Israel marks a new era of peace and prosperity — not only for Israel — but for the entire planet."

THI☈TY

Edinburgh, Scotland

Bishop Dibold Kora was at the podium in the outdoor arena, just off
of the Royal Mile and within a stone's throw of Edinburgh Castle, the
dark medieval structure perched up high on a solid rock cliff, over-
looking the city.

On the dais behind him was the Archbishop of Canterbury and
the head of the Church of Scotland, along with the young Dalai Lama,
two Hindu priests, a special emissary from the Vatican, an American
Indian chief, the president of Wiccans International, several representatives from tribal South American and African religious groups, and
the Chancellor of the Gnostic Church of the European Union. Seated
directly behind the podium was the head mufti of the Waqf, the Islamic trust that had, up to that day at least, exclusively controlled the
Temple Mount plateau in Jerusalem.

The arena was filled. Special box seats had been constructed for
royalty from Jordan, Saudi Arabia, England, Morocco, Belgium, and
a dozen other nations. The international press was granted access to
the first ten rows. Two television platforms had been set up to accommodate the Internet television coverage that was being disseminated,
live, over every network on the globe.

Kora, the special advisor to Coliquin, was finishing his introduc-
tory comments.

"Last night, Israel signed the historic peace treaty that has been
painstakingly forged by my hero and my good friend — Alexander

Coliquin, secretary-general of the United Nations. This was an astounding achievement of historic proportions: Israel, the Palestinian Authority, and the entire Arab League, all in agreement, all in good faith, walking together, into a future of peace. But as significant as that is, the Charter of Common Belief signed here at Edinburgh Castle today is equally monumental — a document that will go down in history as a stunning, evolutionary development — a Magna Carta, if you will — of jointly held values. A pledge of the world's religions to preserve earth from the ravages of carbon emissions that cause global warming; to insure the rich will be held accountable to provide for the poor through an internationally uniform system of enforced cooperation and equalized property ownership; to oppose the spread and dissemination of absolutist religious dogmas and rigid doctrinal beliefs that damage the spiritual harmony of our world; and most importantly, to rejoice because we have discovered a common god that everyone, everywhere, can now worship in peace and tranquility."

After the echoes of the ovation in the arena ceased, Bishop Dibold Kora motioned for a priest from the New Aztec Tribal Union to approach the podium. The priest lit a "unity" torch and waved its flame back and forth in front of him as he chanted.

The crowd, excited by the idea of a new world dawning, rose to its feet and cheered — and kept cheering for several minutes, clapping and voicing their approval in a sea of many languages.

Annapolis Junction, Maryland, Headquarters of the Security and Identification Agency (SIA), Near the National Security Agency

At the SIA headquarters, Jeremy, the night-data manager, had just sent an insta-memo to the assistant managing director for the Division for Exigent Requests for the TagWatch Surveillance Program. Jeremy knew his boss was at home, probably finishing his dinner, but this was urgent. The message simply said:

> Have received Red Notice from AG, seconded by Homeland. Please call.

Jeremy's line rang a minute later. The assistant managing director said, "What's this about a Red Notice?"

"Yes sir. Signed by Attorney General Hamburg."

"Homeland Security wants this too?"

"That's what it says."

"Who's the subject?"

Jeremy hunted for the name on his screen. "Female. Married. U.S. citizen. Abigail Jordan."

The assistant director took a moment to respond. "Why does that name sound familiar?"

"Don't know, sir."

"All right, then. Start trolling. When you get a good fix, alert the SIA agents or maybe the FBI for an apprehension."

Jeremy clicked off his Allfone and whirled in his chair until he was in front of another screen. He placed the palm of his hand on the screen for two seconds until a green light lit up in the corner. He typed the Red Notice case number and Abigail's name, date of birth, social security, driver's license, and passport numbers into the blank. Then touched the screen where it said Extrinsic Data Location Commencing.

After thirty seconds, he received a message that read, "Subject's Last Verified Location — Mayflower Hotel, Washington, D.C."

"Okay," Jeremy said to his computer screen, "let's go trolling." His screen lit up with ten smaller screens arrayed along the margins, five on each side. Each image was in grainy black and white, the kind produced by remote video cameras.

A female face appeared in another small box on the screen. It was the District of Columbia Sector clerk speaking. "Jeremy, this is the D.C. Sector here. We've got a black vehicle we believe to be a private limo — Lincoln Navigator — driving the subject down Constitution Avenue. Video will follow."

"Copy that," Jeremy said.

□□□

Inside the Lincoln Navigator, the driver, silver-haired attorney Harry

Smythe, glanced up at the green light of the traffic camera that had just captured the image of his vehicle as it passed through the intersection. He spoke aloud but didn't turn around to his occupants. "Abby, after all these years you've known me to play it close to the vest, cautious, careful, I bet you're shocked to see me aiding and abetting a public enemy like you." He guffawed. "I read your affidavit from Harley Collingwood. Finally I told myself, that's enough. The Gestapo kind of tactics I've seen from the Tulrude administration is the last straw. So — I guess I've just become an honorary member of your Roundtable."

In the rearview mirror, Harry could see Cal turn to his mother and say, "Deb said they probably located you at the Mayflower Hotel through the extrinsic data system ... public records, like hotel registrations. So we can assume they're already following us with the traffic cameras here on Connecticut Avenue."

Abigail looked ahead, and Harry followed her gaze to the sign for the National Zoo on the right. "Harry, try going in here," she said, pointing to the sign. He took a sharp turn into the zoo entrance.

Moments later, Harry was wheeling the Navigator back onto Connecticut. After several miles, he turned sharply off to the right, heading toward Rock Creek Park. But the cameras at the intersection caught the vehicle again.

□□□

At SIA headquarters, Jeremy spotted the image of the Navigator speeding through an intersection, then turning toward the park. He touched the SIA agent button on the screen and then the FBI button. A message flashed: "Closest agents — 35 minutes."

So he touched the Metro Police square on his screen. The message flashed — "5 minutes." Jeremy touched the button on the screen that read: "Authorize Metro Police Stop."

□□□

Four minutes and twenty seconds later, a D.C. metro police car, with its blue lights flashing, pulled the black Navigator over.

Two patrolmen with their guns drawn ran up to the car, yelling for the driver to put his hands up. When Harry Smythe calmly lowered his electric driver's side window, one of the officers screamed, "Hands up where I can see them. Step out immediately!"

Harry stepped out of the car, and the officer slammed him face forward against the side. The other officer was already on the other side to arrest Abigail. As he swung the passenger door open with one hand, grasping his sidearm in the other, he screamed into the vehicle, "Come out with hands raised — now!"

A few seconds passed. From the driver's side, the officer who had Harry Smythe pinned against the car called out to his partner. "Officer Baker, confirm that you have the subject in custody." Several more seconds passed, and the first officer repeated, "Officer Baker, confirm apprehension!"

The other officer appeared at the driver's side now with his revolver holstered. "No subjects in the car, sir."

The officer stepped back, and Harry Smythe lowered his arms and brushed off his silk shirt. "Do you know who I am, officer?"

"I was about to ask for your driver's license — "

"No need. I'll tell you. I'm a lawyer who has personally represented two former presidents and half a dozen U.S. senators and congressmen. I've also had one other client you ought to know about — your boss — the chief of police of the District of Columbia."

The officers gave each other a quick look. Then they tipped their hats and began to walk away. One of them added, "Sorry to have troubled you."

On a bus that was now leaving the National Zoo, Abigail and Cal sat next to their suitcases on the bench seat in the back. They glanced up at the camera above the driver's head. Cal whispered, "In two blocks we'd better hop off, get a cab. I don't think they're all equipped with cameras yet."

□□□

At SIA headquarters Jeremy was on the cell phone with his boss, explaining that the apprehension had not been successful — yet.

"I wouldn't worry sir," he said. "We'll get our subject eventually. First, she'll hit the trip wire of our BIDTag scanners and register a nontag alert. Then she'll be tracked with facial recognition cameras in every public place — restaurants, gas stations, airports ..."

"Yeah, yeah," the assistant director bulleted back. "I help run this outfit, remember?"

"Just saying," Jeremy replied, "she's in the matrix now. Just a matter of time."

TH1RTY-ONE

On the Campaign Trail Somewhere in the Northeast

Special Agent Ben Boling was ordering a sandwich at the outside counter of a roadside deli. "I'd like the pastrami on rye. No chips with that, but I'd like it heated."

Senator Hewbright was next to him. His entourage of staffers were milling around the campaign bus, out of earshot. "Don't mean to hurry you, Agent Boling, but we have an incredibly tight schedule. What can you tell me so far?"

"First — I don't have much on Perry Tedrich's death — yet. We just don't know if it was connected to your run for president. The autopsy indicates he was poisoned. That's all I know."

"I'd like to reach out to his family …"

"I know you would. But I recommend that for the time being you let me express your heartfelt regrets. There'll be time for you to talk to his relatives when our investigation gets a clearer picture of why he was killed."

"And my Allfone being hacked?"

"That's a different story, though it may be connected. Just can't tell. What our IT forensics people say is this — it was hacked through a source in China."

Hewbright was nearly speechless. "What in the world …"

"Do we have any reason to believe that China has any particular interest in your campaign?"

"Certainly. I've traveled there several times, spoken out against

186

their abuses of human rights and violations of religious liberties of Christians and other religious minorities. And I've argued against President Tulrude's attempt to expand our national debt that's owed to China. I've publicly argued that she's enslaving us financially to that nation."

"Anyone on your staff have any special relationship with Beijing?"

"No, sir, other than my foreign-policy advisors being knowledgeable about China in general."

Agent Boling threw some cash onto the counter and plucked up his pastrami sandwich, wrapped in paper. "We'll keep looking at this," he said. "Meanwhile, be careful who you have around you. I've talked to Agent Owens, your Secret Service man. He'll help you keep your circle tight. Can't afford too many people getting close to you. Limit yourself to those who are air-tight, as pure as the driven snow."

Ben Boling smiled at his own comment as he took a bite of his sandwich. How pure could anyone be who was knee deep into the dirtiest blood sport of all — a run for the presidency of the United States? On the other hand, after being around Hank Hewbright for a few days now, Ben had a feeling about him. There was a kind of common decency about the guy. Maybe he was the exception.

"You know, Agent Boling," Hewbright said strolling toward the campaign bus, "you want me to restrict my circle, but that's impossible. People want to — have a right to — shake your hand. The voters ought to be able to look you in the eye, find out what makes you tick."

"Sure," Boling said, walking beside him and using a paper napkin to wipe the mayo off his chin. "But I'm not talking about that. I mean your staff," and he tossed a nod toward the campaign workers by the bus. "They're the ones who know your every move."

Cairo, Egypt

U.N. Secretary-General Alexander Coliquin stopped at a glass case containing the mummy of an ancient Egyptian prince. He gazed into the display and studied the smooth facial features, worn by thousands of years but still preserved enough to give the impression of his brow, nose, and jaw line. The tour guide droned on about the collection in the Museum of Antiquities, lecturing his audience — representatives from the Arab League nations and the OPEC countries who had gathered to celebrate Coliquin's great coup in negotiating the treaty agreement with Israel. Meanwhile, the tour guide gushed enthusiastically about how the museum had been gloriously rebuilt since its desecration during the so-called Arab Spring revolts of 2011.

U.N. Deputy Secretary-General Ho Zhu was standing next to Coliquin. He looked at the mummy too. "Once a ruler of a great civilization," Ho remarked. "Now, just some bones in a glass box. A museum piece. How is greatness measured, truly?"

"By becoming more than even that," Coliquin replied.

Ho Zhu wondered at that. "More than what?"

"Than merely a ruler of a civilization."

Before his deputy could pursue that further, Coliquin changed the subject. "Did you get the polls after the Tulrude speech on economics in Nebraska?"

Ho smiled and bobbed his head up and down. "Yes. She gained twelve points. The bump probably won't last, but it's a good start. An excellent speech. This is good momentum leading up to the convention. Meanwhile, Senator Hewbright's party will have its convention first."

"In politics," Coliquin added, "a few days, or weeks, is an eternity. Anything could happen to Hewbright. Don't you agree, my friend?" The two men shared a knowing look.

As the crowd was led to the other end of the hall, Coliquin and Ho Zhu dropped back. The deputy whispered to the secretary-general, "Also, you should know that we have been contacted by Faris D'Hoestra's people. The World Builders."

Coliquin stopped in his tracks. "Concerning what?"

"They want a meeting."

"You still haven't answered the question."

"Concerning your 'agenda for the future.' That is how they put it."

Coliquin took a few steps and then turned to Ho Zhu. "Arrange the meeting."

"Really?"

"Of course. And I want Faris D'Hoestra there personally. Is that understood?"

Ho Zhu gave a tight-faced nod of understanding. "It will be done."

Philadelphia, Pennsylvania

President Tulrude had just finished a photo op and a quick public appearance at the Liberty Bell. Nearby was her former chief of staff, Natali Traup, who had taken a leave of absence from her White House job to help with the campaign. Traup had her Allfone in her hand and was waving it at Tulrude, as her Secret Service entourage led her to the limo. "Madam President, this has to be addressed."

"I don't see why."

"Because there are allegations that your speech was stolen from Hewbright, as a result of the Chinese hacking into his computers."

"I have no personal knowledge about Chinese computer hackers. Do you?"

Traup followed her into the backseat of the limo. "No, but it's going to look bad."

"Screw what looks bad," she replied. "How do they know that Hewbright didn't try to steal the speech from me—but I just happened to deliver mine first? That's the story that needs to get out."

"But there isn't any evidence of that."

"Then find it," Tulrude said. "Look, in the melee leading up to Nebraska, we go into a prep meeting before my speech. And when we come out, I've got a five-point plan to save America from a final, devastating financial depression. That's the fact, Natali. Now, who gave me what regarding those five points for my speech I honestly don't recall. My staff is gathering research, data, and policy ideas from the four corners of the earth. That's what they're paid to do. I'm simply not going to agonize over this. Oh, and another thing," Tulrude said, remembering a PR idea. "Get Coliquin to set up his schedule to do a public event with me while he still has the glow on from this peace deal with Israel. He may be the hero for the day, but he needs me and he knows it. Time to pony up."

"Speaking of Israel," Traup said, "Attorney General Hamburg said to tell you that Colonel and Mrs. Jordan will soon be in custody. Israel will extradite Colonel Jordan back to the U.S. and Mrs. Jordan is being arrested for violation of the BIDTag Act."

"I smell baseball in the air," said Tulrude, a die-hard White Sox fan, with a smile. When Traup flashed a confused look, the president added, "You know, a double-play."

Jessica Tulrude nursed a satisfied grin as the limo gunned away from historic Independence Hall.

THIRTY-TWO

Reagan National Airport, Private Jet Hangar

Cal paced in the lounge as he waited for the pilot of the Jordan family's private jet, the Citation X, to finish his preflight check. While waiting, he put a call in to the Roundtable's media leader.

The voice of Phil Rankowitz finally came on the other end. "Cal, buddy, what's up?"

"I'm in D.C., about to leave on a trip with my mother."

"Anywhere interesting?"

"Yeah, but I can't tell anyone where or why."

"Now you've piqued my curiosity."

"I have something even more important."

"Shoot."

"I got a story that, if we can back it up, will blow the roof off this presidential campaign."

"Sounds like a category-five hurricane news-wise ..."

"At a minimum. This is going to make Watergate and Monica-gate combined look like stuff that belongs in the lifestyle section."

"Spoken like a true tabloid journalist," Phil cracked.

"Okay," Cal continued, noticing that the pilot was exchanging pleasantries with Abigail. "I got to talk fast. You need to find some high-caliber forensic pharmacologists who are not afraid of stepping on political toes. No — strike that. Make that — not afraid to amputate some political feet."

"Ouch."

"I made a few inquiries into the National Institutes of Health and just sent you a qwiktext with the name and contact information of one doctor in particular. According to my research he did a documentary with this guy, but we may need more than one."

"We'll jump on it."

"Also, we have a blood sample that can be sent to any of them to analyze at a moment's notice."

"All right. So, can you give me a hint what we've got here?"

"Remember the *Wizard of Oz*?"

"Let me guess," Phil said, filling in the blanks. "Uh … let's see. A house is about to land on the Wicked Witch of the West …"

After chuckling at Phil's quick pickup, Cal said, "Yeah, something like that." He began to stroll in the direction of the pilot and Abigail.

"Makes me think," Phil said in a voice that was now changing tone, "that God might be moving the chess pieces in a huge way. This is all child's play for the Lord, of course. I was in the book of Haggai recently. Not where I usually spend my Bible-reading time. I'm kind of a New Testament guy. But it pays to keep one foot on each side of Malachi, I think. Anyway, I ran across a verse in chapter two. Just a few words, but it struck me in a powerful way in light of what's going on in America. The dark days we're in. The election. And the tidal wave of change around the world … It said, 'I will overthrow the thrones of kingdoms and destroy the power of kingdoms and nations …'"

"I need that reminder," Cal said, "about who's really in control. Especially now, in the middle of this chaos. And listen, Phil, Mom and I need prayer. Like right *now*. I'll fill you in later."

Cal clicked off his Allfone, greeted their longtime family pilot, and climbed into the Citation X.

When he and Abigail were buckled in, he turned to her. "Did our backpacks get loaded?"

"Check," she said, nodding. "Did you contact Phil?"

"Yes. He's going to line up some medical experts with steel in their spines."

"By the way," she said with a smile, "nice of you to finally fill in your mother with the news story of the century you've dug up — 'Vice President Poisons President and Steps into Oval Office.'"

Suddenly hearing it phrased like that, the full weight of the revelation bore down on Cal. "Almost sounds like a Shakespearean tragedy, doesn't it?"

As the jet slowly turned toward the runway, Cal glanced back and caught a glimpse of the tiny green light of the surveillance camera mounted on the top of the hangar. He said aloud, "I wonder who's watching us now."

TH1RTY-THREE

Through the jet's windows, Abigail and Cal could only see the pitch black of evening. The pilot clicked on the intercom, "Jackson Hole, Wyoming, folks, straight ahead."

ooo

Down at the airport, just out of sight, an SIA field agent sat in one vehicle, and four local police officers were in two squad cars, all poised in the shadows to rush toward the incoming jet. The plan was to wait until the plane had taxied to a stop, and then to roar up to it from three directions, pinning it in, so the jet couldn't attempt a turnaround and a quick takeoff.

"Remember," the SIA agent said to the two squads, as he leaned toward his dashboard audiofone, "I take Mrs. Jordan into custody. You four take the pilot and her son. Keep your subjects in custody in separate squads for interrogation. I'll take Mrs. Jordan to the plane that I've chartered and have standing by. Remember, I won't be able to hang around your lovely city. I'll have my charter take off immediately for Washington — just me and my subject in cuffs."

"Anything else we ought to know?" one of the local deputies asked.

The SIA agent flicked on his dash light and glanced at his digital data pad. He tapped on the little window of his screen that said Extrinsic Data Field and answered, "It says here the subject may have picked Wyoming to land because she is believed to have personal contacts here, maybe people who will aid and abet her. This is Senator Hewbright's home state, and she's a supporter. Extrinsic database says she gave money to his campaign and has met with him personally. She and her husband have visited here three times in the last five years for recreational purposes."

The SIA agent clicked off his dash light and radio, then said to himself, "Looks like we've got you figured out, Mrs. Jordan."

□□□

The pilot started the descent.

"Citation X," the tower called in, "you're cleared to land."

"Roger," the pilot responded. Then he brought the private jet perfectly in line with the airstrip ahead and continued to drop.

Ten seconds later the pilot clicked on his transmitter again. "Stand by."

"Tower standing by."

"Okay ..." was all the pilot said at first. Then, a few seconds later, he said, "Landing gear ..."

"Sorry, Citation, didn't catch that. Say again ..." Silence. The tower radioed again. "Say again, Citation. We're tracking you, and you're cleared for landing."

"I said, landing gear."

"Oh, okay. Landing gear," the man in the tower responded with a lighthearted laugh. "That's always a good idea."

"No," said the pilot, "landing gear light ... not up yet ..."

Down below, just off the tarmac, the SIA agent who was looped into the tower's conversation was staring at the little audio screen on his dashboard.

"Clear to land, Citation," the tower barked again.

"My landing gear light isn't lighting up," the pilot explained.

"Toggle it," came the sharp reply from the tower.

"Did that."

"Do a flyover," the tower responded. "With our big spots we'll give you a visual of your underside, to make sure your landing gear is completely down and in place."

The pilot of the Citation X clicked off his external radio control and calmly announced over the intercom, "Abigail, Cal, hold on tight now ..."

Suddenly, the Citation jolted upward at forty degrees. The jet soared off in a westerly direction, over the mountain range that ringed Jackson Hole.

"Citation, this is tower. Please make a flyover immediately! This is the tower. Bring your jet ..."

But the pilot was no longer listening. "Folks, we'll be getting some slight turbulence over the mountains," he said to his two passengers. "You can sit back and relax. Next stop, Washington State."

SIA Headquarters

The sun had not yet risen in Maryland, but it would be up in another twenty minutes. An early-shift Tag Enforcement officer was standing over Jeremy's screen, drinking from a large paper cup of coffee. He was looking at the big red box with two Xs in it in the upper right-hand corner of the monitor.

"Hey," he said to Jeremy, who was hunched over the screen, "I see you got a big fat double-failed notice on your locator status window ..."

"Gee, thanks," Jeremy grunted. "'Cuz until you mentioned it, I hadn't noticed the huge red Xs staring me right in the face ..."

"Maybe you need Sheila to come down here."

"Negative. I can handle this," Jeremy snapped back.

Fifteen minutes later, the director strode in with a Red Notice Status Memo in his hand. He usually didn't arrive until well after dawn. Jeremy had been frantically swishing his hand across the screen, moving from menu to menu to try to insure the location of his subject. But when he saw the director, his hand froze.

The other Tag Enforcement officer slinked out and down the hall to his cubicle, clutching his mocha latte.

The director approached Jeremy, holding a crumpled email in his fist, his face radiant with flushed heat. He stood directly over Jeremy.

"This is a major malfunction, Jeremy," he growled.

"Yes, sir."

"You will consummate positive location and apprehension of the subject Abigail Jordan — and I mean in a hurry. You understand?"

"Absolutely."

"Which is why I've instructed Sheila to come down from master control and make sure it happens. The efficacy of our BIDTag protocol is on the line. The White House is watching me, and I am watching you. And you know what else?"

Jeremy shook his head.

"I'm watching your descending career path. I'll make sure the odds of your holding onto this or any other meaningful job for the rest of your life will be about the same as a porpoise playing first base for the Nationals if this snafu doesn't get turned around."

The director stormed out.

Five minutes later, a woman with stringy, slightly disheveled hair, came strolling into Jeremy's room while munching a candy bar.

When Jeremy spotted Sheila he was about to make a crack about her eating a Snickers bar before six in the morning but decided against it.

Without expression, Sheila shooed Jeremy out of his swivel chair by wagging the fingers of both hands like the maître d' in an expensive restaurant might do to a homeless visitor.

Once planted in the chair, which she first adjusted to her taller height, Sheila proceeded to display programs on Jeremy's screen with lightening speed.

"I've never seen those properties before," Jeremy muttered as he watched the master at work.

After another fifteen minutes or so, Sheila tapped a lower quadrant of the screen that read, "All National Systems Synced."

Then the red X box in the upper right section of the screen disappeared. It was replaced by a display that said, "Reboot Completed — Advanced Search Commencing."

"You know," Sheila said with mild irritation, "I told the guys here at SIA I didn't have time to train you humanoids on the second floor." Then she sighed and got up from the chair.

Jeremy pointed to his computer. "What did you do?"

"It's what you *didn't* do," she said with a lilting whine, "like integrating all the systems. What good does it do for us to spend billions on all this stuff — voice- and facial-recognition monitors, BIDTag scanners, the Personal Profiler EX-3, All Extrinsic Database and Likely Route Estimator programs, and all those cameras and mics planted in every corner of the country — when morons like you forget to synchronize them during your subject location search?"

When Sheila reached the door she tossed one last comment over her shoulder. "Now hit Start," she said. "Your Red Notice subject, whoever she is, won't have a chance."

TH1RTY-FOUR

Olympia Airport, Washington State

As the Citation X rolled to a stop on the tarmac, Abigail and Cal had already unbuckled themselves and were reaching for their backpacks. Abigail tucked her legal file in the center zip pocket.

"You didn't catch any Zs on the flight over, did you?" Cal said.

She shook her head. "I had to go over my notes, getting ready to argue your father's case." Then she looked down at the atomic-clock function of her Allfone. "Which is now less than forty-eight hours away." She closed her eyes, contemplating the enormity of the mission ahead of her. She muttered something aloud — a prayer, mixed with exasperation — "Dear Lord, all things are possible with You. But this is really coming right down to the wire ..."

As they deplaned, the pilot shook their hands. "I'll take care of the FAA and SIA inquiries. But just remember — there are four webcams here on the tarmac. So you've already been logged into the system. The clock is ticking. It won't be long before SIA catches up to your location here. A personal car, not a rental, is waiting for you in the parking lot," he added, "courtesy of your friends at the Roundtable." He handed Cal a piece of paper with the parking-lot location and the make and model. "The car's unlocked. The keys are wedged between the retractable headrest and the top of the passenger-side front seat." The last thing their pilot said before disappearing into the hangar, was, "Godspeed, Mrs. Jordan. And you too, Cal."

Abigail and Cal lugged their backpacks through the small regional airport, leaving through the security exit doors. They knew the cameras up at the ceiling were catching them from several angles. All they could do was to hope and pray that they would be able to arrive at their destination before the SIA agents tracked them down. The blessing was that the little airport was not close to any major federal law enforcement offices.

While the element of time was not on their side, something else was — the primeval kind of environment ahead of them. The long arm of government scanner surveillance had not yet reached the remote wilderness area they were about to enter.

In the parking lot they located the green Land Rover. As planned, the car was unlocked, and the keys were under the passenger headrest.

Cal jumped behind the wheel, and Abigail sat in the passenger seat with Cal's micro laptop open. They headed north on the 101, toward Skokomish. After forty minutes, they were surrounded by dense forest and mountains. While Cal pushed the Land Rover as fast as they could afford to go, Abigail opened the extensive trail of emails between Cal and the clandestine group they hoped to meet.

"Cal, you've been connecting with them for five months. No," she corrected herself, paging down more emails, "almost six months."

"Ever since you started talking about not getting BIDTagged," Cal replied.

"And you did all that for me?"

"I had a feeling you were going to need something like this. Without your BIDTag, I knew this was your only chance."

"Thank you," she said, reaching over and squeezing his arm. Suddenly she was aware of the strength in his arms. He hadn't shaved, and his face had the same kind of dense bristles that Joshua would get. And there was a rugged maturity now to his profile, no longer the baby-faced teenager.

"Your dad would be so proud of the man you've become," she said. "He *is* so proud, Cal."

Cal tightened his face and didn't respond. After a while he said, "I miss him. We have to get his case turned around so we can all be together again." Then he added, "For however long we've got down here."

That took Abigail by surprise. She and Joshua were the ones who had been talking about the approaching apocalypse. They never hid their strong belief that Jesus Christ was poised, any minute now, to enter human history once again — to whisk his believing flock off the face of the planet, just before the beginning of the end.

But now, hearing Cal open up about that same thing — about the imminent return of Christ — it brought home what she had always believed in her heart, that the truth that had so spiritually revolutionized the lives of the parents had been quietly observed and absorbed by their son and their daughter. She silently spoke it in her mind. *Your word never returns void, O Lord. It always bears fruit in the right season.*

Then she went back to the email trail on the screen.

"Who is this Chiro Hashimoto they're talking about?"

"A software technology genius," Cal said. "I've read about him over the years. He was hired by Introtonics in Seattle when he was only a sophomore at Stanford, put in charge of high-tech research for the corporation. According to one article, he was developing a really advanced laser process for encoding and storing information when he left Introtonics."

"Why did he leave?"

"He found out that the White House had cut a deal with Introtonics to use his laser process to create the human BIDTag process. He's a privacy freak, totally against information systems collecting data about people. So one day he packed up his personal stuff from his impressive glass office on the floor just below the corporate president's suite, grabbed his little sculpture of Rodin's *The Thinker*, and walked out. Totally disappeared. Like vapor."

"And you know for a fact he's up here in the Olympic National Forest?"

"Not *in* the forest. Right on the edge. In a private compound."

"And you tracked him down?"

"Took several months. I had to send some fishing bait out. Posted some things on obscure, hi-tech computer networking sites. The kind of ultra-advanced technology blogs I figured that a guy like Chiro Hashimoto might be reading from his hideout, wherever that was. A lot of rumors about him — some said that he was dead. Others said he had been hired by China to hack into American security systems. Another said he brought down Wall Street's digital trading system a few years ago."

"He sounds like an anarchist," Abigail said.

"I don't believe all the rumors, but one thing's clear — he's not your average computer geek."

"Why does he trust you?"

"I'm not sure he does."

Abigail had a stunned look on her face. "Wait. I don't understand."

"I've only communicated with his group — they call themselves the Underground. A super-secret group that protests the BIDTag program — and they don't use the new international currency — the CReDO — either. But I haven't connected directly with Hashimoto."

"Why would they trust you? How do you know they're not just taking you for a ride?"

"I told them my father developed the RTS system and that my mother was the ringleader of the group that singlehandedly tried to stop the terror plot to detonate a nuke inside New York City."

"*Ringleader*? You called your mother a 'ringleader'?"

"Hey, Mom, don't be such a ... a *mom*. I had to make you sound exotic. You know, rebellious."

"I consider myself a patriot — not a rebel. There's a difference."

Cal laughed.

"It's not funny," Abigail said. "What kind of impression do they have of me anyway?"

Cal laughed louder. "I love the way you are always Miss Manners, Mom — except when you're on the other side of a legal argument, and then you really go for the kill. You forget, I've seen you in action."

They fell into a comfortable silence.

Two hours later they saw a sign: "Skokomish 10 Miles." Cal checked his odometer and turned it to zero. Two and a third miles later, he saw a fire trail cut into the deep forest on the left.

"That's it," he said.

"You sure? It looks like it leads up the foothills and into a dead-end."

"This is exactly what they told me."

Cal checked his rearview mirror to make sure no other cars were around. Then he wheeled the Land Rover across the highway and onto the rough fire trail.

They began to bump their way up the path, jiggling the car so violently that their voices quivered when they spoke.

"I was just thinking about Dad," Cal said, "wondering how he's doing, whether he's safe."

"This may sound odd," Abigail said, "but I've learned not to worry about your father. At least not too much. God gifted that dear man with an uncanny ability to get out of the worst kind of trouble." Then she added, "I've actually been sitting here thinking about something else."

"What's that?"

"I've been wondering, down to my soul, what in the world has happened to my country."

The screen on Cal's Allfone, which was lying on the dashboard, lit up with a video email. He pulled the car to a halt. "This could be important," he said and tapped the Receive key. "This may be our rendezvous."

But it wasn't. The image of Captain Jimmy Louder was on the screen. The text said,

> Thanks for friending me on Facebook, Cal. I'm trying to connect
> with your dad but can't get any intel on his current whereabouts —
> for obvious reasons now that I know all about his situation. Any
> suggestions? Capt. J. Louder.

Cal handed the Allfone over to Abigail who glanced at the message and smiled. "Okay, give him Ethan's email. He's screening incoming communications for Josh."

After tapping in Ethan's email address, Cal hit Reply. "I wonder what that's about," he asked aloud. Abigail shrugged.

Cal redirected his attention to the steep path through the woods ahead, and he hoped, after all this effort and risk, they would be able to meet with the secretive Chiro Hashimoto and his Underground. He put the Land Rover into low gear and continued the rough, jostling drive up the fire trail that cut deep into the wilderness.

TH1RTY-F1VE

Headquarters of the Central Intelligence Agency, Langley, Virginia

That same morning, as usual, William Tatter, director of the Central Intelligence Agency, had been picked up at his brownstone mansion in Old Town Alexandria by his sedan driver. Now the black sedan was pulling off of Dolly Madison Boulevard and into the familiar entrance leading to the two-hundred-and-twenty-six-acre intelligence compound.

But one thing was utterly unusual — the encrypted iGram message he had received in the early morning hours on his digital Com-Pad from one of his inside sources. He had to read it twice while shaving just to make sure he wasn't dreaming; then he swore so loudly that his wife thought that he accidentally sliced his neck with his razor. From home, Tatter immediately called his special liaison to the National Security Council and, after that, his deputy in charge of communications with the congressional intelligence oversight committees. Tatter was not a man to be blindsided. Apparently, on that day, he had been. An embarrassing realization for a spy chief. The classified iGram message proved what William Tatter had been famous for saying among his colleagues privately — that domestic spying was now the primary province of SIA, Homeland Security, and whoever happened to be Jessica Tulrude's pal.

When Tatter blustered into his office suite on the top floor, directly above the entrance doors of the agency building, he was informed by

TIM LaHAYE AND CRAIG PARSHALL

his executive assistant that the secretary of state would be visiting him that morning. Fifteen minutes later, the secretary arrived.

"Vance," Tatter said to him with visible distress, "I already know about this outlandish development. It's absurd. Maybe even treasonous."

"Oh, come on, William," the secretary said, "you had to know this was coming."

"Tulrude is — excuse my bluntness — stark raving crazy if she thinks that the CIA is going to be subject to international control of the Security Council of the U.N. This is insane."

"It's nothing new — "

"I really thought this was just some nutty idea of a bunch of radical political scientists who must be doing dope on the side — "

"You're overstating it," the secretary said calmly. "All the treaty requires is that the U.S. government must disclose to the U.N. security council, in advance, any American clandestine operations of the CIA prior to actually taking hostile action against any other nation that is a member in good standing of the United Nations."

"I got the memo. It doesn't change my mind. Well ... okay, maybe. I'll retract my comment about the proponents of this absurdity doing dope on the side. Instead, how about this — they must be on hard drugs. How about that?"

The secretary rolled his eyes. "We may not be able to do everything over at State," he said, "but we can do one thing well. We can count. And we know we've got the votes in the senate to ratify this treaty. We both know it."

Tatter's face expressed no displeasure, but his voice told a different story. His tone carried a message of total disdain. "Where is Roland Allenworth in this discussion? The secretary of defense should be here right now. He'll be equally disgusted at this act of total betrayal of America's interests."

"As for Roland," the secretary of state said as he rose to leave, "he is announcing his resignation later today."

Tatter was a Washington veteran. He knew the rules. He shot back, "But that's not what's *really* going on. What's really happening is that

Tulrude is cleaning house before the election, kicking the honest ones out of her administration so they can't spill the gory details of what has really gone on during her tenure in the Oval Office. Honestly, Vance, is there anything our president would not do for political gain? Does she have any honor left at all?"

As the secretary of state strolled toward the door he stopped long enough to ponder William Tatter's indictment of the president. "Honor? Yes, that noble, if not antiquated, value mentioned in the Declaration of Independence. *Our sacred honor* ... Well, Bill, I'll tell you what's sacred. Global peace and harmony. We are witnessing a new world unfolding before us."

Tatter had a look of resignation now, as if he had just glimpsed the future. Behind the happy placards and politically correct billboards, he could see the black smoke rising up from a dawning empire of destruction. "A new world order?" he called out to the secretary of state. "Maybe. But still guided by human corruption. That's what is going to be pulling the levers behind the curtain."

Georgetown, Washington, D.C.

Deborah Jordan was hustling breathlessly down the sidewalk along the shopping and restaurant district. She had been given the message about a secret rendezvous point, but she wondered, *I don't remember a magazine stand in front of Charley Beck's Restaurant.*

She strode down the sidewalk from the parking garage until she approached the restaurant. "Can't believe it," she said under her breath as she brushed past pedestrians. There, off to the side of the entrance to Charley Beck's, was an old-fashioned magazine and newspaper stand. Ever since the migration of all news publications to the Internet, those relics of the old print world had slowly become extinct.

The guy manning the booth was middle-aged with sunglasses and a Washington Redskins cap.

Deborah remembered the routine given to her by Pack McHenry, the shadowy black-ops manager of private intelligence services. His group — known only as the Patriots — was the stuff of legend among the members of her parents' Roundtable. She got the drift from her father that Pack McHenry, a former CIA foreign operations director, had really never left the Agency, that he and his team of special operations veterans were still assisting the United States government — but very discreetly. Not just under the radar — but practically invisible on the map.

After talking to her mother in her suite at the Mayflower the day before, she did as she was asked. She had called McHenry's number. He had answered with one word: "Patriots."

Deborah had introduced herself and said she was carrying a request from Abigail Jordan.

"Anything for the Jordans," he had replied.

She put in the request for a passport check on Zeta Milla and gave all of the background information she had about the Cuban beauty.

"Done," he said on the other end.

Then Deborah broached the other request. "I need a reliable, authentic-looking driver's license ID for myself. My picture and address. But identifying me as Deborah Shelly."

"Who's going to be checking it?"

"Some very official people ... who carry guns."

"Gotcha." Then, Pack McHenry sobered. "I have such respect for your dad and mother. Worked on some pretty important projects together behind the scenes. Saved lives. Protected the country. Tell them that I wish them God's speed, won't you?"

There had been a final good-bye kind of tone to his comment that sent a chill up Deborah's spine.

"I certainly will, Mr. McHenry," she simply said in return.

"My friends call me Pack," he had said. "Young lady — I know your position over at the Pentagon. How hard you worked at West Point to get where you are. And I also know how you must be risking all of that with what you've got planned. Your parents will be very proud."

That struck home. She stammered for just an instant, then recovered. "Yes ... sir. I appreciate your thoughts."

Before clicking off, Pack had issued a final word. "The daylight is waning, Deborah. Night's coming. A long, terrible night, I fear. What your parents believe — the coming end of days. Wrapping up of human history. The coming hand of God Almighty. Victoria — my wife — and I ... haven't been the religious type, but the more we look around, we find it pretty hard to deny it now. It's all coming to pass. Josh and Abby have been right all along, you know. The Bible. The prophecies. Everything."

"Yes, sir. I believe it too."

"Well," he said finishing the thought, "you can tell your folks that I said that. I'm doing a lot of thinking lately."

That was yesterday, and now Deborah reflected again on his words as she approached the vendor on the sidewalk, the guy with the Redskins cap.

She recited the script. "I'm looking for a Superman Comic book from 1985. The one with Supergirl."

"I'm all out," the man grunted, "but I thought you'd like to see this."

He handed her an old tattered tour guide for visiting Cuba, which must have been printed before Castro came to power. Deborah smiled. Pack McHenry had a sense of humor, that was clear.

She reached in her purse, but the man frowned and shook his head. "It's on the house."

When Deborah reached her car, she opened up the book, and inside was a pristine-looking driver's license for "Deborah Shelly" with her photo on it. She drove out of the parking garage and back onto M Street North West. But when she drove by Charley Beck's, the guy with the Redskins hat was gone. And so was the magazine stand.

TH1RTY-S1X

Israel

Joshua had been talking about risk at the beginning of their ride out of
Jerusalem. Now Ethan, sitting in the back seat, listened as Josh mentioned it again.

"You're taking a big risk," Josh said, turning to Joel Harmon who
was driving the Volvo. "Or did you forget that in Israel I'm now an
enemy of the state?" Ethan saw Josh's face grow momentarily solemn.
He knew how weary his friend had grown over his troubles in the U.S.
Now Israel, his so-called safe harbor, had turned against him too.

Joel didn't look worried. "I may be a freshman legislator in the
Knesset, but I know my way around these Shin Bet security issues.
We'll get you to a safe house, Josh. If I'm asked by anyone where I'm
going, I've got an answer handy."

Ethan said, "I'd like to hear that one."

"Simple," Joel shot back, "I'll tell Shin Bet, thanks to me, they
don't have to worry about Joshua Jordan being inside Israel anymore."
Joshua and Ethan waited for an explanation. "I'm taking you to the
Palestinian Authority side," Joel added. "Because of the deal cut with
the U.N. by our prime minister, that area is becoming part of the new
Palestinian State — off limits to Israel."

Josh had a curious look on his face.

Joel laughed. "You think I'm taking you out of the pot and throw-
ing you into the fire?"

"Now you're sounding like an American. I would have thought
you'd have a clever Hebrew phrase for that," Josh tossed back.

"We do. But now that Sol Bensky is forcing Israel to be absorbed into the international community," Joel said with a sneer, "I'm working on trying to sound non-Jewish."

Joshua nodded. "You did a brave thing, Joel, opposing the prime minister on his U.N. plan, but I still don't know how smart it was bringing a flame-thrower like me into that meeting."

"I wasn't trying to be smart," Joel remarked, "just right. And true. When I think of those two qualities — who else besides you could I possibly bring to that meeting?"

In the back Ethan was smiling. In his private moments he had thought about the unique chance he had been given to follow Joshua through his travels, watch him in action, to hear firsthand the respect he had engendered from other men — men who were themselves accomplished and courageous. It made Ethan feel a flush of shame — for just an instant — about his potential plan to leave Joshua and head back to the U.S. He thought he had settled the issue, but lingering doubts kept popping up. He had just helped rescue his mentor back in Jerusalem, and he felt good about that. On other occasions, he felt like a piece of excess baggage on Joshua's bullet train, but not then.

Then Ethan was struck by something else. *Here I am, an ex-Air Force pilot, out of work, and what happens? I get onto a flight and run into Deborah, the daughter of Joshua Jordan, the man who is the envy of the entire defense industry and my own personal hero. The next thing I know I meet him and he offers me a job. So, am I supposed to think this is all coincidence?*

That triggered another thought, something that Joshua was always saying: "In a universe governed by God, there are *no* coincidences."

Why did it always come back to God? For most of Ethan's life, he hadn't given Him much thought. But then the Jordan family swept into Ethan's life, and ever since then, it was as if he was on one of those bumper cars at the carnival — constantly bumping into the Bible, sermons about Jesus, and Joshua's talk of his own encounter with Christ. Now Ethan was living in Israel, tripping almost daily over ancient places where Jesus walked, that Christians point to and say, "*Here* is where God did this . . . or that." Ethan felt surrounded by it all, and he didn't know whether it was that bad a thing or not. Was this some kind of "Custer's Last Stand" for him on the religion issue, with the hostiles all around him with their arrows? Or was it simply a surprising turn of events, where he had a chance to smarten up and maybe learn something about himself or discover something much bigger than even that?

As they drove northeast through the remote desert suburbs of Israel, Ethan had one more question — one that had been pestering him nonstop. *Why do I get the feeling that Joshua brought me with him for reasons he hasn't bothered to explain yet?*

Joel Harmon pulled through a subdivision of Jewish homes in a desolate area. The signs on the outskirts read, "Nablus." The sun had just set.

Joel put the car in Park and turned to face Joshua and Ethan. "We're about fifty feet from the wall separating Israel from the Palestinian Authority. Obviously, you can't exit from the Israeli side through one of the regular checkpoints. There's an alert out on you, Joshua, and it's being passed through all the channels. They'd grab you immediately."

"Let me guess," Joshua said, eyeing the twenty-six-foot-high concrete wall. "We're going to leave Israel *creatively ...*"

"That's the plan," Joel replied.

"These old joints of mine aren't what they used to be," Joshua said. "Haven't scaled a wall like that in a while."

"Oh, don't worry. No repelling. No ropes. Nothing like that. That's not the dangerous part."

Ethan jumped in. "Then what is?"

"See that part of the wall — that concrete slab — that juts out a little?" Joel pointed to a point in the wall about seventy feet away. "See how it's not flush with the rest?"

They nodded.

"That's where two big concrete slabs were dropped into place by the IDF contractors. But the two ends don't exactly meet. There's a space about two-and-a-half feet wide."

"I can't believe they'd leave that open," Ethan said.

"They didn't. Razor wire's been bolted into the gap — but it can be unbolted too ... if you know the right people."

Ethan thought he had it figured out. "So, that's the hard part?"

"Afraid not. Time was when Israel would have roads on the other side of the wall where IDF patrols would cruise. But Sol Bensky ordered those stopped. So now, once you get through our wall, there is DMZ strip about one hundred feet wide until you get to the Palestinian side. You'll have to run like wild men across that strip. It's open ground. When you get to the other side, all they have is a chain-link fence with barbwire on the top. I'll give you some big wire cutters."

Joel glanced in his rearview mirror then checked his side mirror. "Okay, all clear. Everybody out."

There was only one part of the plan that Ethan didn't feel good about. As he climbed out, he asked, "Joel, we're about to enter an area riddled with Arab terror groups, and Josh's RTS system has been used to wipe out a number of those kinds of groups who have launched Stinger missiles and who ended up swallowing their own missiles — like Iran, when they got nuked by their own warheads. So, you're sending us to the Palestinian side ... Why?"

"You'll be staying with Ibrahim Kalid," Joel said as he popped open the trunk, seeming to ignore Ethan's comment.

That didn't sit well with Ethan. Not hiding his sarcasm, he kept it up. "Oh, great. You've got us under the control of some Arab guy?"

Joel reached in and pulled out two red-and-white-checked Arab headdresses and handed them to Joshua along with the wire cutters. "I know we've already gone over this, but here's the plan one more time. You will wait about ten minutes. As it starts to get dark, crawl through the open space. I've arranged for the spotlights to stay off for a few minutes to help you get across." Then he bent into the trunk and pulled out something that looked like a modern version of a long Roman shield, with a handle grip on the backside.

He gave it to Ethan. "High-impact Kevlar riot shield. You're going to want to hang on to this," he added.

TH1RTY-5EVEN

Joel told Joshua and Ethan to wait until he gave them the signal by flashing his headlights. As promised, the gap between the slabs of concrete had been left open. The razor wire had been unbolted from the concrete and pushed aside. They squeezed into the space, while Ethan clumsily clutched the bulletproof shield and Joshua held the wire cutters. It was almost dark.

Then the headlights flashed.

"Go time," Joshua whispered hoarsely.

They bolted out of the space and began to run. Ethan knew he was faster than Josh, so he slowed down a bit to let him keep pace, while holding up the Kevlar shield to protect them from any shots being fired from the right, where Palestinian border guards might be watching.

As they dashed across the first twenty feet, the big floodlights were still out. Better still, no shots were fired. Then, about thirty feet in, the lights blazed on. The whole DMZ strip lit up like a department store.

At forty feet, shots rang out from the guard tower on the Palestinian side. They pinged off the rocks and stones, then started raining down on the shield.

Fifty feet from the goal line, there was a loud boom and a large chunk of dry ground exploded three feet beside them.

"Fifty caliber," Joshua grunted as they kept up the sprint. Ethan hoped the sharpshooter wasn't too sharp. *Will this shield hold off a fifty caliber?*

Ethan kept the shield high enough to guard Joshua's upper body and head. One shot could blast his skull wide open.

Then, twenty feet from the goal line, they heard it.

Boom!

The fifty-caliber bullet struck home, punching into the center of the shield. The force knocked Ethan sideways into Joshua, and they both tumbled to the ground with the shield clattering on the hard sandy soil next to them.

Now someone on the Palestinian side began firing an automatic weapon at them. The bullets raced up the sand in a line toward them.

Ethan picked up the shield and planted it on the ground lengthwise and pulled Joshua up close. A hale of ping-pings sounded as the bullets struck the Kevlar.

"Now," Ethan yelled when the shots stopped momentarily. But as they leaped to their feet, the floodlights shut down. The DMZ strip was plunged into shadows.

The two men ran pell-mell toward the chain-link fence. More shots were fired randomly all along the strip. Ethan worried that a stray bullet would find its mark. He wondered if they were simply going to spray the fence line with bullets, knowing that it was their destination, shooting at that spot until the two reached their goal.

So Ethan decided to take Joshua farther down the strip of sandy ground. "Don't go to the fence yet. Keep running away from their sentry tower." Ethan now held the rear position, keeping the shield high and slightly upward to protect Joshua who ran a few feet ahead of him. They sprinted parallel to the fence for another twenty feet. Three more bullets pinged off the shield. Ethan's arm was getting tired. *Keep holding it up. Don't let it down.*

Then the shots stopped. The two men veered toward the fence. With his wire cutters, Joshua snipped through the metal link until he had opened a space big enough for them to squeeze through.

They dropped the cutters and the shield and donned their Arab headdresses. They ran between two concrete-block houses, trying to tread as softly as they could. Somewhere a dog started barking. Ethan swore quietly under his breath.

"Don't worry," Joshua said. "The Lord has brought us this far."

But Ethan was thinking something else. Like — what's so great about where we are now? In enemy territory — crawling with assassins.

Chased by the Israelis and shot at by the Palestinians. Supposedly, they were here to find refuge in a safe house, but for the life of him, Ethan could not see a safe place anywhere.

As they hit the street leading through the Palestinian suburb, trying to look calm as they strolled, a car approached with its headlights on. It slowed, training the beam on the two of them.

Ethan wished they had taken the time, before meeting up with Joel Harmon, to arm themselves. Now they were sitting ducks.

The late-model Citroen pulled up next to them. With the engine still running, the driver turned off the headlights and said, "Good evening, Colonel Jordan and friend."

Joshua strode up to the driver's side and reached his hand into the car to shake.

The driver was an older man with a close-cropped beard. He enthusiastically took Joshua's hand and said, "I am Pastor Ibrahim Kalid. In Jesus' name, I welcome you to the safety of my car and to the sanctuary of my home and to the friendship of my family."

The men looked at each other with a shared look of surprised amusement, as they jumped in the back of the car.

Pastor Kalid turned around and grinned at Ethan but said nothing. He just kept smiling as if he was waiting for Ethan to give him a greeting, but none came. Finally, Ibrahim Kalid said to Ethan, "And I welcome you also, my friend." As he turned his headlights back on, he added, "My wife has prepared a good meal. We must not be late."

TH1RTY-E1GHT

City of Jenin, Within the Territory of the Palestinian Authority

Anwar al-Madrassa's route from his headquarters in Islamabad to this particular patch of former Israeli geography — now in the hands of the Palestinian Authority — had been a long and tortuous one. His reputation as a major figure of Islamic terrorism made it necessary to take a circuitous route, first in the back of a freight truck to Turkey, then into Syria, and over to Lebanon. That is where a Hezbollah cell rolled him up in a Persian rug and loaded him into a van owned by a carpet store. The van then crossed into an area of Israel now controlled by the PA.

The city of Jenin was a good choice for his new center of operations. It had been the site of bomb-making for suicide terrorists. But now they were working on something that would have been unimaginable in scope so many years before and would make the former efforts of men with their bulky explosive belts under their shirts quite obsolete.

The day after Joshua and Ethan had reached the safe house in Nablus and not far from that city, in an underground laboratory beneath the basement of a children's clothing store, Dr. Ahlam was getting ready to demonstrate his weapon to Anwar al-Madrassa. In his younger years Ahlam had been one of Saddam Hussein's many chemical-warfare researchers. Now he was waiting for al-Madrassa to arrive. When he finally did, Ahlam could hardly control himself.

"Such an honor, may Allah be praised!" he gushed.

But al-Madrassa was in no mood for pleasantries. He wanted to see the experiment.

217

Dr. Ahlam shuttled him into an adjoining room with a glass-enclosed sub-room that contained a wire cage with a dog in it, a German shepherd. Dr. Ahlam offered al-Madrassa a chair, but the chief of the al-Aqsa Jihad terror group waved it off. He stood right up to the glass. He could see everything that way.

Dr. Ahlam donned a triple-layered haz-mat suit and screwed down his protective helmet connected to an oxygen tank. He typed the password into the airlock, and the thick glass door clicked open. He entered the glass room and pushed a button to close the door behind him. Once inside, he stepped over to an iron pipe, which was closed at one end and open at the other, which extended into the wire cage.

On a table was a heavy metal tube, and Ahlam unscrewed it and removed an interior steel lining. Then he took an unusual, industrial-looking syringe and he drew out a single drop of a yellow chemical fluid from the inner container. Ahlam then connected the tip of the needle into a pin-sized hole in the closed end of the pipe, and squeezed the end of the syringe to express the single drop into the pipe.

Two seconds later, the dog gave a worrisome look, then immediately began convulsing in pain, yelping, and vomiting blood. Within ten seconds its fur and skin began to emit smoke as it burned off of the dog's frame, falling away from its skeleton.

Dr. Ahlam looked at his watch. He held up ten fingers and flashed them twice to signify the twenty minutes he would now wait.

Al-Madrassa wasn't overly impressed. VX gas was known to have similar ghastly effects. But this little demonstration had two acts. It was the second act that he was waiting for. He strolled back and forth in front of the glass, hands behind his back.

When the twenty minutes was up, Dr. Ahlam strode up on the other side of the glass, directly in front of al-Madrassa. Then he spread out his arms dramatically, to signal his next move. With a flourish, like the impresario at the center of a miniature circus of horrors, Ahlam pointed the index finger of each hand toward his helmet.

Taking a step closer to the glass, al-Madrassa was transfixed and dropped his hands from behind his back. He stared at the chemist in the glass room.

Ahlam placed his hands on his helmet and began to screw it off the collar of his protective suit. Until the very last turn. When he was at that point, the chemist half bent a knee down as he turned the helmet one last half turn, then popped it off his suit, fully exposing his face and head to the air of the enclosed toxic room. Dr. Ahlam flashed a ghoulish grin. He then scurried up right next to the wire cage that contained the smoldering remains of the dog and placed his face against the wire, holding his hands up into the air for effect.

This was what al-Madrassa had come to see — and he was not disappointed. The implications were staggering. Whole populations of Jews, infidels, and other undesirables could now be gassed in Tel Aviv, even in Jerusalem, and almost immediately the city could be occupied without toxic effects to the Islamic conquerors who could then march in and take over. Buildings, cars, businesses, even food and water supply, would be untouched by the gas — and after twenty minutes of exposure to the air the toxin was designed to completely dissipate.

Al-Madrassa was not one to lavish praise on his deputies. After all, only Allah deserved that. But this — the triumph he had just witnessed — nearly overcame him. On the verge of tears of joy, he slowly clapped his hands together in celebration.

On the other side of the glass, Ahlam took a slow bow and threw a kiss to the terror chief who was applauding.

"Genius," al-Madrassa whispered. "Genius."

Now they could move to the next stage. He would talk to his missile men, after which the planning would begin. He had not forgotten the faces of the people he had planned to be his first two victims. The infidel Jordans from America. Indeed the Jordans, America's most zealous patriots with their detestable Roundtable group and enemies of the great Islamic Jihad ... they would be the perfect targets to start with.

TH1RTY-N1NE

Jerusalem, Temple Mount

The sun was shining, and Alexander Coliquin enjoyed the feeling of warmth on his upturned face. He was standing next to Prime Minister Sol Bensky, who had the aged chief rabbi of Jerusalem next to him. Bensky's two main staffers, Dimi Eliud and Chad Zadok, were hovering in the background.

Because of the threat of an Islamic intifada from a few of the non-cooperative Palestinian groups, the mount had to be ringed with soldiers that day for the ceremony. The security measure was a joint effort by the IDF and the blue-helmeted United Nations troops. That was more than symbolic. It was a preview of the new Jerusalem under Secretary-General Coliquin's peace treaty with Israel. That city would be a truly international province, jointly ruled by both Israel and the U.N.

On the other hand, Coliquin had much to be happy about. Most of the Islamic clerics were on board with his treaty because of the designation of the Palestinian Authority territories within Israel as sovereign, and the international status of Jerusalem, which took it out of the exclusive grasp of the Israelis. After all, the Arab leaders felt assured that when conflicts broke out — which were certain to happen — the U.N. would side with them against Israel.

On the other hand, giving the Jews control over a portion of the Temple Mount was a sticking point, even with the wall that was being constructed to keep them entirely separate from the Muslim Dome of the Rock and from the Al Aqsa Mosque that had been on the plateau for centuries. But then the Palestinian leaders and the Arab League took comfort from the private assurances of Coliquin, though he knew they were not quite sure how he was going to be able to accomplish his audacious plan. He was glad for that.

Coliquin gave the signal and an international band struck up the Israeli national anthem.

When the music stopped, an old rabbi among twelve Jewish leaders at the ceremony watched as Sol Bensky stepped up to the raised podium laced with wireless microphones from every major news organization on the planet. He pointed down to the large cornerstone that was the star attraction for the final and most dramatic feature of the monumentally historic event.

"For two long millennia," he said, "the Jewish people have waited for the rebuilding of their great temple. It was destroyed in AD 70 by an act of violence, during a time when the Roman Empire was at war with the Jewish people. But today," he said, his voice ringing out from the Temple Mount and echoing down on the city of Jerusalem, "today we see the rebuilding of that temple taking place in an epoch full of promise — of peace, not war — of cooperation, not enmity — with two great faiths each agreeing to worship God side-by-side, with mutual respect on this sacred piece of ground. As in the days of Ezra, we raise our hands in praise for the construction that is taking place — and it is marvelous and wonderful in our sight."

The twelve Jewish leaders then strode to the industrial lift that held the white stone monolith. The construction had already begun. Backhoes and tractors had been busy in the Jewish sector of the plateau digging the foundation. Cranes had lowered the first row of stones, all but one — the cornerstone. Now the twelve men stepped back to allow the old rabbi to totter forward to the lever on the industrial lift.

And as in the days of Ezra, the old rabbi covered his eyes and wept. He did not weep with grief. He did not see this as a time that might soon be ripe for mourning, like the fig tree bearing fruit that was pleasing to the eye yet poisonous to consume. Instead, he wept for that which he believed had been fulfilled from the dark, dusty corners of time forgotten.

The rabbi pulled the green lever, and the engine of the lift began to grind and whir as the great stone was slowly tilted with hydraulic precision at the perfect angle so that it would slide down the smooth steel rollers. As it did, the cornerstone dropped into the space between the adjoining stones. A ground-shaking thud was heard when it found its resting place. But there was half an inch of space between the cornerstone and the neighboring stones.

The rabbi and his fellow Jewish historians and engineers and experts in the Talmud had disputed that fact bitterly with Sol Bensky. The engineers had told the Prime Minister that this was the most efficient method to accommodate the ceremony, as the project had been rushed by Bensky, with the first row of stones being laid in a tireless effort with contractors working around the clock. Bensky had ordered that the foundation be laid in a hurry, before any kind of uprising occurred from Palestinian protestors. The religious scholars told him that this design would require that mortar be placed around the cornerstone to fill in the space, something the ancient engineers two thousand years before had avoided, having brilliantly placed the stones of the Herodian temple in perfect symmetry without the use of mortar.

"But back then, thousands of years ago, they didn't have the political problems that I have," Bensky said in reply. And that was that.

The group of twelve rabbis, together with the chief rabbi, each recited a portion of Scripture and prayed over the row of mammoth white stones that were the foundation for the new global center of Jewish worship. With the foundation now laid, the rest of the construction could be finished with lightning speed. The engineers had assured Bensky of that.

But in the midst of the honored guests on the Temple Mount that day, Coliquin was not thinking about engineering details or Bensky's political problems. He had his own agenda. As the last prayer was being recited, Coliquin heard in his Allfone earpiece the chimes of an incoming message. He tapped the tiny ear bud to listen. It was the Deputy Secretary-General Ho Zhu.

"Mr. Secretary," he reported, "I have been in personal dialogue with Faris D'Hoestra. It took some time. Many layers of protection surrounding him. But I got through and spoke with him about your desire for a meeting."

Coliquin, in a hushed voice, asked to hear the specifics.

"D'Hoestra wanted to meet on neutral ground. I expressed your similar thoughts."

"You'd better have done this right, Ho."

"I said you wanted Abu Dhabi. Specifically Dubai."

"Perfect."

Coliquin tapped his ear bud to turn it off. It had been a very satisfying day. The U.N. secretary-general's agenda was far bigger than some temple building on a hill in Jerusalem. And now Coliquin could see that it was getting very close to completion.

FORTY

Washington State, on the Edge of the Olympic National Forest

Two miles up the rough forest trail, Cal pulled the Land Rover to a sudden halt. He had spotted something. He got out and trotted to a large tree just to the left of the lane. After studying it and running his finger along a marking on the bark, he said, "This is it!"

Abigail was reading something on her Allfone, but she clicked it off, hopped out, and joined him. She stared at the bark where someone had carved an intricate image — the shape of a light bulb. Inside the outline, a lowercase *i* had been cut into the center. She asked, "What is it?"

He gave a knowing nod. "The logo of IntraTonics, the software and laser logistics company where Hashimoto used to work. Must be an inside joke. We've got to be close."

Abigail wasn't convinced. "I know you emailed your contact that we were coming, but we can't wait for them to find us. I'm running out of time. Josh's case is being heard in a federal court on the other side of the country tomorrow, and I'm the only one who can handle it. I had hope that Harry Smythe would be my backup, but I just got a text that he's been hospitalized. It may be his heart again. I hope not. So, I have no other legal counsel who can pitch in. I'm it. We have to find these people *now*."

They climbed back into the Land Rover and drove up the trail a quarter of a mile. Cal slowed the car again, then stopped. He gazed out at the woods to the left. "Not exactly a road," he said, pointing to a spot where the underbrush looked less dense, "but wide enough for a four-wheel drive ... maybe." He rolled down the window and clicked off the ignition so he could listen.

"I hear something," Abigail said, "like some kind of vehicle approaching."

"Someone's coming," Cal said, pointing to the cleared space. Moments later, a black Hummer bounced into sight, winding slowly around trees and hitting ditches and rises in the forest floor. It stopped. Four men with beards, sunglasses, and stocking caps on their heads jumped out, mostly decked out in dirty lumberjack shirts and overalls. Two were carrying shotguns.

Abigail had a sudden, fearful thought. *What if these men have nothing to do with the Underground? Maybe they're simply thugs living in the wild, running from the law.*

One of the unarmed men approached them first.

"We've been looking for you —," Cal started to say.

"Shut up," the man barked, "until we ask you to talk."

"What's your name?" he asked Abigail. She identified herself, trying not to tremble.

He stepped up closer, grabbed her, and forced her to the ground as he pulled long plastic zip ties from his pocket. He looped them around her wrists. Cal leaped at him, jamming his forearm under his neck and locking it until the man started gagging and let go of Abigail. Cal then yanked him off of Abigail and tossed him sideways to the ground and shouted, "What are you doing? You know who we are and why we —" But Cal didn't have a chance to finish his sentence. Two of the other men jumped him from behind, and one of them slugged him twice in the side of the head. Abigail screamed, but they ignored her. The two men pinned Cal and zip-tied him while the other secured Abigail.

At that moment a small all-terrain four-wheeler came rushing out of the woods and slammed on its brakes next to the Hummer. Another bearded man hopped out, this one dressed in dockers and a clean sweatshirt. He had a photocopy of the headshots that Cal had emailed the group when he had first set up the meeting. The man compared the faces in the picture with Cal and Abigail on the ground. He said, "Okay, men, no need to get rough. These are the ones." He bent down to Abigail. "Sorry about the inconvenience, Mrs. Jordan, but we can't be too careful. The government would love to know our location." Then he ordered the men to cut the zip-ties.

As Abigail and Cal stood up, the leader added, "But I'm going to insist that you wear hoods over your heads until we reach the compound."

An hour later, Abigail found herself sitting across from the mysterious Chiro Hashimoto in a forlorn camping lodge. The front yard was filled with tall weeds, and the main building, constructed of split logs, had moss creeping up its outside.

Hashimoto was a slim Japanese man in his early forties, but he looked younger with his head of wild, untamed black hair, which seemed to sprout in all directions. Now that Abigail had her personal audience with the iconoclastic computer genius, she was going to give him a piece of her mind. "You men are outrageous! Cal gave you notice that we were coming, and why. Roughing us up was uncalled for!"

Hashimoto seemed nonplussed. "You're the one who needs me, not the other way around. So we can treat you any way we want."

"You should be ashamed of yourself!"

Hashimoto laughed loudly. "So, you're going to act like my mother now?"

She glanced around at the dirty dishes stacked on a table in the corner. "You clearly need one around here."

"Look," Hashimoto shot back, "the way your son went after my guy, you should be glad that neither of you got shot. And you know what else?" Hashimoto stiffened his back and tilted his head slightly. "I think your son is a punk."

Abigail went snake-eyed and blurted out, "You may think he's just a computer geek because he managed to hunt you down, but if it was just the two of you in a fair fight, he'd break both your arms."

Hashimoto grinned back. "And what makes you think I fight fair?"

He gave a loud guffaw as he sat cross-legged, jiggling his foot. His face turned. "Okay. Chitty-chat is over. I know what you want. You got a problem. No BIDTag. And you want Chiro Hashimoto's magic solution."

"I'll be frank with you," Abigail said, "because I'm desperate. In about — " she glanced at the atomic clock on her Allfone — "nineteen hours, I've got to be in a federal court of appeals in Washington, arguing my husband's case."

"You're not going to make it, lady. How you going to get there in time from here?"

"Don't worry about that. I've got my travel plans set. But what I can't do is pass through a BIDTag scanner without your help. I'm a nontagger."

"When chips are down, you need Chiro Hashimoto," he said with a sly smile.

"That's right," she said, "but first I want to make sure Cal is okay. Where did they take him?"

Hashimoto waved to a man standing outside who had been peering in through a dirty window. The man disappeared, and in a minute Cal was led into the room. Hashimoto dismissed his man and pointed to a chair next to Abigail. He asked Cal to sit. "I've read up on you guys," Hashimoto said, "all of you. You Jordans are some kind of wild, wacky family." He tittered. "Don't really know, though, if I like your Roundtable. Maybe some of your agenda is okay. Other stuff, not quite so sure. But I like the way you tell the big fed power tyrants they got to watch out."

"I think you're the real rebel here," Cal said. Abigail could see that Cal was trying to win Hashimoto over. "You masterminded the biggest global computer network hacking job ever accomplished. If, in fact, that was you — "

Hashimoto grinned. "Kid's stuff. I just used some advanced spearphishing emails contaminated with malicious software and spread through botnets — my own design — aimed at worldwide organizations and several countries. They click onto my infected link and — presto — I get an open door into their entire network. I was on the verge of an attack even bigger — an instant entrée into all thirteen root servers that control the entire Internet."

"So, why'd you leave China?" Cal asked.

"The IT bureau guys in Beijing said they would hurt me bad if I didn't do everything they wanted. That was like a big poke in the eye. I kind of woke up, you know? I decided to get out fast. Next stop, Seattle, and IntraTonics." He turned to Abigail and added with a grin, "Also lady, I don't really think Cal is a punk. I was just playing with you."

Cal jumped in. "Chiro, can my mother get one of your masking BIDTag facsimiles?"

He rubbed his chin and turned his attention to her. "So, your husband, Colonel Jordan ... I've read some of the tech journals on his RTS invention. Nice little system he's developed. So, this legal case he's got ..."

"He's been charged with treason. The real story is he's a patriotic American hero who has done nothing wrong, but President Tulrude is bent on using the attorney general's office to destroy him. This goes all the way back to when Tulrude was vice president. Josh's AmeriNews Internet service started to expose her corruption. She knows that the Department of Defense is resentful of her sellout of our country and sympathetic to what the Roundtable is trying to accomplish — to educate the American people about the garage-sale giveaway of American national security and sovereignty by Tulrude's administration."

"Okay, yeah," Chiro said, "interesting. But I don't get why you need my help, lady."

"I'm my husband's attorney. I've got to plead his case tomorrow. If I don't, he and I will be forced to stay on opposite ends of the earth, and Josh will never get a fair trial. Ever. But I can't take a single step into that federal court building — through the scanners — unless I've got something that looks and acts like a BIDTag on the back of my hand."

"I guess you and I have something in common," Hashimoto said. "Neither of us wants to be a tagged chicken in the government's henhouse. But I always wondered why the government wouldn't let people get tagged after the deadline ... you know, for people who change their minds. Just make them pay a fine, that kind of thing. It didn't make sense."

"I could speculate," Abigail said. As she looked at Hashimoto's widening eyes, she could see he was interested. "It's my guess that Tulrude's tough, no-amnesty for nontaggers was part of some deal she made with international leaders. Part of a global plan she's tied into. There's somebody at the very top — higher even than the president — who needs every human on this planet to be controlled through BIDTagging."

Hashimoto leaned back in his chair. "Yeah, yeah. The big plan. Right. The worldwide game. I've been thinking about that." Then he broke into a big grin. "But I got my own plan. I can outsmart the global people. I have a plan for gaming their own game."

"I came to you for help," Abigail said. "So, in return, I'm going to help you. I'm going to tell you something important. You may be a computer genius, Chiro, but you need to know that some systems can't be gamed. The prophetic events that God is about to unfold can't be sidetracked or avoided. I'm here because I believe God is about to allow Planet Earth to be shaken in a very dramatic way. Titanic events — horrible catastrophes — human suffering, yes, all of that is about to come to pass. But in the midst of it all, a chance for everyone, including you, Chiro, to consider the most important figure in the history of the world — Jesus Christ. What He did for us in the past — His death on the cross for your sins, and His promise of eternal life for everyone who believes in Him and receives His forgiveness as Savior and Lord. And then there's what He's going to do in the future — when a few years of worldwide suffering have passed, Jesus will come back to establish His reign on earth. His kingdom. I'm telling you this because, when these events are ready to burst upon the scene, my son, Cal, and I, and many, many others — all of the followers of Jesus Christ, we will all be taken off the earth."

Chiro gave a funny look, jutting his head backward. "You taking a space ship or something?" And then he gave a nervous laugh.

Abigail gave him a warm, mothering smile. "Jesus is calling His

TIM LaHAYE AND CRAIG PARSHALL

own, His true followers to Himself, those who have believed in Him and whose spirits have become born again as a result. In one, fleeting blink of an eye, we will be gone and will be in the presence of the King of Kings. I hope by that time you will be one of those, Chiro. But if not, then just remember what I told you today. If you find yourself left behind, surrounded by an unbelieving world full of chaos, and violence, growing cold, and loveless, and dark, then remember this conversation. Whatever else you do, remember what I just told you."

Chiro was now wrinkling the side of his mouth, not smiling, not sneering, but considering the unthinkable. "You're talking about the end, aren't you? The end of the world."

Abigail nodded and smiled in a way that looked into his eyes and way beyond. Then Chiro jumped to his feet. "Okay, lady, I'll help you. Quick, quick. Follow me."

FORTY-ONE

Special Agent Ben Boling was in his office, finishing up reports at his desk. He was summarizing his investigation into the possible threat against Senator Hewbright. He had been walking a razor-thin line with John Gallagher, collecting tips and dropping hints himself, but just short of violating Bureau rules.

When Boling was in Wichita, he scoured the records of the Better Body Health and Fitness Club where Perry Tedrich was a member and had worked out the day of his disappearance. Boling learned something intriguing. On the day that Tedrich had been there, a woman member said that, after her workout, her membership card went missing, apparently when she was in the shower. At first she thought she had misplaced it but realized it had probably been stolen. While the locker rooms were open to the public, a card was required to get into the gym itself. For some reason the owner had set up a system where the membership cards had RFID chips and ID numbers in them but no other identifying data — no picture, no name. According to the fitness center, that was to protect the privacy of their members.

When the manager of the center found out about the possible theft, he made a general announcement over the PA, warning the people in the gym to make sure their cards were secure. Boling figured that Tedrich must have heard that and placed his card in his shoe for safekeeping.

Boling asked the owner to check the computer registration log. It showed that the woman whose card was stolen entered the gym at 12:30 p.m. that day. She left at 1:20 p.m. when she had finished her workout. But someone, using the same card, went back to the gym at 1:28 p.m., about three minutes after Perry Tedrich had arrived.

One thing that had not been made public was the fact that Perry Tedrich wasn't just the head of Hewbright's Wichita campaign. He had also been an integral part of Hewbright's Washington senate staff for several years, before returning to his hometown of Wichita to run that city's campaign headquarters. He knew Hewbright as well as anyone in the capital, including a lot of personal contact with Hewbright's late wife, who had died of cancer two years earlier. Did Tedrich have some personal or political information about Hewbright that his enemies wanted to learn?

That was when Boling put in a city-wide request for hotels, restaurants, bars, and movie theaters — all of which now were using RFID scanners as well as BIDTag scanners — to see if the computer chip in the membership card registered a hit at any one of them that day. He received one result. The card carrier had entered the Red Steer Bar and Grill at 3:00 p.m. At the exact same time, the RFID chip in Tedrich's membership card also registered a hit as he also walked into the restaurant. At 4:50 p.m., Perry Tedrich's credit card was hit for a lunch for a party of two. No one at the Red Steer remembered Tedrich or the mystery woman, but the cards showed that they left together.

Boling felt he was closing in. He was about to put it in writing when a flag showed up in the corner of his computer screen. It read: "Assignment Status Report."

He read it over, groaned, and shot back an insta-memo to the sender. "Is this true?"

The reply showed up on his screen five minutes later. "Yes. Effective immediately."

Boling sat at his desk, staring out the window for nearly half an hour. Then he called his wife. "Hey, it's me. Okay, honey, how about dinner out tonight? Your choice of restaurant."

"Sure, but I've already thawed some pork chops."

"Feed 'em to the dogs."

"Something wrong?"

"I just need to get out and get my mind off my job."

Wichita, Kansas

That same day, John Gallagher had managed to persuade the manager of the Better Body Health and Fitness Center to let him roam among the clients in the gym. Gallagher had simply explained that he was "working the case with FBI Special Agent Ben Boling." Technically true, he mused. Sort of.

He arrived on the same day of the week — at the same time — as when Perry Tedrich had last been there. Gallagher interviewed every woman in the gym, but none of them could remember a thing about that day. He strolled over to a man on the elliptical machine. He flashed a picture of Perry Tedrich, and the man stopped his routine and took a look. "Yeah, he looks familiar. I've seen him here."

Then Gallagher asked whether he recalled the day of the incident and gave the date and added, "The desk records say you came in that day."

The guy became a little ill at ease, but Gallagher assured him he wasn't the focus of any investigation and had nothing to worry about. So he started opening up. He said he vaguely remembered Tedrich being there that day.

"Do you remember any new faces that day?"

The man smiled. "Oh, yeah. A real looker. A really fine-looking woman working one of the ellipticals down the row there."

Gallagher asked for a description, after which he pulled out pictures of some of the women on Hewbright's staff, together with a few wildcards thrown in for good measure. He showed them to the man and told him to take his time.

"This one," he said, pointing to one of the photos. He picked that photo out in an instant, and Gallagher knew why. He thanked the man, trotted out of the fitness center, and immediately speed-dialed Ben Boling.

When the FBI agent answered, Gallagher skipped the pleasantries. "Ben, hot off the press. I know you don't want any official help from us Roundtable types, but I also know the politics of the new FBI since Tulrude took over — and how you guys have your hands tied behind your back. So I'm about to give you some really sweet unofficial help on this Hewbright case. You can thank me later. I've just made a positive ID on one of Hewbright's national advisors — Zeta Milla — as the woman Perry Tedrich was with on the day he vanished."

Boling was in the lunchroom of the FBI field office where several other agents were milling around. He asked Gallagher to hold on as he went back to his desk.

When Boling got back he said, "Okay. That fits with what I've got. I found out that our victim was with the same person both at the gym and then at a restaurant later that day."

There was silence on the other end. Finally Gallagher replied, "Awfully nice of you to share some information with me, Ben. Really appreciate that."

Now Boling was the silent one, as he was figuring things out.

"So, listen," Gallagher continued, "I've also found out something else. Zeta Milla's got this cover story about being a heroic survivor who escaped Cuba as a little girl, but I believe she stole the identity of that Cuban girl."

When he didn't get a reply, Gallagher added, "Still there, Ben?"

"Yeah …"

"Anyway, I know the really rotten-to-the-core politics in the Bureau. One of the reasons I left. But Ben, I'm telling you, watch your backside. You don't know where this will lead. One thing, though — if you get the pink slip telling you you're off this case — you can pretty well guess that something is really rotten in Denmark, so to speak — and in Washington too."

"Thanks for the tip, John."

"So — where do we go from here?"

"Nowhere in particular."

"What?"

"Yeah, look," Ben said, "I gotta go. Good talking to you."

After clicking off, Ben Boling scrolled his screen up to the Assignment Status Report he had just received and read the notice again:

Please be advised that Special Agent Ben Boling is being transferred from the Hewbright Investigation — Case No. WK-1377 — SA Boling's authority to inquire and access investigative data on this case number is hereby terminated.

FORTY-TWO

Charleston, South Carolina

Outside the barbecue joint, the parking lot had been rigged up with a platform that had "Hewbright for President" banners everywhere and was filled with long tables heaped with food. Deborah Jordan was waiting patiently off to the side. She had been standing there for two hours, first listening to Hewbright's stump speech, then watching him shake hands under the watchful eye of his Secret Service agent. A parade of well-wishers lined up to fill their paper plates with barbecued chicken, baked beans, and cornbread.

Finally, she spotted Katrena Amid with her staff credentials swinging around her neck. Deb strode up to her. "Sorry to bother you, Ms. Amid, but I'm Deborah, and I spoke to you earlier today about working as a volunteer on the national staff, remember? I came recommended from Abigail Jordan. She's a personal friend and supporter of Senator Hewbright. I've got Pentagon experience in information services, and I graduated from West Point."

"Yes," Amid said, "I remember. You're Deborah Shelly. We were waiting for our security folks to clear you. I haven't heard back. Sorry."

Deb persisted. "I've got my own car. I'll pay my own expenses — "

"That's nice, but we've got a lot of folks who want to work in the campaign, and we can't fit all of them in. Perhaps you can work for us in your local precinct — that would be a great help to the senator."

Just then, Deborah noticed that Senator Hewbright had worked his way down the end of the food tables and was shaking hands with a couple. He was just twenty feet away. Deborah excused herself and hurried off in his direction before Amid could protest. The Secret Service agent stepped in front of her when she was about ten feet from Senator Hewbright.

Deborah stopped, smiled cordially, and called out to the senator. "Senator Hewbright — Abigail Jordan says hello!"

Hewbright turned and squinted in her direction. He started moving toward Deborah as Katrena Amid stepped quickly in her direction to play interference. But Deborah beat her to the punch. Hewbright was next to Deborah and tossed a relaxed nod to his security guard. Deborah explained, "Abigail Jordan recommended me as a volunteer on your staff."

"Oh? So, how is Abigail these days?" the senator said as he shook Deborah's hand.

"Doing well, Senator. Working on her husband's case, I believe, trying to reverse the nonsense caused by the Tulrude administration."

Deborah pulled a letter out of her pocket and handed it to Hewbright. "Here's Mrs. Jordan's letter of recommendation."

Hewbright scanned it while Katrena Amid grimaced.

"This young lady is Deborah Shelly," Senator Hewbright said, holding up the letter and handing it to his staffer. "It says here you graduated with honors from West Point and work at the Pentagon."

"Yes, sir. I applied for an extended leave with the hopes of being able to help with your campaign."

"Of course, security is getting tighter these days. They'll have to screen you."

"Ms. Amid has already put my name in several hours ago. I filled out your security form. We're just waiting now."

"I'll tell you what," Hewbright added. "I have great admiration for Abigail and Joshua Jordan. If they say you should be on my national team, and you get clearance from security, then I say come onboard." He turned to his assistant campaign chief of staff. "Katrena?"

She smiled tightly. "Yes, Senator, we could use her, absolutely."

"Well, this is the last whistle-stop for me before our national convention, which starts tomorrow in Denver. I'm flying there tonight."

"And you have the sufficient delegate count from your primary victories," Deborah said brightly, "to sweep the convention." She was silently thankful she had done her homework.

"On the other hand," Hewbright said, "anything can happen at a political convention." He waved to her and started to step away as his national campaign director beckoned to him. Hewbright stopped and took a step back toward Deborah. "I'm sure you know I'm an old military guy myself and a member of the armed services committee for more years than I can count. I'm really happy to have someone like you onboard."

After stopping for a moment to say something to George Caulfield, Hank Hewbright headed to the big campaign bus to get some down time.

ooo

In the campaign bus Zeta Milla was pouring a cup of coffee for Senator Hewbright. She mixed in some creamer and a packet of Sweet'N Low. "Hank, here's your coffee, just the way you like it."

"Wow, that's real service. Thanks, Zeta."

He dropped into a soft swivel chair and loosened his tie. "I know your focus is South and Central America and the island nations, but that briefing book you put together on the Russian Republics and China for my future debates with President Tulrude was exceptional."

"Glad it was helpful. I've told you a million times, I'll do whatever I can to help. You're very special."

He nodded humbly. "It's been a long primary season," he said, rubbing his eyes, "but now the convention. Then the debates, and then the home stretch to the election."

Milla sat next to him in the other swivel chair. "If you allow me to say so, Hank, I know that Ginny, from what I knew of her, would have loved to have been here to see this. She would have been so proud of what you've accomplished — and all that you will accomplish as the leader of the Free World. This is your time, Hank. Relish it."

"Funny you should mention Ginny. I haven't said this to many people — but she's been on my mind because of what she said shortly before she died, about her wanting to see me run."

Zeta reached over and rubbed his hand. He squeezed back. He looked her in the eyes, then broke the gaze and slowly released her hand. "We have to be careful, Zeta. About mixing the personal with the political. Sometimes the lines get blurred. It's not about Ginny either. She told me pointblank that I would need a woman in my life when she was gone."

Zeta smiled and nodded, but she wasn't surprised to hear Hank's confession. She replied, "Whoever that woman is, she'll be very lucky. I've never met a man like you, Hank." Then she pulled his hand to her lips and kissed it. Standing up to leave, she said, "You need time. Today was a long day. I'll be around … anything you need … anything. Just ask."

As she walked out of the bus, she ran into George Caulfield who asked where Hewbright was.

"In the bus," Zeta answered. "We were having some private time together."

The campaign director stopped in his tracks and gave her a withering look. Then he mounted the steps into the bus.

Zeta continued on. There was a lot of work to do.

□□□

An hour later, Katrena Amid, holding her Allfone, strode up to Deborah. "Right. Just heard. Got an expedited approval from the security people. Looks like we'll be seeing you in Denver. You'll have to get your own transportation though. We'll have your credentials by the time you arrive."

Deborah breathed easier and thanked Katrena. In her peripheral vision Deborah caught Zeta Milla. As Katrena hurried off, Deborah casually jogged over to Milla, who was putting some papers into a briefcase. "Excuse me, but aren't you Zeta Milla?"

The Cuban woman smiled politely. "Yes, I am."

"I'm Deborah. New campaign worker. Volunteer. I know you're one

TIM LaHAYE AND CRAIG PARSHALL

of the shining lights among the senator's foreign relations advisors, and I just wanted to introduce myself."

"Kind of you to say so," Milla said, going back to her papers.

"I'm a West Point grad with a strong interest in foreign relations. So I'm thrilled I might be able to work with you."

Zeta Milla turned quickly to face her. "I'm afraid not. Campaign staff — especially volunteers — don't consort with professional policy advisors. Now, if you'll excuse me …"

Milla gathered up her reports, stuffed them in her briefcase, and walked quickly away.

FORTY-THREE

Abigail and Cal were in the Citation X, winging their way through the darkness back to Washington, D.C. Abigail was relieved she might be able to get to her court appearance on time after all. She glanced over at Cal, who was fast asleep and snoring loudly. But she couldn't sleep. Her mind kept clicking despite the fatigue that threatened to overwhelm her.

The reading light above her head was on. She was cramming for the oral arguments that would commence in just a matter of hours. She knew the laws related to the issues in the case, of course, and she had the facts down cold. But she didn't know what was on the mind of the three appellate judges who would be hearing the case. She wouldn't know that until she was standing at the podium in the federal courtroom. The green light would flash on, signifying her turn to start her argument, and then — if everything had gone perfectly up to that point — she would argue the wrongness of the case against Joshua and field a raft of questions from the judges.

Before getting to that point, however, she had to get inside the courthouse, which meant getting past the security guards with their BIDTag scanner just inside the entrance. She lifted the back of her right hand to the light. The laser tattoo was invisible — just like the real BIDTags.

When Chiro Hashimoto had escorted her and Cal out of his lodge and down a path through the woods to a lonely cement building that had a huge satellite dish mounted behind, he assured them his system would work. "My BIDTag facsimiles are the closest counterfeit you will ever see," he bragged, "perfect in every detail. I was able to duplicate the government's laser imprint system. You know why?"

Before Abigail or Cal could respond, Hashimoto answered, "Because I'm the one who designed it for IntraTonics, who then sold it to the government!" And with that he laughed raucously. "I consulted with bioengineers and medical experts about using nonlethal lasers to imprint permanent, invisible code matrices on human skin. Not easy. But I did it. You have to admit — the idea was pretty cool, right?"

"Now the question is," Cal replied, "will your counterfeit BIDTag, created out here in the forest, simulate the government's system? Is it close enough that the tag screeners at the courthouse will give her a pass?"

"I've built my own scanners," Hashimoto said as he unlocked the door to the cement building, "very close to the ones the government uses. So I can test the result. Passes every time."

Once inside, he flicked on the florescent overhead lights. What Abigail and Cal saw was a fully functioning tech lab, complete with rows of computers linked together, laser guns inside glass tubes, and a table with microscopes. But there was more. Cal drifted over to the other side of the room where a row of chairs were lined up behind a long metal table. On the table there were rows of zephyrs, receivers, shortwave transmitters, voice analyzing screens, cryptographic cipher machines, and monitors — all cabled together in a massive tangle of electrical cords.

"This is your own listening station, isn't it?" Cal said, pointing to the strange collection of electronics.

"We're not finished yet," Hashimoto said, "but when we are, I'm going to watch the government's surveillance just as closely as they watch the citizens of America."

"Why?" Abigail asked.

"Well, why are you here, right now with me, in the Olympic National Forest?" he shot back. "Because we don't trust how our government has morphed — turning into a predator, devouring information about everyone in the nation. I don't trust how it's going to use that data. We are entering a new ice age, where freedom will be extinct. The big freeze. And so, this," Hashimoto said, gesturing to his make-shift surveillance laboratory, "is my Ice Station Zebra."

Cal chuckled at the movie reference. Chiro took Abigail over to one of the laser tubes. "The key," he continued, "was to take the basic laser-imprint system I devised and refine it. Changed it so in my version the imprint is only temporary and would fade from the surface of the skin. That was really hard to do, but I did it. That way if we have to venture out into society we can laser-tag ourselves with a little invisible QRC box on the skin that contains harmless basic bits of information that will satisfy the government scanners but won't give away anything. Then, after a few days — poof — the laser tag starts to dissolve."

Hashimoto dumped himself onto a lab stool in front of a computer. He started typing in a flurry. "I'm creating your QRC pattern that will contain only a little bit of data about you, which I will put into the system." When he had finished, Abigail placed her hand into a brace that lined up the back of her hand against the glass-enclosed end of the laser tube. "Okay. Now your own personal QRC matrix has been loaded into the laser for transmittal in the form of a little invisible pattern that will be lasered onto your skin. Don't move," he said. He typed in a code that was connected to the laser and flipped a switch. "In twenty seconds you'll feel it," he said. "Unlike the government's version, you will feel mine, and it'll hurt a little."

The laser whirred — first softly; then, with a minor roar, a stream of light as gossamer thin as a spider web shot through the tube onto Abigail's hand. She winced. Then it was over.

As the three of them walked back to the lodge in the dusk, Cal thought of something the tech genius had said. "You described your scanners as 'very close' to the kind used by the government. Which is fine as far as it goes. But have you ever sent your temporary laser tags — like the one you just gave my mom — through the government scanners to see if they will pass security?"

"Ha, ha," Hashimoto replied.

"That doesn't answer my question," Cal pressed.

Hashimoto's reply left a cloud of uncertainty hanging in the air.

"Do you think I would leave my compound to test it out on the federal government?"

Now, airborne in the Citation X, Abigail stared at the back of her hand, wondering what was there. Would it be her passport into the court building in Washington? The rest would have to remain as it always had remained, in the sovereignty of God. She tried to review her notes for the case, but her eyes were too heavy. Before long she was fast asleep.

FORTY-FOUR

Jerusalem

Pastor Peter Campbell staked out a spot on the Western Wall plaza to preach. He knew it would be controversial, but he fixed his eyes on the earthmoving equipment, tractors, and cranes on the Temple Mount just above the plaza. It seemed clear that the climax of history was rushing up. How could he wait? This was a time for boldness. He had left his Eternity Church in Manhattan in the hands of his assistant pastor so he could come to Jerusalem for exactly this moment. He thought about runners who had trained and prepared all of their life for the Olympics and had one chance to compete. Would any one of them balk when it was time to stride up to the starting blocks?

Forty members of his small Jerusalem congregation gathered around Campbell as he started to preach. Onlookers started drifting over to hear him. Soon the group swelled to over a hundred. Campbell had a small portable amplifier and a wireless mic headset. As he spoke, his voice was calm, unrushed.

"Two millennia ago, a fisherman-turned-disciple by the name of Peter walked into the center of this city. Filled with the Spirit of God, he told the crowd what he himself had seen and heard about the person of Jesus Christ. Peter was an eyewitness. And he gave testimony that Jesus, his beloved friend, rabbi, Savior, and king — the very Son of God — died on a bloody Roman cross not far from here. But he died for an incredible purpose — to take away the sins of everyone standing here today — me and you — everyone who ever trod these stones and everyone who ever lived. He paid the price that only the sinless Holy One of God could pay — the man who was truly God in the flesh and who had dwelled among us. He took on Himself the punishment destined for us and willingly accepted the sentence of torture and death. Right here in this city.

"But it didn't end there. Jesus walked out of the tomb three days later, just as He said He would. And Peter was an eyewitness to that too. Possessing such earthshaking news, Peter could not be silent about it. And neither can I. Many years ago my life was transformed by the power of Jesus Christ who walked out of that grave — it started on the day I confessed that I was a sinner and that Jesus, the Son of God, was my Savior and Lord, and that I wanted Him to live and dwell in my heart — that is when everything changed. And it can change for you. Thousands responded to Peter's message that day in this city two thousand years ago. But God is not interested in thousands or millions or billions. Numbers don't impress Him. He is the one who cast a trillion stars across the universe. God will soon enter this planet and bring an end to human history. His Son, Jesus the Christ, will establish His kingdom. But there is one particular number that does concern the heart of God." Peter Campbell pointed his index finger up to heaven. "That number is the number one. Which means you," and he pointed to a young man wearing a UT Longhorns football sweatshirt in the crowd. "And you." He pointed to a mother with her hands on a baby carriage. "And you, my friend." He gestured to a bearded Hasidim in the very back of the crowd, who was wearing a black hat and long coat.

"Today, you are building a great temple," Campbell said, pointing to the construction on the Temple Mount. The sounds of tractor treads and diesel engines could be heard. "But know this — that God is building His temple. And it is not a thing made by human hands. It is an assembly of people who have chosen to believe in, receive, and follow Jesus. They are His temple, the work of the hands of God. And today God welcomes you to become part of His great spiritual assembly. He holds the door open. And when God opens a door no man can close it. You can walk through that door right now. Jesus is that door. And He wants to welcome you, like a prodigal son or daughter, and to lift the burdens from your soul. But also know this — a day will come when that door will close. And when God closes the door, no man can open it."

□□□

The commanding Shin Bet agent, who was surveying the scene from his position on the edge of the large open plaza, radioed the Jerusalem police and gave his order in Hebrew. "We need armed officers to disperse an illegal assembly at the Western Wall plaza, over."

"This is police dispatch. What is your situation?"

"A Christian religious leader is preaching in violation of the prime minister's emergency order regarding religious incitement of civil unrest."

"Confirmed. Officers are being dispatched, over."

□□□

Beyond the outer ring of listeners, GNN reporter Bart Kingston was ready to do a stand-up with his single cameraman. When he had heard from his sources in the city that Pastor Campbell planned to defy the prime minister's emergency orders to prohibit "public displays of extremist religious language," he rushed to the scene.

His timing was perfect. At the other end of the plaza, a dozen Jerusalem police were entering the wide space, heading directly toward the crowd. A loudspeaker boomed over the area, commanding the crowd to disperse. People moved in all directions. Soon, the only people left were Campbell, a handful of his devotees, and the police.

Kingston motioned for his camera guy to follow him closer to the Western Wall area. Then the unexpected happened — four Jewish men, who appeared to be lawyers or some kind of businessmen, appeared and rushed headlong toward the police.

They held papers in their hands, shouting, "We have a temporary restraining order from the Israeli Supreme Court to protect the rights of these Christian worshipers ..."

Kingston, standing a good distance away, watched as the guards disregarded the paperwork. One of the officers lobbed a canister of tear gas into the air, which fell a few feet away from Campbell, spilling white smoke into the area. A young woman collapsed, coughing and gagging. Campbell stumbled over to her and picked her up in his arms and tried to walk her away from the area. But his eyes were streaming with tears, and his throat was closing as if a boa constrictor was squeezing his windpipe.

From his safe position, Kingston was about to ask his cameraman if he had caught all of this, but the guy was a pro, and Kingston knew it. At some point — perhaps only an instant later — it ceased to be a news story for Bart Kingston.

He surveyed the scene. Pastor Peter Campbell was overcome by gas and down on his knees with a young woman cradled in his arms. Kingston looked up at the Temple Mount, where the construction workers were peering down at the melee on the plaza below.

Apocalypse was one of the words that flooded Kingston's mind.

And he thought of another word, one that Campbell had shared in their television interview a week before. It was a word that he couldn't admit to anyone else. He barely was able to admit it to himself, but he was seriously entertaining it and what it meant. The thought of the ultimate divorce — of some taken and some left. A God who rescues those who have accepted his lifeline and leaving behind those who have refused. As the police with their gas masks waded into the smoke to arrest Campbell's small but disabled group, Kingston could not shake the almost palpable force of that word.

Rapture.

FORTY-FIVE

Washington, D.C.

It was after hours and Supreme Court Justice Carter Lapham was in the back of the limo that was pulling out of the underground parking deck of the Supreme Court building. For some reason his driver turned onto the avenue that ran past the front of the tall marble courthouse with the words "Equal Justice Under Law" chiseled in stone over the columns. After stopping at the corner, the driver turned right onto Second Street and slowly eased into traffic as it passed the Supreme Court building. It looked like a traffic tie-up ahead and some flashing lights from two squad cars.

Lapham peered at the tangle of traffic. "Hey, Brock," he said with a wry smile, "would you like me to drive tonight? I could teach you some techniques on avoiding traffic jams."

Brock, his longtime driver, smiled into the rear view mirror but didn't respond, as if he had chosen this route on purpose.

The justice glanced from the window as the limo snaked past the steps leading up to the Supreme Court. He could see several capitol police officers handcuffing a man and a woman who were holding signs. One read: "Christ = Truth / Allah, Buddha, Sidharta = Liars." Another read: "Jesus Is Coming to Judge the Judges."

Justice Lapham had dissented bitterly in Marquis v. United States of America, but he could only woo three other votes to his side in that case. His dissent went beyond the bounds of anything he had ever written before in a decision — calling it a "constitutional atrocity" for

249

the majority to have upheld the hate speech provisions of the international treaty pushed by President Tulrude and ratified by the senate. He was now witnessing the toxic aftermath of that treaty with his own eyes. But there was something worse, and it made him cringe. Lapham considered the court's decision in Marquis to have been a betrayal of the oath taken by the five other justices who formed the majority in that court opinion. After all, there was that matter of an oath taken by the justices — all of them — to uphold the Constitution. When exactly, he wondered, does bad judicial reasoning drift into treason, like a wayward youth who finally takes up the enticing invitation to join the local gang?

For a fleeting moment he entertained, once again, the idea of retirement. To go fishing in the Gulf on his forty-footer; going after that worthy fighter, the yellow-finned tuna, or the elegantly powerful sailfish that he would catch and release; traveling the world slow and easy, with his wife at his side ... Perhaps he would accept the permanent invitation to become an elder in his hometown Bible church in Wilmington, North Carolina.

Now it almost seemed as if he had the taste of vinegar in his mouth as the limo cruised away from the scene. It was the bitterness of gall, that his own country seemed to be slipping into legal oblivion. But then, this was not just a legal issue, and Lapham knew it. By and large, most judges he knew expressed little compulsion to honor the great Lawgiver. The words of one of his favorite poets, William Butler Yeats, haunted his mind more than ever lately. Its harrowing vision of the disintegration of civilization seemed to be ever before him — just as in Yeats's poem "The Second Coming," which he knew by heart:

Turning and turning in the widening gyre
The falcon cannot hear the falconer;
Things fall apart; the center cannot hold.

FORTY-SIX

SIA Headquarters

In his office, Jeremy was back on duty. Taking tentative sips of his still-too-hot paper cup of French vanilla coffee, he read the tracking report on Abigail Jordan. The surveillance chain had broken temporarily in the state of Washington. Then it was picked up again when the SIA facial recognition software made a match, verified by the Likely Route Estimator program: she had boarded her private jet in Seattle with a flight destination of Reagan National Airport in D.C.

Jeremy tapped in the search for FAA radar results. The jet was now approaching Columbus, Ohio.

The radar read: "Permission to land received by the tower in Columbus."

He took another sip. Better now, the coffee was hot but not scalding.

"Permission to land granted."

Ten minutes later, another posting on the FAA update quadrant of his screen.

"Citation X cleared to land at the Rapid Air commercial delivery hangar."

On the jet, Abigail put down her legal file and stretched. Cal was awake next to her. He looked out the window at the Ohio landscape. "You know they'll be waiting for you," he said, still gazing out the window. There was a resignation in his voice.

"Yes. They won't give up." As he turned his face from the window to face her, she added, "And neither will I."

"Abby and Cal," the pilot said, adjusting his sunglasses and donning his cap, "we'll be landing shortly. We're going into our final descent."

Abigail knew what that meant. And what she had to do.

At his tracking desk Jeremy touched the screen to view all the camera shots at the Columbus airport. He saw three angles. A small Rapid Air jet was being loaded with boxes. Some members of the ground crew were hovering around the jet, finishing the preflight check.

Jeremy hit the local police alert. A few minutes later the Columbus airport police said they would dispatch two squads to the hangar as soon as they finished the execution of a warrant on a fugitive who had just entered the passenger terminal.

The Citation X was rolling down the runway into view. It taxied up to the hangar and stopped.

"Better hurry," Jeremy said into his voice monitor. "They've landed."

The airport security officer responded, "Your subjects will not be leaving the airport — at least not on the ground," the officer replied. "We've relayed your request to every road leading from the commercial hangar. Tollgates are all shut now. Your subject can't get past any of them."

One of his fellow SIA staffers strolled in and began asking him about the upcoming agency bowling tournament, but Jeremy's eyes never left the screen. He shot his left hand up in the air. "Can't talk. Following a Red Notice here."

"Oooh," came the cynical response, "excuse me, Mr. Bounty Hunter of cyber space," and he left.

The camera shots on Jeremy's monitor showed the door of the Citation X opening. He saw the pilot, in his sunglasses and cap, and his flight case in hand, walking down the steps and darting quickly into the hangar.

"What's this?" Jeremy shouted. He waited a minute, then decided to hit the speed dial number for the hangar desk clerk. But before he could, the pilot, with his flight case, came striding back out of the hangar and quickly mounted the stairs and entered the Citation X, closing the door behind him.

"What's the matter," Jeremy said, questioning the image on the screen, "don't those expensive private jets have their own bathrooms? This doesn't look right."

The two pilots and a navigator of the Rapid Air commercial jet walked out and climbed up the stairs. The pilots could be seen strapping themselves into the cockpit. Jeremy hit the airport tower alert line. "Request a stop on a private passenger jet on the tarmac."

The Citation X was already taxiing down the runway.

"SIA, you need to give us the FAA stop order number" came the response.

"Forget it," Jeremy grumbled, "too late. Bathroom break completed. Or whatever ..." It was the *whatever* that bothered Jeremy.

"Say again?"

"Never mind. The private jet is already back in the air." Then Jeremy said to himself, "Okay, now I'm bringing it, Mrs. Jordan. The full force of the SIA's coming down on you at Reagan National. Last stop. We'll be waiting."

Jeremy touched the All Agency Enforcement tab on the screen. Boxes for FBI, SIA, Homeland Security, D.C. Police, Secret Service, and Airport Security appeared. One by one, Jeremy touched every box on the screen. Each time, he typed the Red Notice file number to authenticate his request.

It took only fifteen minutes for each of the agencies to respond. All but the Secret Service and Homeland Security verified that officials were on the way to the private charter flight section of Reagan National Airport. Two FBI agents, two SIA officials, two squad cars full of D.C. police, and an armed airport security officer had been dispatched. The full fire power would arrive at the tarmac within thirty minutes. More than enough time. The Citation X would not land for at least forty-five minutes, maybe longer.

FORTY-SEVEN

Nablus, Palestinian Authority

Ethan sat exhausted at the dining room table. He slept little the night before, tossing and turning as if electric currents were racing through his body. He couldn't shut his mind down. Pastor Ibrahim Kalid and his quiet, pleasant wife and their two daughters had all been cordial — overly accommodating, in fact, during his stay in their modest cement-block house.

The pastor's wife was now serving Ethan another enormous meal, this time a midafternoon snack of tea, falafel, hummus, dates, and olives. Joshua was in the other room with Pastor Ibrahim, praying. Ethan gave the woman a weak smile.

"Eat, please," she said. "You are a big man; you need much food."

"Any more, Mrs. Kalid, and you will make me too big." He patted his stomach, and she smiled and shook her head.

He reached out and picked up a soft date and popped it in his mouth, pulling the sweet fruit away from the seed with his tongue and then plucking the seed out of his mouth with his fingers and putting it on the brightly painted plate in front of him.

"Good dates," he said.

She smiled. Ethan felt awkward alone in the room with this woman, so he tried to make conversation. "So, have you — and your family — always been Christians?"

"No," she replied, "we were Muslim, like most here in Nablus."

"So, you changed?"

"Yes, took Jesus into our hearts."

"Has that … caused you problems? With your neighbors, I mean?"

She shrugged and said, "A little, yes."

Ethan was tempted to explore that. He knew enough to understand that these people must be viewed as infidels by others in their town. Now they were harboring Joshua Jordan, a man targeted by Islamic terrorists — in fact, one of their Imams had issued a fatwa against him. He wondered if the Kalid family had ever received death threats for their new faith or had even been the targets of violence because they were now following Jesus.

But Ethan decided not to pursue it. Instead he said, "Mrs. Kalid, you are very brave to have us stay with you. I really appreciate it."

She said something in return, but he couldn't decipher it through her thick Arabic accent. His face must have registered a question because she articulated the comment once again, but much more slowly: "I am being the Good Samaritan, like Jesus say."

"I see."

Ethan felt a flush of embarrassment, though he wasn't sure why. Maybe it was because, looking at this quiet woman now, he was in the presence of an astounding mixture of character traits — simple purity of motives coupled with some incredibly big-time courage. How could he explain that? He didn't know. But it seemed to amplify his own shortcomings.

The door to the adjoining room opened and Joshua and Pastor Ibrahim walked out. Joshua had his Allfone in one hand and with his other shook hands with the pastor. He then glanced over at Ethan. The look on Joshua's face seemed to possess an answer to a question that Ethan hadn't even asked yet.

Josh motioned for Ethan to follow him over to the other side of the room, and lowered his voice. "I just received a message from Joel Harmon," he said. "IDF command wants to talk to me about finishing our RTS refinement after all."

"What? Israel was tracking us down. I thought the prime minister wanted you in custody and turned over to the FBI for extradition?"

"He did. But then things changed, and they're willing to let bygones be bygones if I help them now."

"What happened?"

"I don't have all the details. But it seems the threat level has just been raised."

"What kind of threat?"

"Biological. In the hands of bad guys. That's all I know. The IDF's begging for us to help them to achieve full redirection capacity for the RTS defense system. So, I'm guessing that they anticipate a missile strike with some kind of nightmare biological warhead. They must want to make sure they can redirect the missiles to a full spectrum of alternate destinations — away from population centers."

"That's good news, then," Ethan beamed. "We can come out of hiding."

"Good news and bad news."

"What's the bad part?"

"The RTS tests I've run here in Israel haven't done the trick yet, to accomplish the higher level of control over the guidance systems of incoming missiles. That's what the Israelis want. But I've got an idea on how to get that RTS enhancement to happen. I hope . . ."

"You'll figure it out," Ethan said, worried but trying to sound convincing.

"I just hope by the time I figure it out," Joshua said, "it's not too late."

FORTY-EIGHT

In the early morning hours, around 6:45 a.m., the nurses at George-town University Hospital were making their rounds. One of them was attending to attorney Harry Smythe, who was hooked up to a heart monitor. He had not been a happy patient. He kept talking about a case he might have to argue in court for some lady named Abigail Jordan. The nurse assured him he was going nowhere. He would have to remain in the hospital for several more days at least.

ooo

At 6:45 a.m., Jeremy was looking at his monitor, which was full of video images of the hangar and part of the D.C. Reagan Airport tarmac. The director was standing next to him, and behind him were several SIA staffers who had heard about the upcoming arrival.

Jeremy saw that the area around the hangar where the charter flights and private jets would dock was surrounded by armed federal agents and local police. On his audio hookup, Jeremy could hear the Citation X radio the tower for permission to land. It was quickly granted. The jet was descending. The FBI had taken the lead in co-ordinating the task force on the ground and would soon give the go ahead to approach the jet. "Hold positions," the senior FBI agent said over the radio.

The Citation X slowed as it approached the tarmac apron in front of the hangar. Then it halted.

"Perfect position," the FBI agent said to his team members. "Wait till we verify the engines are off."

The engines of the Citation X were cut, and the roar began to wind down to a whine and then a quiet whirring. The FBI agent counted down slowly from ten. When he got to one, he shouted into the radio, "*Now*, go, go, go!"

Several officers, with guns drawn in point-and-aim position, sprinted forward to surround the cabin of the jet. Over a bullhorn a voice advised the occupants to exit the plane with their hands raised high. Moments later the door opened. The pilot, still wearing his sunglasses, appeared with hands up and slowly descended the steps.

Next came Cal with his hands up as well. When they were on the tarmac, the officers grabbed them and cuffed them. All eyes were on the open door of the jet.

"Abigail Jordan," the voice on the bullhorn announced, "exit the airplane immediately with your hands up or we will come in after you."

In the SIA headquarters, watching the arrest scene play out on the monitor in Jeremy's office, the director was muttering, "Doesn't this lady know the jig's up?"

There was movement in the cabin near the open door. Someone was preparing to exit. A woman's hand appeared through the door and grabbed the handrail.

"Hands up!" the bullhorn boomed. Then the person exited the plane in full sight of the law enforcement team on the ground with their weapons drawn.

"What?" was the first word that came out of the SIA director's mouth. And then several profanities quickly followed.

Descending the stairs was a blonde middle-aged woman dressed in a pilot's uniform with a pair of sunglasses perched carefully just above her hairline so as to not muss her elegant coiffeur. When she reached the bottom of the stairs, she raised her hands but with a maintained gait and look of relaxed confidence, the kind of expression belonging to someone who had grown accustomed to high-stress intrigue.

As the FBI special agent in charge holstered his weapon and approached the woman, he ordered his fellow agent and two D.C. cops to enter the plane and search for Abigail. They scrambled up the stairs.

The agent, now directly in front of the woman, squinted in the early morning sun, shielding his eyes with his hand. "Victoria?" he stammered. "Victoria McHenry? What in the world are you doing here?"

She smiled and replied, "Hi, Fred. Yes, it's me."

"You aren't," he began and stepped closer, "still in the Agency..."

She shook her head. "No. Pack and I've been out of the clandestine services division for a number of years now."

"Then what in the world are you doing here? In a pilot's uniform?"

"Can't a girl play dress-up once in a while?"

From the top of the stairs, the other FBI agent shouted down, "Fred, there's no one else in the plane."

Fred straightened up into a posture of official business. "Sorry, Victoria, but if you're a civilian, then I'm afraid you've just walked into a world of legal troubles."

"And what would those be?" she asked nonchalantly.

He bulleted back his reply without taking a breath. "Assisting a citizen who has refused to submit to federal BIDTag identification procedures as required by federal law."

Cal spoke up. "That's where you're wrong..."

The FBI agent whirled around toward Cal. "And who are you?"

"Cal Jordan. You need to know, agent, that in the rush toward passage in Congress, the federal act making it a crime to refuse to get tagged contained one technical mistake. It was drafted in such a way as to prevent someone — like Victoria McHenry, or me for that matter, or even the pilot of our Citation X — from being prosecuted for aiding and abetting or even being a party to conspiracy to aid someone who has refused to get tagged. In other words, the only person you could prosecute would be someone who actually refused to get BIDTagged. And I presume you think that person is Abigail Jordan, my mother. Am I correct?"

The FBI agent strode up to Cal. "Are you a lawyer?"

"No, but I'll be a law student in a couple of weeks."

The FBI agent narrowed his eyes as his face faded into a scarlet color.

"Wanna bet?"

FORTY-NINE

Dulles International Airport, Virginia

John Gallagher had received the message from the Roundtable that Abigail needed his help. So he flew to the East Coast, having just arrived at the Dulles airport, west of D.C. He used his ex-fed-agent contacts to get a big SUV with tinted glass, hoping that would limit facial-recognition systems from getting a peek at Abigail, who was now sitting in the backseat. The license plates had special reflective plastic covers that made them unreadable from intersection cameras.

In a matter of minutes he would have to pass through the Dulles Toll Road. As part of the BIDTag program, the highway folks had discontinued the quick-pass system. Now, all drivers had to stop at the tollbooths and hold out the back of their hands to the scanners. He half-turned around to alert Abigail. "Okay, tollbooth ahead. We're about to see if I'm Mr. Clean with the feds or not."

Abigail leaned forward with her forearms resting on the seat in front of her. "John, this is the only route that will get me to the federal courthouse in time for my argument. We both heard the traffic report on I-66. The Dulles Toll Road is our only hope. So, friend, you do the driving up there, and I'll do the praying back here."

When they arrived at the booth, Gallagher held out his hand so it could be examined by the scanner housed within the little plastic hood that jutted out toward the driver's side.

The tollgate stayed closed in front of him and the red light was illuminated.

Gallagher waited, shifting in his seat. He could hear Abigail's voice softly speaking behind him. He raised his eyes to catch the reflection in his rearview mirror. He saw Abigail in the rear seat, hands clasped, head bowed, praying.

Come on, come on, Gallagher thought.

Then the gate lifted and the light turned green. Gallagher rolled to the tollbooth. A clerk sat in her little window. He took out a couple of international CReDO coins — the only ones that were accepted at tolls, and handed them to the woman. She counted the coins. The final light was still red ahead of them. The toll woman seemed to be studying her BIDTag scanner screen. Gallagher shifted in his seat, staring at the red light. Another half minute passed. Finally, the red light turned green and Gallagher eased his car forward, and then immediately merged into the crush of traffic on the Dulles Tollway heading toward downtown Washington.

◻◻◻

In the Security and Identification Administration headquarters, Jeremy was working the same Rubik's cube he'd been working on all day. And he was about to twist the last colored square into place.

He reviewed the footage from the cameras at the Columbus commercial hangar. It showed someone — obviously Abigail Jordan, he now knew in retrospect, dressed as a pilot and walking from the Citation X into the hangar. Then, shortly after that, Victoria McHenry, also dressed as a pilot, left the hangar and then headed back to the Citation X.

Jeremy asked the obvious question: Where was Abigail Jordan now?

He was more than a little embarrassed and nervous to have to put in yet another apprehension request. This was his third request for the same violator, and now he had to get the approval of the director. He ran upstairs to the executive level and waited outside his door in the lobby. This particular apprehension was giving him heartburn. After fifteen minutes he stepped over to his secretary and asked her to move things along. Five minutes later, the director stepped out. Jeremy had the order for apprehension on an e-pad and a digital pen in his hand. The director scribbled his signature on the screen, gave him a look of disappointment, and reentered his office.

This was Jeremy's last chance — and he knew it. He returned to his database and tried another search. This time, the computer revealed just the information needed. Abigail Jordan, attorney-at-law, was scheduled to present an oral argument that morning at the U.S. federal court building in Washington, in the case of *United States v. Jordan*. Jeremy typed the courthouse address into the notice and hit Send, delivering it electronically to "all available law enforcement personnel within the District of Columbia." Then he crossed his fingers.

FIFTY

Abigail was as ready as she would ever be.

She clutched the brown expandable case file in her hand as she rode in the back of Gallagher's SUV. During the flight, she had changed into a dark blue suit and white silk blouse — the one she had stored in the flight case that she had carried off the Citation X and onto the commercial delivery plane. It was the outfit she often used for appellate arguments back when her law practice had her appearing in court regularly. That was when she would be able to jog several miles a day and would log three days a week at the gym. She giggled to herself in the jet's cramped bathroom when she put on the suit, skirt, and blouse and realized that they all, mercifully, still fit. Life had become so complicated recently. Almost no time now for the gym or running or so many other seemingly mundane things she used to take for granted. Sometimes she yearned for them.

As she buttoned up the suit, she wondered, *When, exactly, did the journey of life transform itself into such a hair-raising mountain climb?* She used to chuckle when friends would talk about slowing down and preparing for a future of relaxation and recreation. For her and Joshua, the days had sped up, not slowed down. The risks were more dangerous, and the stakes had become almost too high to calculate. In a short time she would be trying to enter a U.S. courthouse with a forged BIDTag to defend her husband in court. It was as if a spider web with the tensile strength of steel had entangled them both.

As she continued to get ready in the SUV, now brushing some lint

263

off her sleeve and trying to work the wrinkles out of her suit jacket, Abigail looked ahead at the traffic on Constitution Avenue. Just a few more minutes and they would be at the courthouse.

She thanked God for the miracles that had popped up every step of the way. That ride from Columbus to Dulles airport on the commercial transport plane had been arranged courtesy of Rocky Bridger, retired Pentagon general and devoted friend on the Roundtable. Rocky knew the president of Rapid Air personally. He hadn't filled them in about all the details of Abigail's desperate plight, but Abigail and Cal had researched the law and knew that Rapid Air employees couldn't get into any criminal trouble by helping her avoid the SIA surveillance. Another Roundtable member, Judge Fort Rice, also checked out the BIDTag authorization act hurriedly passed by Congress. Because of a glitch in the law he had come to the same conclusion. Of course, none of that affected the ability of the U.S. government to come after Abigail.

Gallagher slowed the SUV and pulled into a parking spot reserved for "authorized vehicles only."

"Okay," the ex-FBI agent said, turning off his car. "I'll get a parking ticket here, so I'll have to send you the bill." He cocked an eyebrow. "But it avoids all the cameras and scanners in the public parking area. Also, here's some good news for you. I checked and the facial recognition cameras inside the courthouse had to be yanked out. Got some kind of computer virus. Come on, Abby. Follow me."

Gallagher and Abigail moved along the perimeter of the courthouse building until they arrived at a rear service entrance. Gallagher hit the speed dial on his Allfone. "The agent is outside," he announced into his cell and clicked it off.

"So I'm an agent now?" Abigail asked.

"I know the courthouse security guy. Did him a few favors when I used to be a frequent government witness here in D.C.. Anyway, I told him you're operating undercover. You are, aren't you?" Gallagher half smiled. "Anyway, this'll get you past the front door X-ray machines and cameras, but it won't get you past the BIDTag scanners they've set up on every floor. Which courtroom are you heading to?"

"Courtroom 11, fourth floor."

"You remember the back stairway leads up to each of the floors?"

"Yes."

"It should be smooth sailing to your floor. But from that point on, SIA agents are at the scanners. I'm sorry, but I can't help you there. You'll be on your own."

Abigail nodded, then checked the time. Ten minutes left. She hurried to the stairwell.

A bailiff and a court clerk with her hands full of files stepped into the stairway, then passed by her, complaining about the crowded elevators.

Abigail tried not to look too rushed as she climbed the stairs to the fourth floor. Arriving at the door that led to the open hallway, she prayed, *Lord just give me the chance to argue Josh's case — I will accept whatever happens after that.*

She opened the door. Fifteen feet ahead was the SIA security station, blocking the hallway leading to Courtroom 11, which was halfway down the corridor on the left. Two SIA agents were in position, one on each side of the scanner, which was a larger and presumably more sensitive version of the one that was in the tollbooth on the Dulles Toll Road.

A lawyer with a fat briefcase was standing in line ahead of her. He placed his right hand into the scanner. Ten seconds later the bulb on top flickered green. The SIA agent nodded, and the lawyer strolled ahead, briefcase in hand.

Abigail stepped up. She smiled. "Good morning," she said brightly.

"Right hand please," one of the agents told her.

Abigail inserted her right hand into the open space in the big square scanner, palm down. She was glad it was only a BIDTag scanner and not a facial recognition camera. But that was only cold comfort now as she waited to see if Chiro Hashimoto's substitute BIDTag was as good as he had claimed.

The SIA agent squinted at his screen. A few seconds passed. The light on the scanner was not lit. "Withdraw your hand please," he barked.

She did as she was told, but her heart was racing.

"Reinsert please," he said bluntly.

Abigail placed her hand in again, palm down. Two seconds passed. The SIA agent staring at his monitor gave a nod toward the screen but seemed surprised when he looked over at the unlit bulb. He reached over and tapped the bulb with his finger.

The bulb lit up green.

Abigail, still clutching her file, strode between the SIA agents and picked up the pace. Courtroom 11 was only thirty feet away, but there was a sudden noise behind her in the hall. An FBI agent and an SIA official had just blown into the hallway from the stairwell.

"Stop her!" one of them shouted.

At the opposite end of the hallway, at the other SIA station, the two agents posted there left their position and started charging toward Abigail. She broke into a flash of speed, sprinting with legs churning.

I haven't come this far ...

She skidded to a stop at the open doorway of courtroom 11 and dodged in. A court clerk with an electronic clipboard was standing just inside the courtroom. Abigail could see that a dozen other lawyers were already seated in the benches, waiting for their cases to be called.

"Abigail Jordan, arguing for the defendant. *United States v. Jordan,*" she said hurriedly to the man.

An instant later, one of the armed SIA agents grabbed her by the arm.

"What's this?" the bailiff said with a stunned look.

"Illegal entry into the building," the agent barked, "and an outstanding SIA warrant."

Abigail stretched forward, getting as close to the bailiff's ear as she could, and whispered, "Sir, I am an attorney, and I need to argue my husband's case today. *Please.*"

The court officer held up a hand and looked at the SIA agents. They were immediately joined by the FBI agent, who grunted, "No offense buddy, but you're just a court bailiff. We're federal agents with a warrant. So step aside."

The bailiff's eyes lit up. "Excuse me, what did you just say?"

The SIA agents ignored him and began to tug Abigail out of the courtroom.

The bailiff was fuming. "You may be federal agents, and I may be *just* a bailiff, but you have just stepped inside the courtroom of the United States Court of Appeals. The judges are in charge here — not you. And those judges have delegated authority to me — that's right — to *me* — to exercise absolute control over the conduct of all persons entering this place. So I say to you, gentlemen, please unhand this attorney. Take your seats quietly in the back if you wish, but you'll have to wait until after her case has been argued to execute your warrant. If that's not acceptable, I'll call the U.S. Marshal's office downstairs, and you can have it out with them."

The SIA agent loosened his grip, and Abigail quickly pulled away, striding up to the counsel table in the front of the courtroom.

The opposing attorneys from the Department of Justice were already in their seats. All three government lawyers were bug-eyed, having just witnessed the spectacle in the back of the courtroom. Abigail pulled her notes out of her file and laid them on the table with precision, trying to calm the thumping in her chest. She turned to the three opposing attorneys.

"Counselors," she said with a nod of greeting. She turned to face the door where the three judges would soon enter.

Lance Dunny, the lead prosecuting attorney at the other table, returned her greeting. "Counselor," he replied. And then with a twisted grin added, "This is perfect. A criminal for a lawyer, comes in to defend her criminal husband."

A thought suddenly occurred to Abigail, and she turned back toward her abrasive opponents to share it. "As John Adams once argued in the most famous case of his career — 'Facts are stubborn things.' And just for the record, Mr. Dunny, so am I. I trust you're prepared for both."

FIFTY-ONE

Lance Dunny was the government's choice to argue against Abigail. A smart move, Abigail knew. The DOJ lawyer who was standing at the lectern addressing the three judges was the head litigator in the government's criminal division, and when Dunny won — which was often — he didn't just edge out the opposition by a nose. He would usually crush them. His argument that day in *United States v. Jordan* had been commanding and elegant in its simplicity, perfectly attuned to the three judges, two men and one female, who sat, black-robed, in front of him and peered down from the bench.

Of the three appellate judges assigned to hear this case, none had been appointed by President Tulrude. Abigail considered that a plus. On the other hand, all three had reputations for pro-government toughness when it came to criminal prosecutions. Rarely did any of them vote for reversal of criminal convictions. Agnes Lillegaard, the chief judge on the panel, had been a former federal prosecutor, as had Judge Turkofsky, who sat to her right. Judge Preston on her left had a stint, before appointment to the bench, as counsel to the Senate judiciary, where he helped draft stringent anti-crime legislation.

In his oral presentation, Lance Dunny did an artful job pulling apart what he expected to be Abigail's chief arguments.

During her own opening argument, Abigail made two main points. First, that the "material witness order," which the trial judge had imposed against her in Joshua's case, was improper. That order, she pointed out, prevented her from leaving the United States while

Joshua's case was pending, supposedly on the basis that she was an important witness for the prosecution, and that without such an order she might be a flight risk, leaving the country to join her husband overseas and thereby placing herself beyond the jurisdiction of the court. This, she said, violated due process, constituted cruel and unusual punishment for a witness, and further violated the constitutional right to travel.

Dunny called those arguments "absurd." At one point Judge Agnes Lillegaard, nodding as Dunny continued to denigrate Abigail's reasoning, added her own comment: "Some wives might feel that being forced to join their husbands would be the real cruel and unusual punishment — " The courtroom broke into cordial laughter.

Then Judge Turkofsky asked, "Mr. Dunny, isn't it a fact that the defendant, Mr. Jordan, has already been residing overseas, placing himself outside of the jurisdiction of the United States?"

Dunny nodded vigorously. "Precisely, your honor. In Israel. And he has successfully avoided extradition back to America. So we have already been stonewalled by a criminal defendant who has committed acts of treasonous interference with the U.S. government. It is outrageous that his wife is trying to get this order overturned so she can flee this country too."

Abigail then argued her second point, that the case against Joshua had been based on false and contrived evidence, which, she said, she would soon reveal.

At that point, Dunny's invective became white hot. "Mrs. Jordan comes into this courtroom, telling us that honorable, high-ranking members of the Department of Justice have deliberately manipulated a witness into presenting false testimony. This is astonishing! Does this woman have no shame? But look at what she has produced — an affidavit from a former low-level assistant U.S. attorney, clearly a disgruntled former prosecutor who — for whatever reason — has invented this tale of prosecutorial misconduct. This attorney, Mr. Collingwood, by the way, has now joined one of the most well-known criminal-defense firms in Washington. His affidavit admits that. Apparently, now that he's defending criminals rather than putting them behind bars, Mr. Collingwood is showing a different side of his character — a side that doesn't blink at defaming the very legal agency he once worked for."

But Dunny saved the hardest blow, the punch in the solar plexus, for last. He argued that Abigail was ethically disqualified from even appearing in front of the judges as her husband's attorney "in light of the clear ethical rule prohibiting a lawyer from representing a client in the same case where the attorney is called as a witness. The material witness order recognizes that the government intends to call Abigail Jordan as a witness against her husband," Dunny said. "Case closed. Mrs. Jordan's appearance here is an insult to the rule of law."

When Dunny sat down, Abigail approached the lectern for her rebuttal. As she took a moment to collect herself, she felt the volcano of emotions threatening to be loosed within. She knew the risk she had taken in even defending her husband in the appeal — trying to argue with cold analytical precision a case that had so torn their lives apart and had separated Joshua from her by the full expanse of an ocean. But now she had no choice. She had to become someone else — Lady Justice herself, dispassionate, objective, and truthful.

"As to counsel's argument," Abigail said, "that I am a material witness in the case against my husband, and am therefore disqualified from appearing here, note that the word *material* implies relevance and materiality, that I have something relevant and significant to say in court that would tend to incriminate my husband. Where is that materiality? Where is that relevance? I have filed an affidavit proving that I have nothing whatsoever to say that could possibly show my husband — a true American patriot and hero — to be a criminal. Curiously, the government has failed to advise you judges exactly what they would expect to elicit from my testimony that could possibly be helpful in their case, which leads us to two conclusions: either the government lawyers are sloppy — or they are devious. Sloppy in mistakenly assuming that I have something to add to their empty case. Or, the more likely explanation, devious in deliberately obtaining a material witness order against me just to keep my husband and me separated, thus applying psychological pressure to get Joshua to return to the United States to face a wrongful and contrived prosecution."

Judge Preston, who had been quiet during oral argument, now came to life. "Mrs. Jordan, those are serious charges. Why should we believe you and not the United States government?"

"Because, Your Honor, as I've often said, facts are stubborn things. They call out to our sense of justice and reason and appeal to our moral conscience. So let's look at the following facts. First fact — a respected assistant United States attorney has signed an affidavit — under oath — indicating that the assistant attorney general coerced a witness — a lawyer no less — into making false allegations against my husband, allegations that are the core of the government's case. Fact — the government lawyers have failed to counter that affidavit with one from the assistant attorney general disputing those allegations. Now that is truly astounding. Another fact — Mr. Collingwood, in his affidavit, implicates the Tulrude administration in trying to railroad Joshua into prison for purely political purposes. And a final fact — the government has refused to produce a single piece of evidence disputing those facts."

Judge Agnes Lillegaard took her reading glasses off her nose and stared directly at Abigail Jordan. "You are asking this court to dismiss this case against your husband before it ever gets to trial, based on a single affidavit. As long as I've been on this court we have never done such a thing, Mrs. Jordan. You are asking for something extraordinary here."

Abigail's voice quivered. "This case *is* extraordinary. We live in extraordinary times, when extraordinary injustice has taken place. And in this courtroom we have presented extraordinary evidence of political and legal corruption of the most astonishing kind."

As she prepared to collect her papers, noticing the red light on her lectern, Abigail finished. "There is a reason that in the familiar statue, Lady Justice is always blindfolded," she said. "That is so she will not be dissuaded — not be tempted — by the faces of high and powerful figures, even those in the attorney general's office, and the Oval Office, those who would wink at her, suggesting slyly that their corruptions be overlooked so that they might continue persecuting those who expose their corruption."

Abigail gathered up her papers and walked back to the counsel table. As she did, she saw the contingent of armed federal officers in the back of the room who would soon be placing her into custody.

FIFTY-TWO

Denver, Colorado

The task was to keep Senator Hewbright alive.

Deborah Jordan momentarily thought this was an audacious assignment — bordering on crazy. But with her military training at West Point in clandestine operations, and her desire to work in national security matters, did she really have a beef after all? She would have been happier if John Gallagher was closer, but Abigail had assured her that the former FBI agent was out of pocket. Even if he wasn't, his past government profile and current association with the Roundtable disqualified him from trying to pose as some nondescript campaign volunteer. Besides, he was not the kind to quietly blend in.

As Deborah wheeled her rental car off Auraria Parkway and headed to Chopper Circle to park as closely as possible to Denver's massive Pepsi Center, she wasn't thinking about the frenzied political convention about to take place there. Instead, she thought about her mother's final instructions. "Stay as close as possible to Senator Hewbright — but even closer to Zeta Milla. Milla was the most likely threat against Hewbright, but only when we get clear evidence against her can we afford to blow your cover and reveal it all to Hewbright."

Everyone in the family said that Abigail had the gift of spiritual discernment when it came to people. *Okay,* Deborah thought. *True enough. But the initial facts were sketchy.* A dead campaign director in Wichita. The fact that Milla was wearing a ring that matched the one worn by U.N. Secretary-General Coliquin. Plus Milla apparently lied about being a refuge from Cuba as a child. And Hewbright's economic plan had been stolen by someone, apparently in China, who had hacked into his Allfone. That was all they knew.

Until, that is, Gallagher dug around in Wichita and learned that Zeta Milla was the last person who was with Perry Tedrich at his health club, then at a restaurant for lunch, shortly before his disappearance. In Deborah's mind, that blew everything wide open.

Gallagher had shared the news with FBI Agent Ben Boling, with whom he had been working, but then, incredibly, Boling had gone silent. Maybe it was because the Secret Service had already checked Milla out, along with other staff, and had given her a clean bill of health.

Or maybe it was something else.

So Deborah had decided to do some digging of her own. She checked into Milla's position on the campaign team by making a few calls and using some of her contacts at the Pentagon, hoping to cinch the case against Milla as some kind of saboteur. But the stuff she came up with was pretty benign.

Not surprisingly, Milla's job with the campaign was to help Hewbright bone up on issues relating to Central and South American affairs, including Mexico and the island republics in the Caribbean. She wasn't hired to give immigration advice, however; that was strictly the territory of Hewbright's domestic advisors.

Deborah learned that Milla had a master's degree in international affairs from American University, with credits toward her Ph.D. She worked for a while in the State Department, first during President Corland's tenure, and then in President Tulrude's administration. She was a middle-level staffer, and as far as Deborah was able to determine, she had not distinguished herself. She had kept a low profile. Milla had joined Senator Hewbright's staff just in time for his decision to run for president.

As Deborah made her way through the crowds that swarmed the cavernous lobby of the ten-story glass convention center, and headed toward the Hewbright staff registration desk, she kept asking herself the same three questions. No matter how many times she turned them around in her head, they all seemed hopeless, particularly as she stepped into the monolithic chaos of a presidential convention. *First, why would someone like Zeta Milla pose a threat to Hewbright? Second, even if she is a threat, how am I going to find out about it? And third, if I find out — how am I going to stop it?*

A political volunteer, a tall, blond, athletic-looking guy was behind her in line.

"Hi, there," he said, bending forward to catch Deborah's attention.

She broke out of her mental distraction. "Oh, hi."

"Diehard or newcomer?"

"Pardon?"

"I'm a diehard Hewbright supporter. Helped him in his last senate race. Just local canvassing stuff. My home state is Wyoming. How about you?"

"Oh, yeah I'm pretty diehard. I work in Washington."

"State?"

"No, D.C."

"So you've jumped on board recently, I bet."

"Something like that." She smiled politely but wasn't in the mood for small talk.

"There's already some trash talking from Governor Tucker's group," he said.

That got her attention. "Oh?"

"Yeah, they want to disrupt the ballot and to throw it into a brokered convention. Maybe these lamebrains can't add, but Hewbright's already got the delegates sewn up. He swept almost all the primaries, but the Tucker Troops just won't give up. Just thinking about it makes me sick. What a rotten deal if Tucker actually wrangles the nomination. He's like Tulrude lite, don't you think?"

She was mildly impressed. "Absolutely," she responded.

"The guy's cut from the same cloth as Tulrude ideologically; so why doesn't he just switch parties? And he came across on the TV debates like a college professor. Practically put me to sleep every time he opened his mouth. Reminded me of my history prof at Colorado State.

Anyway, Tucker's so totally unelectable it's tragic. No sweat though. Absolutely no chance of him pulling it out. Hewbright's got this locked up. I mean, really, Hewbright would have to get hit by an asteroid to lose this."

Deborah's head snapped. She thought, *Whoever you are, you have no idea what you just said.*

Then, almost as an afterthought, he added, "I'm Rick. And you're..."

"Deborah."

He shook her hand. He had a strong grip.

"Maybe we'll run into each other during the convention. Tell you what, if we do, I'll buy you coffee."

"Sure, but I have a feeling we may be pretty busy," she said, keeping a poker face. "You know, coming to the rescue of our candidate."

FIFTY-THREE

Washington D.C., Office of the United States Attorney

As soon as Abigail finished her oral argument she snatched up her file and made her way to the back of the courtroom, preparing for the worst. It was every bit as humiliating as she had imagined. In full view of the court, the federal officers jumped to their feet. Then, one agent on each arm, they escorted her into the hallway — where they cuffed her.

Abigail had a single, dismal thought. *Ball game's over. Now we just wait for the score.*

She had expected to be hustled to the federal detention center and booked and put into a cell. And she may have been heading that way. But while she was in the back of the agency car with her hands manacled, the SIA agent in the front seat received a call. When he hung up, he then turned to the driver and said only, "Change of plans. We're going to the U.S. Attorney's Office." On the way they perfunctorily advised Abigail of her Miranda Rights. She knew what that meant. *Here we go*, she thought, bracing herself.

The new U.S. attorney for the District of Columbia, Tanya Hardcastle, was a recent appointee of President Tulrude's. That was all Abigail knew. But that was enough. When they arrived at the building just off of Second Street, the squad drove down into the underground parking. Surprisingly, the cuffs were removed and Abigail was walked through the structure and up into the lobby. She couldn't help but

TIM LaHAYE AND CRAIG PARSHALL

smile when the BIDTag scanner gave her the green light. Her captors were not amused.

She was taken to a small conference room on the same floor as U.S. Attorney Hardcastle's expansive office. She was offered coffee but replied that she preferred tea. They brought her some in a cup with a saucer, and whatever it was, it wasn't bad. Several hours passed. Assistant U.S. attorneys and their staffers scurried by. She caught glimpses of them through the window in the door. And she waited.

When Tanya Hardcastle, a short, bony woman with a smoker's voice, finally entered, she smiled and sat down across from Abigail at the conference table.

Tanya Hardcastle knew that Abigail had no clue that the three federal judges in her case went into their standard closed conference immediately after the morning's oral arguments to consider their votes. And she would not have known how they had made such quick business of the case in *United States v. Jordan*, that it only took one vote to secure a decision among the three appeal judges. It was unanimous. Hardcastle also knew how Judge Agnes Lillegaard had drafted an order. When that judge emailed that order to the court clerk, it was read by another clerk, who called a friend at the Department of Justice. Swearing the friend to secrecy, he disclosed the contents of the order. But the word spread rapidly, and then a deputy attorney general called Hardcastle's office to alert her to the rumor, knowing that she already had Abigail in custody in the high-profile case. So Hardcastle knew the end of this legal story and what the court order said. And Abigail knew none of it.

Sitting across from Abigail, Hardcastle started off with a good-cop routine. "I've checked you out," the U.S. attorney said in an even, pleasant tone. "You have a reputation as a very sharp attorney here in the District. Some impressive victories. And, as you and I both know, it's a man's world, Abigail ... may I call you that?"

Abigail smiled tightly and nodded.

Continuing, Hardcastle said, "It's been a man's world in the practice of law. Back when I graduated from Princeton law, the partner in my first firm had me working in the secretarial pool. Can you imagine? But women like you and me, we've changed things — for the equality of women. Don't you think?"

Abigail took a sip of tea. "Are you trying to turn me into a feminist, Ms. Hardcastle?"

"I think you're already one. You just don't know it."

Pushing the cup and saucer away from her, Abigail replied, "What I am, madam, is a believer in the U.S. Constitution. When the Fourth Amendment says that every citizen has a right to be 'secure in their persons,' it means what it says. It means that the federal government cannot force Americans to receive a laser-tattooed tracking device imprinted onto their skin, even if it doesn't hurt and even if it's invisible to the naked eye."

"Federal courts have disagreed with you, Abigail."

"Only because the Supreme Court has refused to take the issue up. I'm guessing that Justice Lapham can't muster the necessary four votes to grant a writ of certiorari on all those appeals from nontaggers."

"Well, I'm not here to debate the finer points of the law ..."

Hardcastle paused, but Abigail didn't fill in the blanks for her, so the U.S. attorney continued, "I'm here to offer you complete immunity from prosecution if you simply give me some facts."

A brief flash of shock registered on Abigail's face before she returned to a neutral glare. "Such as?"

"Who gave you your fake BIDTag. It's pretty impressive. It passed all our scanners."

"Does it matter? I've been BIDTagged one way or the other."

"Oh, I think we both know you haven't. Not legally. The point is that we know someone out there is minting this counterfeit version. Just tell us who, and we'll grant you immunity."

Abigail had suspected that Chiro's forgery would be of interest to the feds, but she didn't expect they'd offer her immunity in return. Surely, they'd lock her up anyway and try to force the information out of her. But something wasn't right. Abigail thought back to the eccentric Chiro Hashimoto and her pledge to him before leaving his compound that she would keep his identity and his location confidential. "You're asking me questions that are covered by the Fifth Amendment of the Constitution," Abigail replied. "And I recall being given my Miranda rights earlier today," she added.

Hardcastle bristled. "Go ahead and try to play tough with me. But remember — all I have to do is make just one call and guys with guns show up here and lock you in a metal cage."

"Sounds unpleasant."

"Jail cells generally are."

Abigail could smell a rat. Tanya was trying to sneak something past Abigail. Her best guess, and greatest hope, was that Hardcastle had already heard some inside information about the court's ruling in her case. Abigail was banking on that. And she was now also banking on the fact that Hardcastle knew that the government's case against Joshua may have just gone down in flames. "I'll have to respectfully decline your offer," Abigail said.

The U.S. attorney fluttered her eyes. "The thing about smart people," Hardcastle said, this time not trying to hide the edge in her voice, "is that they can sometimes outsmart themselves." Then she got up and headed to the door, but halfway there she halted, as if tempted to try again to manipulate Abigail into yielding information, but then she thought better of it. To cover her abrupt stop, she bent down and scooped up the teacup and saucer off the table. Abigail had to stifle a laugh. She'd made the right call.

"Thanks for the tea," Abigail said brightly.

"Don't move," Hardcastle said, irritation all over her face.

Outside the room, Hardcastle shoved the teacup and saucer into the hands of an assistant and then stormed into her office. She snatched off her desk the hard copy of the Per Curiam Order of the D.C. Circuit Court of Appeals that she had printed out from her email just before talking to Abigail. Now she read its infuriating contents again. One more time. Just to make sure.

Judges Lillegaard, Turkofsky, Preston.

ORDERED: That the Material Witness Order entered against Abigail Jordan by the U.S. District Court, requiring her to remain within the territorial boundaries of the United States during the pendency of the criminal action titled *United States v. Jordan*, is hereby reversed and vacated, on the grounds of the Due Process Clauses of the 5th and 14th Amendments to the U.S. Constitution.

This Court further Orders the government to show cause to the U.S. District Court, within seventy-two hours, as to why the criminal action against Joshua Jordan should not be dismissed on its merits in light of the affidavit evidence of prosecutorial misconduct submitted by defendant's counsel, Abigail Jordan.

Still in the conference room, as Abigail wondered whether she would be spending the night on a metal cot, an agent entered the room and asked her to follow him. Five minutes later, she was outside on the public sidewalk, unaccompanied and smelling the welcoming though automobile-congested air of Washington, D.C. Her only guess was that Hardcastle, having suffered a humiliating defeat in the case against Joshua, was not going to risk charging Abigail with her apparent failure to get a timely BIDTag, especially since she now appeared to have one that inexplicably passed through the federal scanners.

But Abigail was struck with the question she did not have a chance to ask Hardcastle. For Abigail, it was the most important question of all. *Where is Cal?*

But that thought was interrupted by her Allfone. She opened her email and noticed a message from the D.C. Circuit Court of Appeals. The Per Curiam Order was attached.

She took a deep breath and read it with a trembling hand. For good measure, she read it again. That is when, there on the sidewalk, Abigail burst into tears. She continued to cry and laugh amidst the busy pedestrian traffic, murmuring a prayer of thanks about the goodness of God and His love of justice. She didn't care about the passersby who gawked at her. She was finally able to vent the emotions she had carefully managed for so long while she had waited for God's vindicating hand.

Abigail spoke out to no one in particular, "Josh, I miss you." She had been out of contact with him for a while. She knew it was necessary — avoiding phone calls and even encrypted emails while she was dodging the government surveillance — but soon the waiting would be over. "Josh, I can't wait to fly to Israel to see you, darling …"

A voice behind her broke in. "How about your trusty legal intern?" It was Cal. Abigail jumped and even more tears started trickling down.

"Mom," Cal said, "you look surprised. I told you there was no way I could be charged. Victoria McHenry was released too. Man, she's one cool and collected customer. But then, considering her spy background, I shouldn't have been surprised."

"I need to thank that dear woman for sticking her neck out for me," Abigail said, wiping a tear away and not worrying about her messed-up eyeliner. "And yes, you'll join me as soon as we can get our jet ready — and Deborah too."

"I called her," Cal said, "as soon as I was released and gave her a status on what's happening here, left it on her voicemail. I got a short text message back. She said she's in orientation meetings with the convention team in Denver. Doesn't sound promising."

"Give her time. She's the right person for that assignment. We need to keep praying for her too. This could be dangerous."

Cal nodded and then glanced at his Allfone. "I got a message from Phil Rankowitz. Didn't tell me much, just that he needed to talk to us. It's about the two stories he's working on for AmeriNews, both of them shockers — the Alexander Coliquin exposé and the investigation on the possible poisoning of President Corland. Phil reminded me that I need to get Corland to sign an authorization so we can get testing done on that blood sample his family doctor took. His wife had suspicions and ordered the blood draw taken right after that last near-fatal attack he had."

"When was your last contact with Corland or his wife?"

"Last week."

"You may want to double-back with President Corland," she said, dabbing her eyes with a handkerchief. "I'm sure getting his medical consent is no problem, but we need to prepare him. If the tests show he was poisoned, the story will set off a firestorm."

"Right," Cal said, "but first, I'm starving. Let's grab something to eat. Backpacking in the Northwest, escaping SIA agents, and facing federal arrest has given me a monster appetite."

FIFTY-FOUR

Fair Haven Convalescent Center, Bethesda, Maryland

Winnie Corland was sobbing. She stood over the body of her deceased husband, but her knees weakened and she fell against the bed, reaching out and touching his cold face. This was not just a former president she was embracing. It was her husband of fifty years. A nurse came up next to her and helped her into a chair.

"He just passed in the night," she explained to Winnie. "I'm sure it was peaceful. I am sorry about your loss."

She knew his health had been fragile, especially when he collapsed in the Oval Office after one of his worst transient ischemic attacks. But after the succession of power to Jessica Tulrude, and Virgil's transfer to the convalescent center, he seemed to be doing better. Slowly, to be sure, but improving.

The nurse stepped out as Winnie tried to catch her breath in a short, gasping effort. She dabbed the tears from her face and took a deep breath. The Allfone in her purse on the floor started humming. But she ignored it.

She thought back to her time with Virgil the night before. She had spent the evening with him, just talking quietly. She was grateful for that. They had laughed at memories of their life together, like their honeymoon. Being nature-lovers, they had gone rustic, camping in a state park in Maine. They had pitched their tent on the low ground, and when a nasty rainstorm broke in the middle of the night, the waters rushed through their tent, nearly floating them away. Her eyes filled with tears again, but a smile started to break in the corner of her mouth as she remembered that.

She recalled how last night, one more time, Virgil shared with her the story of his devoted Secret Service agent, a Christian man, who had such an influence on him, and how Virgil had made the decision, in his words, to "personally trust his soul into the hands of Christ." It was the day that Virgil had been alone in the Oval Office, shouldering the usual, ever-present burdens of the presidency. But he said that something that day actually outweighed all of that: the burden of his heart, the "empty hole there, and my longing for a touch from God, to repair me, forgive me, and to bring me some peace." So, as Corland related it to his wife, he slowly eased down on his knees, behind the famous nineteenth-century Resolute Desk, and began to pray, pouring out his heart of repentance and faith in Jesus, trusting his soul and his life to Christ, God's "Divine Commander-in-Chief," as he put it in his prayer, "My Savior. My King."

Despite his pleas, Winnie had never been able to make that decision for herself. What was it that had kept it all so distant — at arm's length? Virgil was always such an external person. She, on the other hand, was the private one. She would ponder what Virgil said, but then would silently push it back into the closet and close the door.

Virgil often took her hand gently and asked her, in a voice that, for him, was unusual in its pathos, to "please, please, consider where you stand with the Son of God."

But now he was gone, and there was nothing that would change that. And she was alone.

She slowly fished her hand into her purse, pulled out the Allfone, and hit the voicemail function. The voice message was from Cal Jordan, the young man that Virgil had so enjoyed. He was asking to talk to Virgil or Winnie as soon as possible, and Cal added, "I sure hope you both are doing well. I really appreciated my talks with President Corland. Good-bye."

She clicked off her Allfone so she wouldn't be bothered again and dropped it into her purse. All she wanted to do now was to sit in the room and stay close to the last physical likeness of her late husband. Nothing else seemed to matter.

Pepsi Center, Denver

In the middle of the frenzied political theater unfolding around her, Deborah was obsessing over a question — a very politically incorrect one: *How do I trap our candidate's advisor and slam the cage shut before she bites?*

The volunteers, having paraded to the middle of the cavernous arena, were now seated while the roadies and tech guys finished erecting the sets on the stage. On either side of the presenting area, where a Plexiglas podium had been installed, tall panes of red-white-and-blue-colored glass rose fifty feet into the air. Sparkling banners and a mammoth American flag made of shimmering lights formed the backdrop.

The manager of volunteer services was on his feet at the front with a sports-mic headset. He was looking at his e-pad, getting ready to address the one hundred and seventy volunteers for the Hewbright campaign. Deborah was one of them. A few seats away, Rick was joking with a group of friends. His face brightened when he noticed Deborah.

Oh boy, she thought, as Rick got up from his seat and tripped over knees and feet to approach her. He bent down to the girl next to Deborah and said, "Would you mind switching seats with me? This is a long-lost friend of mine. Gotta do some catching up."

The girl tossed him an exasperated look but changed seats. Rick sat down and stretched out his long legs, pretending nothing had happened.

"Long-lost friend?" Deborah said with a smirk.

"Oh, that? Naw, listen, this is strictly platonic. You don't think I'm trying to hit on you, do you?" Rick's cocky smirk gave that one away.

"Okay," Deborah said, "then hit me with some platonics."

"Right. How about this ... just heard that the Tucker troops are ramping up their smear campaign."

At the front, the volunteer manager was being approached by another Hewbright staffer carrying a digital clipboard.

"Tell me," Deborah whispered.

"They're saying Hewbright's a womanizer. One-night-stands in motels with admirers. That kind of thing."

"That's crazy. Hewbright? Who's going to believe that?"

"Look, his wife's been dead a couple of years. Nobody expects the guy never to go out with women again. He's not a monk. But this stuff they're saying is so vile and false it's incredible. I heard Hewbright's going to haul Tucker before the rules committee, to either prove this stuff — which he obviously can't — or make a public apology in front of the delegates. You wonder where these rumors start anyway."

As Deborah was trying to process that, wondering if it had anything to do with Zeta Milla, the staffer at the front with the e-clipboard broke into a wide grin and waved to someone around the corner. Senator Hewbright came into view, waving to the volunteers, who stood to their feet, clapping and whistling.

After the hall grew quiet again, the senator began his remarks. "You young people who have given so much and asked for so little in return, you are the essence of my campaign. You're here not just for me, although I thank you for that from the bottom of my heart, but you're also here for America. You sense, as I do, that our nation is on a precipice, tottering this way and that — on the brink of an unknown and turbulent future. Possibly catastrophic. But I see, at the same time, another direction — that we can be on the brink of a great restoration, a recovery of something lost, a revival of the American vision. That there can be greatness still in this nation, and we can say that without apology, without embarrassment for who we are, and what we stand for. Leading the world, rather than asking the world's permission. Standing tall, rather than bowing low to international powers, refusing to be financial beggars at the economic table of global masters, but rather choosing to be the brokers of freedom that we were destined to be."

Hewbright stopped and smiled. "All right, enough of my acceptance speech ..." The crowd laughed and burst into more applause. "But," he added, "I do thank you all. Truly. And let me share something I just found out. The first televised debate will be in ten days. I'm hoping and planning to be the candidate on the other side of the podium from Tulrude." More wild applause. "That first debate will be on foreign policy." With that he turned to someone standing just around the corner, blocked by an entryway. "Come on up here, Zeta."

Zeta Milla stepped into view and strode up next to Hewbright with a modest smile. She was carrying a chic black handbag. Deborah, who had inherited her mother's taste for style, recognized the Dolce and Gabbana bag immediately.

The senator looked relaxed and energized. "My chief international-affairs advisor, Winston Garvey, isn't here right now — otherwise I'd introduce him to you. He's up in the war room, as we call it, putting together my briefing books on global issues. But this is Zeta Milla, and she is on our foreign-relations team. She briefs me on Central and South American issues. And she's even smarter than she is attractive …" There was a burst of applause.

Deborah had her eyes on Zeta Milla. As Hewbright waved good-bye to the volunteers, Milla slipped her hand around Hewbright's arm. He moved away from her so slightly that it was nearly imperceptible.

Rick's face lit up. "He's going to make a great president." He turned to Deborah. "So, what's your assignment?"

"Tell me yours."

"I just found out. You're never going to believe it."

"Try me."

"I'm the go-for guy in the war room! Is that the bomb or what?"

"You're kidding."

"Not at all. That Zeta Milla babe we just saw … I met her up in the war-room suite. Met that Winston Garvy dude too. I'm right there, in the middle of the action, even though I'm just a fetch-and-carry guy, but still …"

Deborah tried not to dive in too eagerly. So she waited a few minutes. Then, she looked at Rick and spoke quietly. "Okay, Rick, you can buy me that cup of coffee."

"Hey, sounds great."

"But you have to do something first."

Rick threw her a hesitant grin, "What's that?"

"Can you get me on your team? I'd love to work in the war room. The heart of the action is right where I want to be."

Paris, France

It was 2:00 a.m. in Paris. In his apartment just off Place de la Republique, Pack McHenry was working. The former American intelligence officer had just finished reviewing several surveillance reports on terror cells in the European Union on his encrypted email system. He approved them and sent them electronically — and encrypted — over to the Paris post of the CIA, one of his contract clients. He glanced at his Allfone watch — the one with ten time zones. It was early evening in Cuba.

So he made his call to Marianao, Cuba, which was in the Old Havana section. Carlos picked up.

"Hello, my friend."

"Greetings, amigo. Where are you calling from today?"

"You know I never answer questions like that," McHenry said.

Carlos laughed hard.

"So," McHenry asked, "what have you found out?"

"I am pretty sure it's a match. These two women are the same person."

"You're sure?"

"Yes, I think so."

"Zeta Milla and ... what's the other's name?"

"Maria Zeta. Yes, same woman, I believe. But I had to do a lot of digging, Señor Pack. She's been off the island for about eight years."

"So, the question is, long enough to go to school in the U.S., get a master's degree and some credits toward a doctorate, put time in at the State Department, and then join the staff of a senator?"

"That doesn't sound like a question," Carlos said, "more like an answer."

"Yes, exactly," McHenry said. "Anything else?"

"We call her type *Buta Buts*."

"Meaning ..."

"A poisonous tree. Any contact with it hurts you, blinds you, or even worse."

"Not the kind of girl to bring home to Mom."

"As a teenager, she was recruited by Castro's staff. She was pretty and very smart, but ruthless. Killed two men I know of."

"Why?"

"It was just a test, just to see if she could." Then Carlos added, "She passed the test."

"She's only worked in Cuba?"

"No, I heard she has been reassigned overseas, but I don't know where."

McHenry thanked him and told him he would wire some money to him. Then Pack pulled out the summary of the international travel itinerary his agents had obtained on Zeta Milla, aka Maria Zeta, something he ordered as a favor for Abigail.

As he studied the data, it became clear why Abigail wanted it. The listing documented every trip that the Cuban woman had taken to Romania while Coliquin still maintained a home there during his stint as that country's ambassador to the U.N. And the list of Zeta Milla's trips to Romania — apparently to meet with Coliquin — was very long.

FIFTY-FIVE

On the Edge of the Negev Desert, Israel

The Arab school was the perfect cover for the assembly of one of the world's most grotesque weapons of mass destruction. In that remote area, just off the highway from the desolate Negev, the school was made up of three buildings, mostly classrooms for Bedouin children. There was also a large cinderblock garage fifty yards from the other structures. That windowless building would be the assembly site.

While the children played cheerfully on the playground at the end of their school day, inside the garage, Tarek Fahad, Anwar al-Madrassa's chief of weapons inspected the missile housing and nosecone, which were laid out on a long steel worktable. Then he turned to Dr. Ahlam, the terror chemist who had designed the horrifying biological agent that al-Madrassa's cell was now calling "The Elixir of Allah." "I hear your elixir can melt the skin off a dog, down to the bone. Let's just hope it can do that to humans."

Dr. Ahlam had his own challenge. "Don't worry about my biological material. It will do that and more. My worry," he said pointing to the hardware on the table, "is about your delivery system."

Laying his hand on the shiny steel casing, Fahad retorted, "Very smart missile men have provided this to us. For a very high price, of course. Have you ever heard of a company called the Deter Von Gunter Group?"

Ahlam narrowed his eyes. "Sounds familiar ..."

"Big weapons company. The owner is part of a group called the World Builders."

When Dr. Ahlam gave a blank look, Fahad shrugged. "Not important. Because Anwar agrees with me that this missile will work perfectly to carry your elixir to its target."

"But Israel still has the RTS defense system. I'm afraid it will keep my bio-weapon from reaching its destination."

"You worry too much," Fahad said smugly. "RTS will be of no consequence. We will be burning the skin off infidels one way or another."

Pepsi Center, Denver

Deborah had made a mad dash downtown to do some emergency shopping and was just now arriving back at the convention center and flashed her credentials. Her Allfone rang. It was Pack McHenry.

"Deborah," he said quietly, "I have every reason to believe that Zeta Milla is one bad actor. To the extreme."

Deborah scurried to a corner of the convention center to buy herself some privacy. "Yes, Pack, I copy that."

"I'd stay clear of her, if I were you."

"Can't do that, sir."

"Listen, Deb, this woman is like a coral snake; you don't realize how poisonous until it's too late. Leave her to somebody else."

"Like who? The convention starts tonight. I get the feeling that something is about to break — right on top of us. Maybe even tonight."

"Since none of my people are available," McHenry said, "I put in a call to John Gallagher, but he hasn't called back. Maybe he can do something, push the FBI or local cops to intervene."

"He's tied up in some kind of wedding in Northern California."

"Then you need to confer with your mother. Get someone there to help you."

"Too late. You know the hoops I went through to get inside the campaign. I'm in striking distance. The tip of the spear. I need to finish this."

"All right. I understand. I'll keep calling Gallagher."

"Fine. Just know that I'm getting close."

Then she noticed Rick, who was roaming the lobby, searching for someone. He caught sight of Deborah and trotted over.

"Very close," she added to Pack McHenry and clicked off her cell.

"Come on, Deborah," Rick said in a huff, "we got to get up to the war room suite — like right now. We're supposed to be serving drinks and running errands." He looked down at the big duffle bag on the floor next to her. "What's that?"

"Oh, it's mine. Didn't have time to drop it off at my hotel room." Then she grabbed it by the handle. "I'll just take it with me."

"Whatever," Rick said. "Let's go. I did you a favor getting you in, so let's not blow it, okay?"

IDF Headquarters, Tel Aviv

"I can't seem to get a handle on this. I've worked the problem from every possible angle and still can't get to the bottom."

Over the phone, Ted, the senior engineer at Jordan Technologies, sounded stressed. As well he should.

Joshua was standing off to the side of the R&D conference room with a high-security satellite Allfone in his hand. Several IDF officers were huddled at the other end of the room.

"Look, Ted, they're telling me there's a new threat emerging over here. They've got intel that Anwar al-Madrassa was spotted in Lebanon and may be inside Israel by now. His terror cell is working on a nightmare kind of bio weapon. We can't afford to just turn that kind of incoming missile around one-hundred-and-eighty-degrees. It may be launched from a civilian area. We need three-hundred-and-sixty-degree-capture control. And we need it now."

"I keep telling you, our computer models work perfectly, but something happens in the real-world tests that I can't pick up from here."

Joshua rubbed the back of his neck. He could feel himself tightening like a steel cable. "Well, I've checked the data from this end. Our IDF friends have suggested that we adjust the intensity of the laser beam itself. They think if we scale it down a bit we'd have a better chance at loading our three-sixty controls into the missile's total guidance program."

"Problem is," Ted said, "once you do that, you may lose the capacity to do the initial capture of the trajectory data from the guidance program in the missile cone. If that happens, you may lose all control over the incoming weapon."

"That's what I told them," Joshua said, shaking his head. "I think we keep the laser intensity where it is. My guess is there's something going wrong in the data stream between the laser and the guidance of the incoming missile. Keep working the numbers and see if you can find any anomalies. This may be a software problem. Look at the code we're using and see if that's the issue."

Joshua clicked off and looked over at Ethan, who was sitting at the conference table.

Ethan sat up straighter. "I wish there was something I could do," he said, "but you guys are the tech geniuses. I'm just a former flyboy."

Joshua sauntered over to Ethan and sat down. "This glitch is driving me crazy. But I'm glad you're here."

"I appreciate that, but I still can't help you with your RTS problem, and I've got no political clout with the Israelis."

"On the other hand," Joshua replied, keeping his voice low, "you did some quick thinking in that market, keeping those Shin Bet agents off my back."

"Which turned out to be a moot issue," Ethan said with a smirk, "because they stopped chasing you down anyway — now that they need your RTS system again."

Joshua bent closer to Ethan, and lowered his voice to almost a whisper. "Listen to me, Ethan. I know you wonder what you're doing here, but I know you're meant to be here with me. There are things that have yet to be revealed. You're in a time of preparation, I think, and I know you balk when I talk like this ... but I can see in your eyes that you're starting to believe me. The role you are meant to play is not about me. It's much bigger than that. I get the feeling you are going to be a major player in events to come." Then Joshua felt his countenance fall. "Which means, necessarily, that I fear for you at the same time."

Ethan looked confused, but Josh couldn't explain it any further.

"Colonel Jordan?" A voice came from one of the IDF officers on the other side of the room. "We have a message for you to call your wife."

Joshua nodded to them and turned to Ethan. "That's good news. I haven't heard from Abby for the last week. I wonder what kind of trouble she's been getting into."

FIFTY-SIX

While Joshua was on the Allfone with Abigail, Ethan stepped out into the hallway of the IDF headquarters. He thought about Josh's comments, and his gut did a flip. He didn't understand the meaning behind Josh's words. He was used to Josh's talk about the so-called end times, but now things were getting a little too personal.

As he walked down the hallway, he saw something that made his head spin. He tried to look nonchalant but failed. He made an attempt at a polite head nod but ended up breaking into a grin. Rivka was in the corridor, leaning against the wall with her arms folded. She looked unusually professional in a dark suit and tan blouse. She greeted him, "Hello, Mr. America."

"You look spiffy," Ethan shot back.

"Well, I'm on official IDF business."

With an attempt at bravado, Ethan cracked, "I thought you came by for me."

"And what if I did?"

Suddenly he knew this was one of the nanosecond moments — in the cockpit, stick in hand, incoming aircraft sighted. Friend or not?

"Well," Ethan said, not realizing he was blushing, "I'd say that was good to hear. Really good. If it's true."

"Let's take a walk," Rivka said, motioning them away from the cluster of Israeli officers who were mulling over something out in the hall.

He thrust his hands in his cargo pants. "The last time I saw you,

Rivka, you weren't so dressy. In fact, you were decked out like a fish-monger at the Mahame Yehuda Market, tossing a pan of oily fish guts on the floor, right in front of those Shin Bet agents."

She muffled a laugh. "Have to say I enjoyed that one. I knew that HQ here would eventually get that extradition decision of Bensky reversed, talk some sense into the PM — particularly now that the threat level is sky-high again and they need you guys."

Rivka stopped and looked around. No military staffers were in earshot. "And I noticed the neat little trick you pulled with the forklift at the Souk. Those Shin Bet guys were so ticked ..."

"Brought back memories. I operated a forklift in a warehouse, working through junior college, before the Air Force." He and Rivka leaned against the wall now. It felt good to be close to her again. She smiled but didn't respond. He kept talking. "That was you, giving me the text message that day in the market, wasn't it? Warning us about the two agents."

"I told you once that I was the best friend you could have."

Ethan looked down the hall, where the IDF officers on the bio-threat task force had finished their huddle and were going back into the conference room. "Are you in on this deal too?" he asked, nodding down toward the conference room at the end of the hall.

She answered with a simplicity that Ethan recognized. It was her resolve to do her duty to Israel. "Yes," she said. "I'm involved." But then, with equal calm, she added, "And so are you."

That was a comment Ethan wasn't ready for. He took a breath and was about to dive into it with Rivka, but before he could, Colonel Clint McKinney came hustling down the hallway. "Ethan, where's Josh? I've got to talk to him, stat, about taking a little trip with me."

Ethan pointed to the open door down the corridor. "He's taking a call down there, sir. In that room."

McKinney thanked him and quick-stepped his way to the conference room. He disappeared through the open door.

Ramat Air Base, Israel

On their drive from the IDF headquarters to the airbase, Colonel McKinney briefed Joshua on what he was about to see. The idea electrified Joshua's attitude about finding a solution. Joshua said he had been working hard to use a "left field" approach to solving the RTS problem — thinking beyond the parameters of the problem — which had to do with the inability of the RTS laser system when fired from a defensive rocket, to take hostage the entire guidance program of the other, hostile, incoming missile.

"Yes, Clint, absolutely," Joshua said with a burst of enthusiasm, "this could be the answer."

Clint eyed him with a smile as they strode into the experimental-aircraft hangar.

The IDF officer finally had to ask, "Josh, for a guy tormented by your RTS problem, you seem to be in a good mood all of a sudden. What's up?" Then he flashed a grin. "Is it just my brilliant suggestion?"

"Not to take anything away from you," Joshua shot back with a smile, "but I just called my wife. I'll tell you, Clint, God is good. Abby's been punching away at that phony criminal case the DOJ brought against me. Now she's got the other side up against the ropes. And the court order keeping her from joining me over here just got kicked. She's making plans to round up Cal and Deborah and fly over here."

Inside the hangar, Joshua saw what he had come for. He walked slowly around the gleaming fighter jet and studied it. Another officer joined them.

"Josh, this is Dr. Jacob Chabbaz," McKinney said. "He's in charge of our R&D RTS in-flight program."

Joshua pointed to the fighter. "So, this is it?"

Chabbaz nodded. "The F-35 Laser Variant. We weren't planning on manning this one yet, but with the newest threat, I think we can prep it for you. You'll notice the orbital laser housing where the weapon bay door used to be. The LV has three-hundred-sixty-degree optics, capable of locating any incoming missiles. Excellent capacity also to strike them with your RTS laser."

Joshua peeked under the fuselage at the laser mounting. "I've read the specs. Very impressive." He stood and looked over at McKinney. "You know what I'm thinking ..."

"Yep. That's why I brought you here. You've flown our F-22s over here in the last few months. Our test pilots can run you through the operational stuff for this F-35 variant on the ground. But it's a canopy built for only one pilot—and that pilot has to be able to decipher the RTS laser readings during the test runs. Nobody can do that like you, Josh."

"Okay," Joshua said, "I'm in. Once your guys walk me through the drill I think I can handle taking it up for some test runs. Clint, this may be the way to crack the problem with our RTS data-stream. Starting with in-flight use of the RTS aimed from the jet at an incoming missile at a close range. If I can capture the guidance program of the enemy bird completely that way, then we just work backward to refine the ground-to-air system."

Clint McKinney nodded in agreement. But he and Dr. Chabbaz exchanged glances. Then Clint spoke up. "Our intel says that this bio-threat is imminent. So, I need to start your operational briefing immediately. That's one phase of our defensive response—but there's another."

"Am I involved in that?" Joshua asked.

"No," Clint said with a penetrating look, "but your assistant, Ethan March, is."

FIFTY-SEVEN

Pepsi Convention Center, Denver, the Hewbright War Room

Secret Service Agent Owens, wearing the usual dark suit, white shirt, and light blue tie, was munching a cookie in the corner of the five-room suite while Deborah cleared the soda cans and coffee cups from the long buffet table. The Hewbright staff had decided they couldn't trust the convention hospitality workers to set up and tear down the food service, not since the hacking of Hewbright's Allfone, and Agent Owens had made them aware of the need for heightened security.

Deborah was tossing the trash from the buffet table into a big garbage bag. She glanced over at the meeting taking place in the adjoining room, where the senator, in shirtsleeves, was leaning back in his chair, arms crossed. Beside him stood George Caulfield, his national campaign manager, and across from him was Zeta Milla, holding her black D&G handbag. Winston Garvey, the chief foreign-policy advisor, was somewhere out of sight, and Deborah could hear snatches of their conversation. Several American companies in Bolivia, they were saying, had just been forcibly taken over by government forces, and the executives had been taken hostage. President Tulrude was deferring to the United Nations to intervene. Now Hewbright was formulating his public response.

The opening ceremonies of the convention would start that night. Deborah knew that would involve a military honor guard and a musical number by a large community choir from Colorado Springs. That would be followed by a video presentation on the JumboTrons, giving a retrospective of American history, called *Our Legacy of Liberty*. Later, at the end of the evening, Senator Hewbright would appear on stage and formally present the big ceremonial gavel to the chairman of the party, who was presiding over the convention. As she thought of all this, Deborah had a feeling of impending dread — it was the timing of it all, right before the climax of the convention. If someone was going to disrupt Hewbright's nomination, wouldn't this be the time? Deborah knew she had to do something — anything — to find out what Zeta Milla might be planning. And she had to do it fast. It was time to try the plan she had formulated earlier.

Deborah tied up a garbage bag and walked out of the common room. Rick had left with a rolling cart of leftover food several minutes before. On the way out, she snatched up an empty garbage bag and tucked it under her arm. With the full bag of garbage in her hand, she jogged down the hall to the service elevator and threw it into the open elevator. She pushed the button for Basement and scooted back down the hall to the women's restroom where, around the corner from the stalls, she had stashed her duffel bag. She opened it and pulled out the handbag she had purchased that morning — identical to Zeta Milla's — which Deborah had filled with empty files and a stack of photocopy paper to give it heft. She dropped the expensive handbag into the empty garbage bag and trotted back to the war room.

Hewbright's group was still in the adjoining room. Zeta Milla was in the same spot, handbag hanging from her arm. Deborah could see Hewbright speaking and looking up at Milla. Milla nodded and walked out into the common area where agent Owens and Deborah were standing. Deborah took her garbage bag and pretended to busy herself, collecting plastic knives and spoons. Zeta placed her handbag on a chair and pulled out her Allfone. On her cell she talked quietly to someone, asking for statistics on the U.S. companies in Bolivia that had just been raided. While she was talking, George Caulfield hurriedly dashed out and told her to come back into the room, to catch the remarks of President Tulrude, who was about to deliver a live televised message from the Oval Office. Caulfield was red-faced, yelling that Tulrude was "trying to co-opt our convention" with this stunt.

Zeta Milla nodded and told the person on the phone that she would call back. She dashed back to the adjoining room with her Allfone in her hand, leaving her black handbag on the chair. A chill ran down Deborah's back. An opportunity. She knew this was it.

Go girl, charge of the Light Brigade!

She stepped over to Agent Owens and said, "Excuse me, Agent Owens, I'm not sure, but there seems to be some strange stuff going on out in the hallway. Thought you may want to know."

"Strange? Like what?"

"Like a suspicious-looking bag in the service elevator." She tried to sound innocent so that later he wouldn't suspect her of having staged a diversion.

Owens swallowed the last bite of his cookie and headed down the hall.

Deborah made her way to the chair where Milla's handbag was. Keeping her eyes fixed on Zeta, who had her back to her, Deborah snatched it up, pulled her identical bag out of the garbage bag, and after placing it on the chair, strode quickly around the corner to the kitchen galley, out of sight. Deborah opened Milla's bag and rifled through the contents. A small makeup kit, lipstick, a calendar. She leafed through it, but nothing suspicious jumped out.

She peeked around the corner. Milla still had her back turned. The group was glued to the television at the other end of the adjoining room, and the president's voice could be faintly heard in the background. Deborah kept digging. Kleenex. Breath mints. She came to the bottom where she found a piece of folded paper. It was a printout of an email from Zeta Milla to FBI Agent Ben Boling. She poured over its content. It confirmed their earlier conversation, in which Milla described to Agent Boling, in detail, her visit to Perry Tedrich in Wichita the day of his disappearance. Milla told Boling how much she appreciated his clearing her of any suspicion in Tedrich's disappearance and tragic death and how heartbroken she had been. She also mentioned that she feared for Senator Hewbright, particularly after the hacking of his Allfone, and that she urged the FBI to increase surveillance for the sake of Hewbright's personal safety.

Zeta Milla seemed to be the epitome of a non-threat. Deborah was numb with disbelief. And something else — she felt utterly stupid. She stuffed the contents back into the purse and quickly moved over to the chair. She grabbed her replica handbag off the chair, tossed it back into the garbage bag, and then placed Milla's black bag back on the chair.

When she turned, she was startled to see Zeta Milla standing in front of her.

"Sorry," Milla said with a smile, "I need to get past you."

Deborah moved out of the way. Milla smiled, casually picked up her handbag, and turned back to Deborah. "By the way, I'm glad to see you on the team. I'm sorry I sort of gave you the brush-off a while ago. Must be the stress of everything that's going on, I guess."

With a nod, Deborah said, "Sure. Understood."

Milla dashed back into the adjoining room, as Agent Owens came strolling back from the hallway. He walked up to Deborah. "I found that suspicious bag in the service elevator."

"Oh?"

"Wasn't that the same garbage bag you just took out of here?"

With a struggle to look confident and undaunted, Deborah replied, "Wow. Yes. Don't know where my head's at. Sorry."

Agent Owens sauntered over to the cookie plate and grabbed a lemon bar, still eyeing Deborah as he did.

Deborah tried to sort things.

An hour later she was standing in the top tiers of the convention arena, looking down over the scene — the human tide of political exuberance mixed with celebratory chaos. Every seat was taken. Funny hats, waving banners. Confetti flying. The signs for each state delegation posted among the crowd.

But in the midst of that massive surge of optimistic energy, she was surrounded by darkness. Doubt, like a storm cloud, had swept over her.

When the house lights dimmed, the crowd quieted. A mezzo-soprano from the Denver Opera appeared on stage in a single spotlight.

Behind her, the entire back wall displayed an enormous American flag made of tiny lights, which sparkled and began waving digitally. The woman began singing "The Star Spangled Banner."

Deborah saluted the flag, but as she did so, something flashed into her mind. Why would Milla carry such an exonerating email in her purse in the first place? In fact, why would she have so carelessly left her purse in the main room if she knew there was a mole inside the campaign? Deborah quickly worked through one explanation in her head. If Milla was a traitor, then perhaps she had left the purse within Deborah's reach so that she could deliberately plant false information about her innocence. But if that was true, that would mean Zeta Milla had discovered that Deborah was suspicious — and maybe even knew that Deborah was a plant herself.

When the singer finished, she made a quick bow, and the crowd roared their approval.

But Deborah's mind was not on what had just been sung — the familiar first stanza of the national anthem — but on what had not been sung. At West Point, Deborah had learned the second stanza as well, and as she recalled the lyrics she felt a chill run down along her spine, as if an ice cube had fallen down the back of her blouse.

> *On the shore dimly seen through the mists of the deep*
> *Where the foe's haughty host in dread silence reposes,*
> *What is that which the breeze, o'er the towering steep,*
> *As it fitfully blows, half conceals, half discloses?*

She mouthed the words to herself. "Half conceals — half discloses."

That was it. She thought about the email in Milla's purse, purporting to be from Milla to the FBI agent. But that was only half the evidence, wasn't it? Milla could easily have contrived that. Where was the evidence that Agent Boling ever received it or that she had actually sent it?

She grabbed her Allfone and typed into the little keypad a question to Gallagher.

Urgent — Did Ben Boling ever clear Zeta Milla as a suspect in the Wichita murder?

Then she hit Send. But Deborah wasn't going to wait for the reply. She was already jogging out of the arena and down to the elevator so she could get up to the war room suite.

◻◻◻

In a small, noisy café in northern California, at John Gallagher's uncle's wedding reception, a homegrown band was playing the blues instrumental "Night Train." Gallagher was one of the groomsmen, but this definitely was not his kind of bash. When he received Deborah's text, he was glad to be able to loosen the button of his starched tux shirt and step outside onto the deck to get a breather.

He glanced at her question on his Allfone. He squinted. He dashed off a reply and hit Send. But halfway back across the deck toward the door, Gallagher stopped and typed another short message to Deborah.

Be careful kiddo.

FIFTY-EIGHT

Deborah was almost to the elevator. A few stragglers dashed past her to get down to the convention hall. In the background she could hear the echoes of the announcer and the crowd cheering in the arena.

She heard the buzz. She flipped open her Allfone. It was from Gallagher.

Her question had been simple enough:

Did Boling clear Milla?

Gallagher's response was even simpler.

No.

In the elevator Deborah punched the button for the floor of the war room. As the doors closed, she knew what she had to do, though it had all the appeal of grabbing a wasp's nest with her bare hands. She had to get Secret Service Agent Owens aside, show him Gallagher's text, and explain the phony email in the bottom of Zeta Milla's purse. She also had to explain the background information that Pack McHenry had dug up about Milla's real connection to the Castro regime and her history as an assassin-for-hire.

Okay, Deborah thought, she would have a lot of explaining to do herself — like why she was acquiring intel about Milla in the first place and how she had joined the staff under an assumed name. Yes, she knew she might even be suspected of foul play herself. But all of that was a calculated risk, well worth it if Zeta Milla could be exposed before something happened to Senator Hewbright.

The elevator doors opened, and Deborah sprinted out just in time to see Rick heading down the stairwell.

"Rick," she cried out, "have you seen Agent Owens?"

"Uh, yeah … awhile ago. He's always hanging around the senator." Then Rick said, "I'm taking the stairs to the arena; it's faster. Don't want to miss — hey," he said as if he had remembered something, "they were looking for you in the private suite." Then he turned and headed down the stairs two at a time.

Deborah jogged into the war room. It was cleared out. No signs of anyone.

She stepped into the hallway. A second buzz on her Allfone. It was the second short message from Gallagher.

Be careful, kiddo.

At the end of the corridor, the door to Senator Hewbright's private suite opened. Zeta Milla emerged, dressed for the evening, very classy. Her hands were thrust in the side pockets of her designer suit jacket, and a Gucci briefcase was tucked under her arm.

"Hey, there," Zeta yelled cheerfully, "we were looking for you. The senator has a quick errand for you."

For an instant, as time stopped, Deborah looked down the long hallway at Zeta Milla and wished she had more time. Thinking of Gallagher's warning, she thought to herself, *Sorry, John. Can't do.*

Deborah caught her breath, manufactured a smile, and strode down the hallway toward Zeta Milla.

Milla let Deborah pass by her and walk into Senator Hewbright's suite. Deb had taken only a few steps into the penthouse suite before she was startled by the sound of the door slamming behind her. Zeta was behind her, her hands no longer in her pockets. She held a briefcase by the handle and wore latex gloves.

Deborah scanned the room. She could see a pair of feet lying on the carpet, extending from behind the cabinets of the kitchenette. She took a step in that direction and recognized the dark suit and light blue tie of the man lying there. In the middle of Agent Owen's white shirt was a small blackened hole and the blood that encircled it.

Deb lifted her eyes. Senator Hewbright was also on the floor of the kitchenette, but from what Deb could tell, he was still alive. His eyes were wide and his mouth covered in duct tape. The cabinet doors under the sink were open and his hands were handcuffed together around the pipe.

When she turned toward the door, Zeta was there, almost touching her, pointing a handgun with a silencer at Deborah's face.

"Sit down, dear," Milla said calmly.

Deborah did as she was told, easing onto the soft chair in the living room but not taking her eyes off Milla.

"You know," the woman said, "I had a plan before I knew that you were coming. Crude. But it would have been effective. But when you walked into this campaign, I knew how very perfect you would be."

"You don't have to do this," Deborah said.

"Oh, but I do."

"Why—"

"Don't bother trying to understand," Milla said. "You Jordans think you can outsmart the world. You—the young West Point graduate—did you really think you were going to outsmart me?" Zeta laughed with a guttural tone. It had the sound of something hideous and evil.

"But you should know something," Milla continued. "How your love for Senator Hewbright will not go unnoticed."

"What are you talking about?"

"How you stalked him and came here under an assumed name. Yes, I know that too. How your romantic obsession with him slowly became psychotic."

Deborah's eyes flashed. "You're crazy."

"Oh?" Then Zeta Milla, with her other hand in her briefcase, pulled out some invoices. "Then what do you think the authorities will say about these ... motel receipts with your name on them—having paid in cash each time, of course, showing your many liaisons with the good senator at those times when I know he would have been alone and without witnesses—except for Agent Owens."

Milla glanced over at the agent's body. "Oh, dear, and he's gone too. Well, they'll find the receipts in your pockets, along with the note about how enraged you were at finding out that the senator had feelings for me. A murder-suicide … a fairly common syndrome, I'm afraid."

"No one will believe it," Deborah spit back. "My father and mother will hunt you down and expose all of this."

"I doubt that, but even if they do, it will be too late. Senator Hewbright will be permanently unavailable as a candidate, because in your rage — you killed him. Before you committed suicide, of course. They will find the gun in your hand, and I will tell them how I witnessed the whole awful bloody ordeal. Which leaves Governor Tucker as the dark horse candidate here at the convention. As you know, he doesn't stand a chance of winning, especially after his political party gets smeared with this grotesque spectacle." Then she added, "Deborah, dear — really — by being here, you really gave me the perfect gift. Thanks, darling."

A knock on the door.

Deborah froze.

Zeta calmly walked closer to the door but kept the long barrel of the gun pointed at Deborah. "Who is it?" she asked.

"Room service. Delivery for the senator."

"No, thank you. He's taking a nap right now. Just leave it outside, please."

"Oh, boy," came the voice from the other side. "My manager's going to throw a fit. All the candidates are supposed to get one of these baskets. I need to say I've passed it off to someone up here or he's going to come up here himself and blow a gasket."

Zeta Milla waved with the gun barrel for Deborah to stand up. Then she said in a hoarse whisper, "Take the basket and close the door. If you do anything I don't like, I'll blow a hole in your back."

Milla stepped to the side, out of range of the door, with her gun trained on Deborah.

Opening the door, Deborah saw a middle-aged man in a white service jacket, holding a basket. He had a pleasant smile. As she reached for it, he pushed his way forward, entering the suite and staring right into Deborah's eyes with a look that seemed to be telegraphing something. "Sorry, but I need you to sign for this," he said and looked around the room as if he were deciding where to set the basket down.

FBI Agent Ben Boling, in the room-service outfit, smiled at Deborah as she signed for the basket, and he looked around the room without moving his head.

When he looked to his right, he saw Zeta standing just around the corner. The glass cabinet across the room had caught her reflection, and Boling could see the gun in her extended hand.

Instantly, he pushed Deborah to the ground, dropping the basket, and in a swooping motion turned the corner toward Milla. He fired a shot but missed. She returned fire and hit Boling in the chest. He collapsed to the floor.

Zeta moved out from around the corner and fired again but narrowly missed Boling's neck. Before Zeta could hit him again, Deborah leaped at the gun barrel and knocked it as it fired. A lamp on the other side of the room shattered. There was a momentary struggle for the gun, but Milla kicked Deborah ferociously in the knee-cap, then in the groin, and stomped her shin, all in rapid succession until Deborah faltered. Then Zeta swung the handgun violently to Deborah's face and pistol-whipped her to the ground.

She took direct aim at Deborah's head as she stood over her.

But a blast dropped Zeta to the ground like a marionette without strings. The bullet to the side of Zeta Milla's head from Ben Boling's Smith and Wesson was fatal.

Deborah scampered over to Boling, who was trying to talk but could only emit a gasping noise because of the hole in his lung. She leaped to her feet and ran into the hallway, where a security guard and a campaign staffer were already responding to the sound of shots.

"Man down, man down!" she screamed. "Get an EMT right now!"

FIFTY-NINE

Abu Dhabi, Domain Tower Hotel

It was evening and Alexander Coliquin was in his top-floor suite, standing before the glass portico, one thousand two hundred feet and eighty-eight floors up from the pavement below. The skyline of the crown jewel of the United Arab Emirates was spread out before him, twinkling like the stars in the night sky.

He was not a man to show inner turmoil. His man servant bowed and presented a cup of jasmine tea on a solid gold platter. Coliquin took it and smiled as the servant disappeared. No one could have guessed the news he had just received. That his dear Zeta — whom he knew as Maria — was gone. Forever. He lifted his left hand and studied the ring on his finger. It was a gold-and-silver replica of a snake with ruby eyes, devouring its own tail. He recalled the day in Bora-Bora when he and Maria had been wed, with these matching rings, in a simple ceremony performed by a local Shaman.

He was not one to commit exclusively to a single lover, and he had assured her of that before their wedding night. But she had only kissed him and playfully replied, "Neither am I."

But even more than her capacity for both playfulness and cruelty, Coliquin treasured her other talents as well: her ability for artful deception and her skillful execution of targets — without hesitation. She had a unique kind of innovation and creativity. For her, the setup, the game, and the killing, was an art form. Few possessed what she had. And now Coliquin's beautiful weapon was gone.

311

But there was an even bigger complication. *What if,* he thought, *despite all my efforts, Senator Hewbright becomes the next president of the United States?*

Coliquin had watched the convention coverage from Denver. Every second of it. He checked every Internet news service, searching for any hint of what had transpired that night in the Pepsi Center when his precious instrument, his beautiful partner, had been shot in the head. But there was nothing. He found it infuriating that his plan, even if it had failed, would not at least have tainted the convention with the bloody tale of near-assassination. Incredibly, they had managed to cover it up, kept it from the American public.

So when Hewbright appeared on stage so repulsively triumphant, confident, and energetic, to deliver his acceptance speech, as if nothing had happened, Coliquin took that as a personal slight. It was as if the idea of a contrived murder-suicide had never existed. Yet even though the scheme failed, Coliquin was convinced that the right kind of media spin about the shootout could have imprinted Hewbright's campaign with a negative image, like an ugly birthmark. But that had been stolen from him.

Now people would have to pay. Those responsible — and maybe even those who were not. Failure never meant having to forego revenge.

When he heard the chimes from the front door of his penthouse, he knew he had business to attend to. It was Faris D'Hoestra and his powerful industrialist associate, Deter Von Gunter, a member of his World Builders group. He buzzed them both into the room.

D'Hoestra was not a man to linger. "I've come all the way to Abu Dhabi," he began, "as you requested. It seems a long trip for a very simple issue."

"You mean the U.N. charter amendment? Not so simple."

"Well, that is why we're here." D'Hoestra glanced down at the couch and asked, "Shall we sit?"

"No need," Coliquin replied. "I said it wasn't simple. I didn't say it was impossible. I know what you want — a restructuring. You want the U.N. Security Council to slowly ebb into oblivion, to be replaced by your super committee, so the World Builders can have a dominant role through your own assortment of international members."

Coliquin pulled an envelope from his suit-coat pocket. "Here's a draft agreement from a number of key nations willing to sign on to your plan and submit it to the General Assembly for a formal amendment to the charter."

D'Hoestra began to reach for it, adding, "And it has your official endorsement, I trust?"

"Of course," Coliquin replied, still hanging onto the envelope.

"And what do you expect in return?"

"Your support. And that of the Builders."

"Is that all?"

"For now."

Coliquin threw a look at Deter Von Gunter who was standing nearby with a blank expression. "Deter," he said waving the envelope, "why don't you have a seat. While Mr. D'Hoestra and I chat privately."

Then Coliquin led Faris D'Hoestra through the glass doors to the sweeping patio outside. D'Hoestra took in the panorama of the night sky and the lights of Abu Dhabi below. "Beautiful," he murmured to Coliquin who was standing on his right side, smiling.

Coliquin, glancing back through the glass toward Von Gunter, said with his hand on D'Hoestra's shoulder, "You and I can be blunt. This U.N. charter proposal was not easy for me to obtain, but I know the leverage you have. You've played the game well. Next time I won't cave in so easily."

He slipped the envelope into the inside pocket of D'Hoestra's suit coat and patted his chest. "Now," Coliquin added, "we have a few loose ends to tie up." Then he glanced down at his own left shoe. "Like an untied shoe."

D'Hoestra looked down and noticed Coliquin's left shoelace was untied. While Coliquin bent down to tie it, D'Hoestra stepped up to the white chest-high stone wall that separated the portico at the top of the sky-scrapper from the thin air beyond. He took a furtive glance over the edge and straight down to the ground over a thousand feet below. Instinctively, he took a step backward. But a hand grasped his right ankle like a vise.

A look of shock spread over D'Hoestra's face as Coliquin, with his right hand still locked on to D'Hoestra's ankle, reached up with his left hand and grabbed the World Builder chairman by the back of his belt.

D'Hoestra awkwardly reached around to remove the hand from his belt, but Coliquin was too quick. In one terrible, swift motion the U.N. secretary flipped Faris D'Hoestra up and over the top of the wall, launching him into the night air.

As he plummeted toward the street below, D'Hoestra shrieked and swung his arms like a child in a nightmare, spinning and doing horrible somersaults on the long ride down.

Coliquin watched until he was sure the body had hit the pavement. Then he stepped back inside. Deter Von Gunter was smoking a cigarette, leaning back in the chair with his legs crossed. He blew out a thin column of white smoke and asked, "That wasn't really a U.N. charter you stuffed in his pocket, I take it?"

"No," Coliquin said, "it was his suicide note."

If his dear departed lover had been in the room, Coliquin would have lifted an eyebrow and instructed her, "That's how it's done."

But he turned to Von Gunter instead. "We have unfinished business. You need to have your World Builders group decide its direction now."

Deter Von Gunter tapped the end of his cigarette out in the crystal ashtray and stood up. "Not necessary. We've already voted." Von Gunter lowered his head to Coliquin's left hand and delicately kissed his ring.

Denver, St. Anthony's Hospital

John Gallagher swept into Ben Boling's hospital room and spread his arms wide when he saw the FBI agent in bed. "My hero!"

Boling gave a head nod. "Hey, Gallagher."

"Sorry I didn't spring for a bunch of flowers for you. Now that I think of it," Gallagher said, "I was just at a wedding ... I could have swiped some on the way out."

He strode over to the bedside table and picked up one of the get-well cards. "Gee, a personal card from the director of the Bureau himself. Nice. But I noticed they didn't include your reprimand slip in it."

"You know the procedure. They'll present it to me personally when I get back."

"Well, anyway, you saved the day."

Ben Boling painfully moved over a bit in the bed to face Gallagher, grabbing the metal railing as he did. "Not entirely. One dead Secret Service agent. Do you know if Owens was married?"

"Divorced," Gallagher said. Then his face took on a thoughtful expression. "You know, there was a time when I would have tried to make a joke out of that. Death vs. divorce. Sound cynical?"

"You're preaching to the choir," Boling said. "We all have ways to cover up the garbage we carry around in this kind of work. Me? I go fishing. You ought to try it."

Then a look of panic spread over Boling's face. "Oh, man, I just remembered. My wife's due here any minute. She's flying in. I needed to keep my intervention at the convention top secret, so I told her I was on a fishing trip."

"You were," Gallagher said, "and you caught a killer — and a half ounce of lead."

"You know where I took it?" Boling said. "Same place in the lung that Ronald Reagan did. So why did he look so much better than me afterward?"

"Speaking of Washington, why'd they yank you off the Hewbright assignment anyway?"

Boling just shook his head glumly.

"There's bad stuff afoot," Gallagher said. "Not just petty infighting, my friend. True rotten, dirty dealing. Starting at the top. Anytime you want to join me in semiretirement, just let me know."

"Naw. Not me. I'm sticking it out. When something's gone bad, there's always a chance to bring back the good." Then Boling's eyes widened. "Hey, you want some inside information?"

"You kidding? It's like Oreo cookie ice cream to me."

"The hacking of Hewbright's Allfone. The FBI cyber guys traced it to a Chinese hacker."

"Old news," Gallagher said.

"What you don't know is the name of the hacker's close associate."

"You got me drooling. Who?"

"Ho Zhu."

"I could make a joke out of that too, like the old 'who's on first' routine ..."

"This one's no joke."

"All right, so what's so important about Ho Zhu?"

"He's the deputy secretary of the U.N., just under Coliquin ... one of his right-hand men."

Fair Haven Convalescent Center, Bethesda, Maryland

Cal had brought the medical authorization form with him to meet Winnie Corland. She had to be there to collect some personal items of her late husband's anyway, she said. Now they sat together in the dayroom. The form was on the side table between them, but looking at Winnie and the sadness in her eyes, Cal was sure he would be leaving with it unsigned. She was grief-stricken, and the way Cal saw it, the last thing on her mind was the desire to expose an attempt to interfere with the health of a sitting President. Not now, at least. Winnie was clutching her purse as if she were ready to get up and walk out any minute.

Winnie didn't talk much. She only mentioned a few details about her husband's time in the Oval Office and the fact that they didn't have any children, but Virgil had always wanted a son.

"He followed that terrible incident you were in up in New York at the train station. He admired your father — but thought highly of you too, the way you were able to stay so calm and courageous in the face of such evil. And I think," she said, and her chin trembled as she said it, "that he would have liked a son like you."

Surprisingly she got around to talking about President Tulrude, and how she had pressured Virgil to use Dr. Jack Puttner, her own physician. Corland received one shot of something from Puttner for his transient ischemic heart condition, she couldn't recall what. Then Virgil's massive attack took place in the presidential limo after a speech in Virginia.

"I never trusted Tulrude or that Dr. Puttner," she said.

"How did your husband end up with a vial containing the blood sample that he gave to us?"

Winnie looked away from Cal, seemingly ashamed. "When we first rushed Virgil into the ER in Leesburg, I told the doctor I thought the attack may have been caused by a medical reaction to the drug that Puttner had used. He must have drawn blood immediately. Because later he gave me a plastic medical envelope with the blood sample tube in it. He gave me a funny look when he did and told me to preserve it by keeping it refrigerated. That I 'might need it as evidence' later on. He said he suspected some strange things going on — the way that federal officials were handling the medical records. That's all he would tell me."

For Cal, the trail seemed to lead not just to Dr. Puttner but to Tulrude as well.

"But now Virgil's gone," Winnie said, her voice faltering, "you have no idea how hard this is, talking about this. I just want to forget. All of it."

A realization hit Cal. If he had done the smart thing while Corland was still alive, and had him sign the medical release back then, he wouldn't be in the tough spot that he was in now. But it was too late for that.

"I think that's all for now," Winnie said and struggled at a smile. "I have to go."

"I understand," Cal said, getting up to leave. "Mrs. Corland, I'm so very sorry about your husband. I liked him a lot. I enjoyed spending time with him. I'm sorry if I've brought up some bad memories for you."

Then he turned and walked toward the entrance of the day room.

"Cal," she said softly. "Please, take this away." Winnie was holding the medical authorization that he had left on the table.

He complied and trotted up to her and took the form, but Cal noticed she was putting a pen back into her purse, and he saw her signature at the bottom of the form.

"And don't worry about my being the one who signed," she replied and snapped her purse shut. "I have power-of-attorney."

SIXTY

Four Days Later, Early Morning, on the Edge of the Negev Desert, Israel

There were no classes in the Bedouin school that day. In the cinder-block garage, Tarek Fahad and his two assistants had finished the assembly of the missile and the portable launching system provided by the weapons division of the Deter Von Gunter Group. Dr. Ahlam had been silently watching them during the process, getting so close that he occasionally got in the way.

Now it was his turn. "I have placed the biochemical agent underground," he said, pointing to a square concrete trapdoor in the floor with the heavy metal handle. "In a protective capsule within a lead-lined container. I am going to carefully retrieve it now. But after that, I will have to put on my bio-suit to load the chemical into the missile. I have suits for you in the back of my truck. You must put them on."

Fahad glanced at his watch. So far they were on schedule.

Dr. Ahlam had a question. "If you will permit me, I have worked so long and hard on this project. The Elixir of Allah is, I believe, my finest masterpiece. I know you have the target selected. You must have. Yes? Down to the square inch."

Stepping closer to Ahlam, Fahad jutted his head up a little, eying the chemist, and said, "What is it? Just say it. What is it you want to know?"

"Your target. Where will my poison do its work?"

"Oh, that?" Fahad said and turned to his two friends. They all chuckled.

"The missile will be aimed at the Jewish Quarter in Jerusalem," Fahad answered. "But as for the location where it will accomplish its most marvelous work," he added with a raised eyebrow, "that I cannot share. It is a secret."

Jewish Quarter, Old City, Jerusalem

Peter Campbell was striding down Bab as-Silsila, the Souk containing shops and restaurants just beyond the Western Wall plaza where he had been arrested the week before. The pastor had always been a fast walker, and GNN reporter Bart Kingston was chugging hard to keep up.

Campbell turned to look for Kingston, then slowed so he could catch up. "I never thought I'd see the day a GNN reporter would help me get out of jail."

"You're an interesting story. My editors had to okay it. You know, all that ethics in journalism stuff. Though we didn't have to post bail. Just had to convince the authorities to release you and the others because of the temporary restraining order entered by the Israeli Supreme Court."

Campbell pointed to a café. "Between the Arches," he said, "let's duck in here, if it's okay. I'm famished."

The two men stepped down the spiral stairs into the subterranean restaurant that had been built into an ancient Roman cistern. As they sat at a glass-topped table, Campbell, who knew a little of the background of the café, launched into a description of the architecture of that part of Jerusalem during the life of Christ.

After ordering sandwiches, Kingston bent forward, leaning his chin on one fist, with one elbow on the table. Campbell noticed he didn't have his notepad out. No tape recorder was running.

"Question," Kingston began. "What do you say to skeptics who say, look, it's been more than two thousand years since Jesus' time. I thought He was supposed to return."

"I'd give the same answer that the Apostle Peter gave in his second epistle. You can look it up in the New Testament. Chapter 3. He explained that mockers asked the same question in the first century.

His answer was twofold. First, God doesn't count time the way we do. With the Lord, a thousand years is like one day. But more important is the reason God is waiting until the last minute to command His Son's second coming to earth. Peter says this: 'The Lord is not slow about His promise, as some count slowness, but is patient toward you, not wishing for any to perish, but for all to come to repentance.'" Campbell sized up the reporter sitting across the table. "Bart, listen, if the Lord is patient, slow to finally break open the heavens and have Jesus Christ appear to His followers and whisk them off the face of the earth, then maybe it has something to do with *you*."

Kingston straightened up. "I don't follow that one."

"God doesn't want anyone to perish into a Christless eternity. Maybe God's been waiting for you — and others like you — to make that one decision that could change your destiny forever."

"Others? You mean members of the press?" Kingston asked with a sly smile.

Campbell tapped his finger on the table, punctuating his response. "Butchers. Politicians. Bakers. Sales clerks. Farmers. Garbage collectors. And yes, even news reporters. Hardened criminals, sure. And law-abiding citizens too. Every tribe. Every tongue. Every nation." Then the pastor leaned back, as he noticed the waiter heading their way. "Bart, I think you are a serious guy who is seriously considering the claims of Jesus Christ. His claim to be God Incarnate — the claim that His blood sacrifice on a Roman cross is sufficient to cleanse your sins and bring you into the family of God — and His claim that He is standing at the door of your heart right now, knocking. And what you need to do is open the door and invite Him in by faith. You have to ask yourself a tough question — am I honest and objective enough to admit that I hear His knuckles rapping on that door right now?"

The waiter laid the plates on the table. As he did, Campbell reached out with his knuckles and rapped them gently on the glass table top.

Tel Aviv

Abigail had taken to holding Joshua's hand everywhere. Shopping, walking in the market, going from room to room in his apartment.

This was only the second day of their reunion, and she didn't want to let go.

"I want to stay with you," she said in the hallway.

In the living room, Deborah was grabbing her purse, and Cal was checking his digital camera. They heard their mother and started to laugh.

"Just don't start kissing in front of us again," Deborah said, rolling her eyes.

"Yeah," Cal added, "rule number one — no parental PDA in front of your offspring, even if we are adults."

"Look, Abby, honey," Joshua tried to explain, "I've got another flight planned in the F-35 LV today. We're getting close to working the kinks out of the jet-mounted RTS system. We'd be separated anyway."

"But we've been apart for two years," she said with pleading in her voice. And she repeated it again. "*Two years.* I had started to feel like a widow, Josh." She knew she was being unreasonable, but she didn't care.

"I know, babe. This has been miserable for both of us," he said. Then he drew her close. As he brought his lips close to hers, he turned toward his son and daughter. "Cover your eyes," he yelled to them with a grin as they both groaned. He held her in a passionate embrace for a while. He pulled back but then went in for another kiss. More moaning from his son and daughter.

"Okay, tell me, Abby," Joshua asked, "what is the name of that legal group you're going to address?"

"The International Society of Lawyers."

"Are you familiar with it?"

"The name rings a bell."

"Who invited you?"

"I received an email from Fort Rice. He forwarded the invitation to me."

"What are you going to talk about?"

She cocked an eyebrow. "Take a guess — your case, of course. I'm the lunch speaker. They want me to address the subject of Wrongful Prosecution and Political Aspects of the American Legal System."

"I can't think of a better expert on the subject," he said. "Now that the Department of Justice has voluntarily dismissed their case against me, thanks to you."

"I think the DOJ just wanted to avoid the humiliation of our judge dismissing it in open court, so they beat the U.S. District Court to the punch."

"You know," Joshua said, "I was just thinking. I can call Clint McKinney and have the IDF escort you."

"Dad," Cal piped up, "what are you worried about? Besides, she's not going to make it in time. We've got to leave right now if we're going to make it to Jerusalem by noon."

"I just want to make sure my bride is safe," Joshua said.

"Really, Dad," Deborah said, "Mom outsmarted the entire federal surveillance system, talked her way into the wilderness compound of one of the world's most secretive recluses — "

"Yeah, thanks to me," Cal added with a grin.

"Oh, whatever," Deborah sniped. "And then she makes it back to D.C. in time to win your case. I think she can take care of herself."

"Well," Joshua said, "she's got you two. Both of you are heroes in my book. You, Cal — getting your mom across country and back again, against everything the SIA could throw at you. And Deborah — putting your neck on the line to face down that threat to Hewbright ..."

"God's hand," Deborah said, with a sudden and remarkable adulthood to her voice. "No question about it, Dad."

Cal was nodding too. "Deb and I have been talking about that, how faithful the Lord has been, watching over us. All of us."

"The sparrow," Abigail began to say, ready to recite the familiar saying of Jesus — that even a sparrow cannot fall without the Heavenly Father's notice. But this time it caught in her throat as she looked at her husband and thought about those words and what he did for so many years as a pilot and what he was about to do again. She began to tear up.

"What's the matter, darling?" Joshua asked.

"Nothing," she said, wiping her eyes. "Just full of emotions. So glad to be with you at last. All of us together. For whatever time we have."

Then she turned to Cal and Deborah. "Okay, let's get moving." As she stepped toward the door, she turned toward Joshua for one last look. "Have a good flight, my precious husband," she said. She went back for one more kiss, then turned with her son and daughter and left.

Two hours later, in downtown Jerusalem on the edge of the Arab section, Abigail was on the sidewalk with a note in her hand that showed the address of the meeting. The green door to the Society of International Lawyers was locked. Cal and Deborah peeked in the windows.

"No lights. The place is shut down," Cal said.

"Some wires got crossed," Deborah said. "I say we take off, start our sightseeing."

"I called my contact person," Abigail murmured, looking at her Allfone and at the number she had called. "No answer."

The neighborhood seemed unusually quiet. Abigail saw only one person, a shopkeeper in front of his corner grocery. In the distance was the sound of approaching vehicles. Suddenly Abigail felt the hair rise on the back of her neck. She turned to move toward their car, and she was about to shout to Cal and Deborah. But not in time.

In a single coordinated movement three vans raced in from a side street. They screeched to a halt at the curb in front of them. Doors flew open. Several armed Arab men poured out. They charged straight at the three members of the Jordan family.

SIXTY-ONE

New York, AmeriNews Network Headquarters

Terri Schultz was bolting out of her office but stopped momentarily to glance at herself in the round mirror on the wall. The news manager didn't like what she saw. *Yikes, I'm a mess.* She ran a brush through her hair, grabbed her e-pad, embedded with her notes, and sprinted down the hall.

The tech assistant outside the recording room waved for her to hurry up. "Come on, Terri, he's on the line."

As she reached the door her assistant reminded her, "Don't forget to get his waiver about our recording him ..."

She halted and gave him a withering look. "I've been doing this for a decade, remember?"

Then Terri scooted into the recording booth and strapped on the headset. "Okay, Dr. Derringer, are you there?"

"I am."

"I can't thank you enough for your willingness to give us your expertise. Phil Rankowitz speaks very highly of you."

"Phil and I go way back. He did a TV series years ago on our work here at the NIH."

"We told you that we're going to record this conversation. I sent you the written waiver. We'd like you to email that back to us, preferably right now, before we start."

"Sure. I realize, you know, how ... explosive this whole thing is. Might be. I can't say I'm excited about getting sucked into what might be the political firestorm of the century. On the other hand, well, it is what it is, I guess ..."

Dr. Derringer excused himself and turned to his office manager to discuss the waiver. He returned to Terri. "We can't email from this desk, the computer's down. Give me just a minute. I'll sign it. We'll get it to you stat. Then we can talk."

While Terri was on hold, she placed her finger on the fingerprint ID of her e-pad, and it lit up, revealing the outline of her questions. She wiped the palm of her hand on her jeans. *Wow, cold sweat. Steady girl. Just because you're about to break a story that's a twenty-first-century version of the Lincoln assassination, no need to unravel.*

Taking a deep breath, she took stock of the moment. Phil Rankowitz had entrusted her with the medical side of this story. She figured that ought to count for something, right? And even being hired by AmeriNews was a great boost for her, after her job at the *New York Times* folded when it shifted to an all-Internet format. And while she didn't share Phil's religious super-zeal about Jesus, they did share the desire to tell the public the truth.

Dr. Derringer came back on the line. He said he was ready. Terri checked her Allfone and saw the email. She opened the attachment. The signed waiver from the doctor was there. She gave the signal to the board operator across the glass from her to start rolling tape. Then, on the record, she asked him if he was consenting to the recording of the interview. He said yes. So she began.

"Dr. Derringer, as head of pharmacology at the National Institutes of Health, you agreed to analyze a blood sample that had been taken from former President Virgil Corland in the emergency room in a hospital in Leesburg, Virginia, shortly after he had suffered a massive episode connected with his medical condition of transient ischemic attack, is that correct?"

"Yes, that's right. I tested the blood sample, determined that it was suitable to yield results. I examined it for several different components and to see what chemical or medical agents may have been in his bloodstream at the time. I reached some conclusions and had them double-checked with my colleagues at the NIH."

"Do you personally know Dr. Jack Puttner, the interim physician for the president at the time?"

"No. I only know of him — that he originally had been the physician for Vice President Tulrude."

"Can you give me a short and concise layman's summary of what you found in the president's blood?"

"Short and concise? I suppose I can."

"Anything I need to know before you explain that to me?"

There was a pause. Terri prodded him a bit. "Doctor?"

"Only this — better buckle your seatbelt ..."

The White House

Inside the Oval Office, Chief of Staff Natali Traup stood stiffly in the center of the carpet's presidential seal as President Tulrude glared at her. The president stood behind her desk, her shoulders hunched and her hands flat on the desk top. Tulrude had a look of contempt mixed with fury as she began to yell. Bits of spittle flew from her mouth.

"What do you mean he won't return your calls? Did you say who you were — that you were calling for the president of ... the United States ... of America?"

"Yes, I told him," Traup said. "I called several times. I said this message is for Dr. Jack Puttner and that President Tulrude needed to speak with him immediately. That it's a matter of grave urgency."

"If our intel is correct, and AmeriNews is trying to do a scoop on Virgil Corland, and they're pursuing some sick, extremist, right-wing plot to tie me to some attempt to worsen Corland's medical situation ... or even ... to cause his ..." But she didn't finish the sentence. Then a thought flashed over her face, and she changed course. "You should have told Puttner in the voicemail that this is a matter of national security. You should have said that."

"But it isn't."

"It is. It's an attack on the credibility of the president — *me*. That's national security."

"No," Traup said quietly but firmly. "It isn't, with all due respect, Madam President. What it really is, I think, is a matter of political security. Yours. And your reelection."

"And that directly affects you. You'd better decide whose side you're on, because you will be called upon to apply some serious pressure on the good Doctor Puttner to play ball with us before the prosecutors sit down with him. Do you understand me?"

Natali Traup took a step backward, just off the presidential seal. "I understand," she said quietly. "And because of that, I will have to do some thinking. About many things."

Launch Site, Edge of the Negev Desert, Israel

Abigail had been beaten. Her left cheek was bruised, and her left eye nearly closed with swelling. Her Islamic terrorist captors had shown her no mercy. Cal and Deborah had been manhandled even worse. From her position strapped to a metal chair bolted to the floor, she could see them both, tied in their chairs next to her. Deborah was bleeding from the mouth and had a gash across her forehead, and both of Cal's eyes had been blackened and it looked as if some of his teeth were missing.

On the other hand, four of the nine members of the Al Aqsa Jihad terror group who grabbed them were now out of commission, thanks to the ferocious struggle put up by Cal and Deborah and the injuries they dealt out: a broken arm, a busted nose, a few fractured ribs, a dislocated shoulder, and a concussion.

But there were still five of them left, and they all had weapons. They captured and tied up the Jordans and dragged them into the van to be taken to the site of their captivity.

Abigail looked up at the roof of the garage that was part of the Bedouin school grounds. Half of the tin roof had been retracted with a long-handled pole and was now open. She could see the blue sky of late afternoon above. She thought about Joshua and prayed that he was safe. She knew that whatever was going on — whatever the horrid plan that their kidnappers had in mind — it must surely have something to do with Joshua and his RTS system. Maybe even retaliation for his system having been used against Iran two years before.

As she thought about that, she also studied an object nearby that looked like a long cylinder on a work bench, draped with a tarp.

A missile.

The five men huddled near a side door as if waiting for someone. Deborah whispered to her mother, though her speech was garbled because of her injuries. "Don't like ..." she started to say, but the rest was inaudible. She tried again. "Don't like that we're *not* blindfolded."

Abigail nodded. The captors were not concerned about being recognized. They were clearly not planning on leaving witnesses. Then the door swung open.

The terror cell leader popped in. The other men smiled and bowed from the waist. Tarek Fahad spoke to them in Arabic. The men scrambled. Several headed to the work bench where they pulled the tarp off the missile containing the Elixir of Allah. The others scampered to a corner of the garage where they retrieved a satellite television camera. They set up the camera directly in front of Abigail, Cal, and Deborah. The savage broadcast would be linked to a television station, set to broadcast the live feed of their grisly fate.

SIXTY-TWO

Israeli Airspace, over the Northern Sector of the Negev Desert

In the cockpit of the F-35 LV fighter jet, Joshua peered through his helmet visor. He focused first on the forward screen on the flight deck, then the one on the left, and the lit-up LCDs on each. "I'm checking the threat warning prime and the auxiliary right now," he reported. "They're both operational. I'm still getting used to the layout. A different configuration than I'm used to."

The voice of the test pilot on the ground at the control tower responded, "That's because it's been adapted for your RTS system. Just maintain your current airspeed. Our guys down here are going to tee-up the unarmed bird to send your way for the first test."

There was another voice. This time it was Colonel Clint McKinney. "Hey, Josh, Clint here."

"Good to hear your voice, man. You down there in the tower?"

"Yeah, stopped by to make sure these guys don't go too easy on you, you know, on account of your advanced age."

Joshua laughed. "You don't know the half of it."

"By the way," Clint added, "got a message from command that I was supposed to pass on to you."

"Oh, from who?"

"A friend of yours — Judge Fort Rice — says that Phil Rankowitz is ready to bust the big story wide open. Said you'd know what that means."

"Yes, sir," he said, "I sure do. Thanks."

To Joshua, it was a long time coming. Now it sounded as if Phil had gathered enough information to break the story about President Virgil Corland's illness, and Tulrude's complicity in a plot to take him out. Finally, he thought, the truth about her rotten administration might get out to the American people.

Clint added, "He also mentioned something about your last message to him ..."

"Right," Joshua replied, "I thanked him for passing on the invitation for Abigail to speak to that international lawyer's group in Jerusalem today."

"Well, that was why he was trying to get hold of you."

"What's up?"

"Judge Rice says that he doesn't have the faintest idea what you're talking about. He never passed on any such invitation."

Joshua spent only two seconds processing that. Then his heart sank. "Clint, do me a favor. You've got Abby's number. Give her a call immediately and make sure everything's okay. Something doesn't sound right."

"I follow you," Clint said. "Will do."

When Joshua had first lifted off in the F-35 that day, he had felt the weight of two burdens. The first was the reason he was in the sky at that moment, trying to engineer a fix for his RTS system. But the other was down on the ground—knowing that Ethan was out there somewhere acting as a decoy on a dangerous mission. Joshua's prayer that morning as he climbed into his flight suit had been for the safety of his protégé. But Clint McKinney's message had just shoved all of that to the back of the line. Front and center, now, was the wellbeing of his wife.

Abby—are you safe?

Northern Bethesda, Maryland

Winnie Corland sat in the den in her Symphony Park brownstone, the one she had purchased because it was close to her late husband's convalescent center. She was alone, sifting through some of his personal effects. She had waded through the political paraphernalia. Now

Winnie was looking through the intimate things, like Virgil's college yearbook and a love letter he had written to her during their undergraduate days. And his brown leather Bible.

His absence was overpowering. Not hearing his voice. Not seeing his face. It was as if their life together had been as fragile as a dry leaf, and a powerful wind had just rushed in and carried it all away in an instant.

That made her remember something that Virgil had read to her aloud many times. She tried to cling to it. She flipped open his Bible, which she had almost never opened herself. There was a thin silk ribbon placed at the first chapter of the gospel of John. She scanned through the first chapter but didn't find what she was looking for. It wasn't in the second chapter either. But in the third chapter she found it, the part where Jesus speaks to Nicodemus, the great Jewish teacher, imparting the secrets of the Spirit. She read it aloud. "'Do not be amazed that I said to you, 'You must be born again.' The wind blows where it wishes and you hear the sound of it, but do not know where it comes from and where it is going; so is everyone who is born of the Spirit.'"

She closed the Bible but noticed the edge of a note card sticking out, just under the back cover. She pulled it out. She recognized Virgil's handwriting immediately.

It was entitled simply, "A Prayer."

Lord forgive me, a sinner,
By the Holy blood of Jesus Christ, Your only Son,
Which He shed on the cross in Jerusalem
*   for all of my transgressions,*
And who was proven trustworthy and Divine
*   by His miraculous resurrection from the grave;*
You, Jesus, I declare to be
*   the Commander-in-Chief of my soul,*
*   my Savior, my King.*
You have set eternity in all our hearts, Oh God,
*   so that we would search for You.*

And now I want You to fill that empty space
with the presence of Jesus the Christ, who is my Lord,
and whose glorious coming is my most blessed hope.

Winnie closed the Bible and put it on the table. But she still grasped the note card firmly in her hand. Her eyes were open but filled with tears. She remembered Virgil's funeral, his closed casket, and the sight of it being lowered into the ground. In a strange way, she felt she was in a casket herself, suffocating. Entombed by her failure of will. How long would she ignore the whispering in her heart — the call of the Spirit for her to be reconciled with the God she had deliberately kept at arm's length?

It wasn't for Virgil that she now reread the note card through hot, streaming tears. Instead, it was for herself, for her own destiny. This would have to be her own act of faith. She knew it was time to move out of the shadowy tomb in which she had lived. She wondered about the sunlight she longed for, which she knew awaited her. She read out loud each word in Virgil's prayer now — no longer just his, but hers as well.

And when she was done, she closed her eyes and wept for the wasted years she had spent neglecting the call of God to her heart. But she also wept for something else. Funny, she thought, but her tears were also for the joy that she felt washing over her like a flood. Winnie suddenly realized that what had just filled her mind like a flash must be true — beyond any debate.

I think that something glorious is coming . . .

In the Streets of Nablus

Ethan was behind the wheel of the armored IDF Jeep, heading slowly down one of the main arteries of the city. His hands gripped the steering wheel with white knuckles. For months he had griped to Joshua about not having a direct hand in any missions. Now he had his chance. He was silently giving himself a pep talk. *Just don't blow it, Ethan. Keep everything under control. Don't let things go haywire.*

That location in Nablus had been chosen because Israeli intel showed that messages about an impending bio-threat had been shuttled back and forth by members of a known terror cell in that Palestinian-controlled area. It was decided that some of the terrorists behind the bio-attack must be there. The plan was to lure at least one of them out in the open, take him alive, and use extreme measures to extract the details of the attack from him.

Ethan glanced at the man sitting next to him, an IDF soldier posing as Joshua. After eye-balling him again, Ethan said, "Not a bad resemblance. But the nose is all wrong."

This prompted a response from Rivka, who was lying in the back of the Jeep holding a Jericho .9mm handgun against her chest. "If they get close enough to see that this guy's nose is different from Joshua's, it'll be too late for them anyway."

Gavi, also armed with a special weapon, was lying next to Rivka in the back, once again acting as her mission partner. He cut them off. "Stop the chatter folks. Ethan, pay attention to your earbud."

Ethan nodded and adjusted the earpiece in his left ear. "Just checking in," he said. A voice came back in his ear. "Head's up, Ethan. You're in the zone now."

Traffic was moderate. A grocery truck ahead of them. A single, older model Renault behind them. A few cars way up ahead. Shops on each side. A woman with a stroller on the sidewalk to the left. A café up on the right, where several men were having coffee at outdoor tables.

A false message had been deliberately disseminated saying that Joshua was being driven by his partner, Ethan, to a testing site for his RTS system, but that gunfire had been heard along the route, forcing them to quickly divert through Nablus. The sound of gunfire was real—it had been supplied by the IDF. They also made sure that the message was leaked to a source they suspected to be a sympathizer of the Al Aqsa Jihad group headed by Anwar al-Madrassa.

The trap had been set. Now they had to hope that the members of the terror cell would take the bait.

The truck ahead slowed. Now the café was almost directly to their right. Ethan glanced to his left. The woman with the stroller was gone.

In the window of an appliance shop two men stood, looking out. Ethan looked up at the second floor. Someone was holding something to his eyes, maybe binoculars. Then the figure quickly stepped back.

"I think I see spotters, folks," Ethan said. "Stay alert."

The truck ahead jerked forward a few yards and stopped.

It happened with lightning speed. Several men with weapons poured out of the shop on the left. The men at the café jumped to their feet, and one of them fired at Ethan, fracturing the bulletproof windshield.

While the men rushed the Jeep from both sides of the street, two Mossad agents in a van parked along the curb jumped out and fired at the assailants from a crouching position.

Rivka was up and shooting to her right. Gavi shouted, "Man in the green T-shirt." He had already picked his target—from a photo array in prep for the mission. He fired the dart and it struck the young man in the chest. The man, who seemed to be about eighteen years old, started shaking, dropped his weapon, and collapsed to the ground while other shooters around him were dropping. The Mossad guys at the van gave covering fire while Rivka and Gavi leaped out of the Jeep and dragged the young man into it.

"Go, go, go!" Gavi screamed. Ethan did a three-sixty, bumping up onto the sidewalk as bullets banged against the armored vehicle, and then he headed back down the street, straight at the Renault. The driver jumped out and started to run away, so Ethan slammed the Jeep into the left front headlight of the little car, knocking it out of the way and then speeding down the street.

In the back seat, the young man was limp from the neuromuscular agent that had been injected into his body, designed to temporarily paralyze his large muscles but not the vocal chords. Then Gavi took out a small black case, slipped out a hypodermic needle and stuck it into the man's jugular vein. Then Rivka turned him on his side so he could vomit. Ethan glanced in his rearview mirror to see what was going on. Gavi told Rivka to keep watch over him as he leaned over the front seat and began shouting out directions to Ethan.

"We need to get out of the Arab areas quick," he yelled. "Turn here!"

Ethan took a sharp right onto a road that he could see led out of Nablus.

"What was in the needle?" Ethan shouted back.

"Our own upgraded brand of SP-117," Gavi said. "We can thank the Russians for coming up with it. But we improved it considerably, speeding up the brain-blood absorption process. Only takes a few minutes now to get the subject ready to chat freely."

When Ethan flashed a blank look, Gavi said, "Hypnotic drug. Disarms psychological restraints. Especially," he added, "under conditions where the subject is experiencing a deep fear for personal safety." Then a second later, Gavi snapped, "Okay, take the highway to the left, and keep going straight. You're on the right track." Then he turned back into the rear of the Jeep.

A few minutes later, Ethan noticed Gavi again in his rearview mirror. Rivka was propping the man up, and Gavi was holding the unloaded dart gun against his forehead and yelling into his captive's face. Rivka was adding to the effect with a mock effort to dissuade Gavi from shooting. "No, no, don't!" she was saying, waving her arms at Gavi. But her partner kept the dart gun pressed against the man's head, shouting in Arabic. "Where is the biological weapon? Where's the poison? Where's the Elixir of Allah?"

The young man's eyes darted around wildly. He muttered something.

"Speak!" Gavi screamed again.

He muttered again. And Gavi brought his face down closer into the young man's face and demanded that he answer the question.

"Madrasah," the young man murmured.

"Yeah, we know you work for Anwar al-Madrassa," Gavi screamed back. "But we want to know where the Elixir of Allah is, and we want it right now."

"*Madrasah,*" the young man said again.

Now Rivka was pushing Gavi away, playing her part in the good-cop, bad-cop routine. "Say again?"

"*Madrasah hassah,*" the man muttered, a numb expression on his face.

Rivka sat up and looked at Gavi. "That's not a name," she said. "*Madrasah hassah* means 'private school' in Arabic."

The Jeep roared out of Nablus, while Rivka yelled into her earpiece, loud enough so that her commanders back at the headquarters would not miss it.

"The bio-weapon's in a school building somewhere."

Gavi grabbed the man by his shirt and screamed in his face, "What school? Where?"

But the man shook his head violently and in a pleading voice cried out in Arabic, "Don't know. Don't know."

SIXTY-THREE

A voice came over the headset in Joshua's helmet. "Colonel Jordan, we have an update on Ethan March."

Joshua had put the F-35 LV fighter in a slow circle over the northern sector of the Negev desert, waiting for the "go" sign for another missile test. But his mind had been on multiple crises. Ethan was one of them.

"What?"

"He's safe. The mission hit the mark."

Joshua breathed out, *Thank You, Lord.*

"In fact," the tower continued, "it was more successful than we planned."

"How?"

"We've narrowed the site. The bio-threat is emanating from a school building somewhere. We received that from a captured cell member. Our intelligence people are putting together a scenario of the probable locations."

"What about the delivery mode?"

"We've got that too. After further interrogation, he admitted it was airborne. Colonel Jordan, we are dealing with a missile carrying a biological toxin. And it's unlike anything we've seen."

Flying a mile over the desert, Joshua didn't want to hear that. He still hadn't been able to use the in-flight RTS laser on the modified F-35 to capture the entire guidance system of incoming dummy missiles during the testing phase. Which meant that his RTS system was drastically limited — it could still only perform the original design task — a mirror-reversal of the trajectory of enemy missiles, returning them to their launch site. His new laser-guided data-capturing program to redirect enemy warheads in any direction, at will, wasn't working.

"Tell me," Joshua asked, "what does that do to our test today?"

There was a pause from the command tower. Then the answer. "It means we wish it was last week, rather than today. Our intel indicates this threat is imminent."

"Do we scratch our test up here?" Joshua asked.

"We're checking on that. But I have some other information — about your family."

A strange feeling washed over Joshua, as if he had half-expected what was next, as if this day had already been scripted.

"A witness in Jerusalem, a shop owner in Nablus, called the police, says he saw a woman matching your wife's description, accompanied by a young man and young woman, being dragged into three vans and driven away at gunpoint."

Joshua had the air momentarily sucked out of him. All he could mutter was, *"Oh, dear God."*

The voice in his helmet continued, "We have a partial description of one of the vans. It's been matched to one belonging to the jihad group headed by Anwar al-Madrassa."

Joshua was stunned. The tower asked, "Still with us, Colonel?"

"Roger that," he could barely say. He was crushed.

"Stay with us for further instructions, sir."

"Roger."

Joshua could now hear only the sound of his own breathing in his helmet. In and out. Inhale. Exhale. In the upper corners of the inside of the helmet were the green illuminated vector screens that he would use to site incoming enemy missiles. He wanted to pray, but somehow it was too much, and he couldn't. He knew the groaning inside of him would be heard. God was listening. It was just that now, circling high above the brownish desert, feeling that his guts had just been ripped open, he couldn't put it into words.

After a few minutes, the voice came into his helmet again. But this time it wasn't the same. It wasn't the usual measured, in-control monotone he had been used to hearing as a pilot from the tower. Now it was hurried. Almost frantic. "Colonel Jordan. Stay in your pattern. I repeat, stay in your pattern. Do you read?"

"Copy. What news?"

"Radar shows an incoming heading to Tel Aviv. One of our F-16s was dispatched, but it blew past him before he could shoot it down. Our ground-to-air defenses have been launched, but this thing has a very advanced avoidance program."

"Where was it launched from?"

"We're trying to determine that. Also — " The voice stopped. Some shouting in the background. Joshua thought he could hear Clint Mc-Kinney's voice. Yes, it was him.

Now Clint spoke into the headset. "Josh, this is Clint. You have a right to know. We just launched the standard RTS-equipped missile to turn this in-coming warhead around."

"I copy that."

"But, Josh, there's video footage on the Internet. Live-streaming. Abby and Cal and Deborah. All of them tied up in some location. And ..."

"And what? Tell me, Clint. Tied up and what?"

"The message says that all three are at ground zero of the launch site of the bio-weapon. If your RTS is successful, it will turn that monster on your family. Josh, I'm so sorry ..."

"Have you reverse-engineered the flight pattern of the incoming, to find the site and get them out of there ..."

"Somewhere around the edge of the Negev. There are several Bedouin schools in that area. We're trying to isolate the location and helicopter the IDF guys out there ..."

Joshua was yelling. "At four hundred miles an hour that missile's going to get there first!"

In the background Joshua heard a voice say, "RTS just made contact with the enemy bird; it's turning around."

Inside his helmet Joshua tried to slow his breathing. *Think. Be precise. But be quick. You only have one crack at this. Oh, Lord, help me.*

Then he said, "Tower, Jordan here."

"We read you."

"Give me the flight pattern of that enemy bird and the coordinates."

"Doing it now."

Joshua checked his radar-warning receiver. It lit up in the corner of the screen, and he now saw the flight pattern of the warhead containing the Elixir of Allah heading his way, high above the Negev desert. He punched the autopilot matching control so he could intersect the trajectory and the altitude of the incoming missile.

"I'm climbing," Joshua said, jamming his side-stick controller on the right and putting the jet into a steep climb. Then he pushed the throttle grip on the left to send him streaking nose-up into the sky as fast as he could squeeze power out of the turbines.

His screen showed the blinking cursor for the incoming missile.

"Waiting for it to come into range," Joshua called out. "Waiting ..."

The blip on the screen was closing in. The missile was getting closer.

Joshua hit the button for the RTS-360 guidance capture system, and a laser beam blew out from under the fuselage. He read the RTS integrated control panel. It illuminated.

Contact.

The data-controlling laser hit the nosecone of the enemy missile.

He waited for the reading — the terse LCD that would read either "Full Capture" or "Failed."

"Come on. Come on. Come on ..."

Then the message flashed on the screen. But his world rocked.

"Failed."

A half second passed — but enough time for Joshua to calculate it. There was only one option now. He had to insure that his family was protected. His F-35 LV had no weapons other than the RTS, so now his only weapon was the jet itself. It was the only way to stop the bio-warhead streaking back toward his wife and son and daughter.

"I'm going to hit it on the run. I'm intercepting," he said.

The tower squawked back, "Colonel, wait. We have no secondary verification that your family is at ground zero."

"I can't take that chance. I'm going in."

Joshua lined the nose of the F-35 with a point along the intersecting trajectory of the missile on his screen. He would have to hit the warhead on the pass. With his left hand he jammed the throttle and headed to the intersection point, and with his right hand he used the side-stick controller to arc the jet toward the endgame. There was only one chance to knock that missile out of the sky. He knew what that meant. No way to bail out before the collision. He had to ride it into the point of contact. Then a fiery crash with a missile loaded with a nightmare toxin. That was the terrible best-case scenario. But at least his family would be spared.

The blip of the missile was closing in on the intersecting vector on his screen. And so was he. Each blip approached the other. Joshua gave his final message to the control tower. "Tell Abby and the kids I love them … and …" His voice caught.

"Tell 'em we'll all be together in heaven."

There it was. He saw it glint into view, the nosecone of the missile approaching like a flash of light. He aimed at it by leading it perfectly, gauging its superior speed to hit it on the pass-by. He banked the F-35 directly toward the oncoming warhead.

He yelled two words.

"Now, Lord …"

With supersonic speed, the missile's nosecone tore through his left wing. The missile exploded and the percussion ripped open the fuselage of the jet, spraying the toxic gas over the ravaged skin of the F-35. The jet began to spiral down, twisting at two hundred and fifty miles an hour, covered in deadly toxins.

He reached for the release for the ejection seat. Where was it?

In the sickening, dizzying spin toward earth, Joshua saw something, heard something, and he could only say one word at first.

"What …"

The tower was calling to him in his helmet. But that didn't matter now.

Somewhere there was a sound. Piercing. Heart-thumping. A trumpet sounding? Incredible. Unfathomable. It had the power of the sound of a cosmos being birthed.

"Oh!" Joshua exclaimed, as a boy might say if he witnessed something awesome, as the sky seemed to fill with a golden note, like the unison of all the world's trumpets. All around him. Thrilling, thrilling. And there was a voice above even that, and the voice had the thundering power of ten thousand oceans.

"My dream," he heard himself say. But it was not a dream. Not this time.

Somehow he was outside of the F-35, watching it as if he were a spectator. The jet had no pilot, yet its canopy was still intact — the ejector seat had never activated — and it was spinning and smoking and careening farther and farther away from Joshua on its gravity-bound descent toward earth. And it kept falling. Until it hit the earth. A tiny red flash of an explosion could be seen far below.

Joshua had never ejected. Yet he had not gone down with the jet. He was not in the debris of the crash. Or anywhere on earth.

SIXTY-FOUR

If he hadn't already been transformed, he wouldn't have understood it. While his jet plummeted to earth without a pilot, Joshua rocketed up through the atmosphere, confounding the laws of nature. Yet his mind was able to fully comprehend it. It had been changed too.

What was happening was not a matter of science. It couldn't be contained in the theories of man. What Joshua was seeing at that moment, and where he had found himself, had reduced all of those things of earth, the human achievements, the fanfare, the struggles for glory and power, to a pale world of shadows.

Joshua was walking in a place that seemed warm and familiar, yet surprisingly spectacular. There was the instant experience of belonging there. This brilliant pavilion was the home of God. And Joshua was part of it. There was calmness inside. Peace. No racing heart. No sweating palms. No gut-wrenching decisions to make. Not anymore. Everything around him seemed so new, like the birth of a new world, yet not bound by the old laws of nature of the old world he had come from. There was a light more radiant than the sun and it was brightening the landscape. It seemed to be coming from a focal point in the distance. Yet it illuminated everything, while at the same time cast no shadows.

Joshua looked around and was suddenly aware that there was a vast ocean of people all around him. Millions and millions of them. From ages past to the present. Their faces, like his, reflecting something. But he didn't have to guess what that was, for he knew what they knew — a miraculous kind of understanding and an expectation of what would happen next. And a joy that surpassed any method of calculation or description.

And here was the amazing thing — Joshua was able to visualize everything around him, both near and far, simultaneously, things in the closest detail and yet at the same time able to take in a bird's-eye view of the entire assembly. Joshua laughed and shouted out in astonishment at the miracle of it. And at the fulfillment of it — God's promise — that at just the right moment in human history the Lord of the universe would rapture — would call to Himself — every follower of the Son of God, and remove them from Planet Earth in an instant.

Joshua looked to his left. There was a woman, no longer aged, and no longer weeping and mourning from a broken heart. She was smiling and hugging someone. Joshua looked closer. Her joy became Joshua's. And he delighted in it as if it were his own.

The woman he was watching had the blush of a newlywed, and she was smiling and touching the youthful face of Virgil Corland, who looked then to be only in his thirties. The former leader of the Free World was now a humble citizen of heaven.

"I saw the glory of it," Winnie Corland said gently as she stroked Virgil Corland's face. "God gave me a tiny glimpse after you died, when I opened my heart to Christ that day at our brownstone condo. A snapshot of what was ahead for us. Oh, Virgil, you were so right, my dearest."

Virgil was beaming as he looked in her eyes. "All of the waiting. The aching joints and the endless medications. The flesh that didn't cooperate and aged. And the trials that tested our hearts and our bodies. All that is over now."

Joshua refocused. There was a voice of another woman, and he recognized it immediately. The one who had taught his Sunday school class when he was a wild, reckless, wayward boy.

"Josh-a-boy," the voice said. And then he knew. She was the only one who had ever called him that nickname, the name that caused him to wince in embarrassment when it was mentioned in the presence of his buddies. Joshua turned to her. He had never truly thanked her for the seed she had planted in his soul. As it turned out, she had not lived long enough to see it bloom.

Standing in front of him, the woman was now youthful and vigorous. The face bore an image that had a slight similarity to Joshua's, the eyes, maybe. That's what family friends had always said. In the final years before her passing, Joshua had only known her as the frail, bent frame that needed a walker. *There is so much to say*, Joshua thought as the flood of memories rushed through his mind, of the house in Colorado with the willow tree and the woman in the apron on the front porch calling to him to come in for dinner.

Joshua now spoke the one word that seemed to contain all of those powerful memories.

"Mom," Joshua called out to her. Then he added with a tender astonishment, "You were so young. I had forgotten how young you were."

"But you, son," his mother said as she reached up to pat his cheek, "you were always the same boy to me."

Joshua put his arm around his mother and surveyed the scene. Not far away, he recognized three members of the current U.S. Supreme Court — all of them whisked away from the conference chambers in the marble court building in Washington in the middle of a heated debate over a pending case, while the rest of the astonished justices who remained behind were left to stare, slack-jawed, at the empty chairs. Joshua noticed one of them, Justice Lapham, close to him and now shaking the hand of John Jay, America's first chief justice, who had taken up that post shortly after the nation's founding in the eighteenth century.

Beggars and billionaires greeted each other like long-lost brothers. Martyrs for the gospel who had been burned, beaten, ripped apart, and beheaded for their faith were now whole. Persons lost at sea, buried in avalanches, ravaged by hurricanes, killed in war and in peace time, victims of disease and hunger, builders of empires who, in paneled offices, had bowed their heads to the call of Christ, and vagabonds who had responded to tent revivals in the wilderness.

They were all there.

But Joshua was searching for other faces. He knew they must be there somewhere. His heart, mind, and soul told him so. His eyes kept searching. Until — right there — he told himself, there they were. He had spotted them. The three of them, calm and joyful, now almost within reach. Joshua held out his arms toward them and pulled Cal and Deborah into a crushing hug. Then he held them both at arm's length to study their faces. "You look older a bit, but only slightly," he mused with a smile. "And most certainly wiser!"

Both of them laughed.

"How proud I am of you both. You were so brave," he added. "And faithful to the Lord, right up to the end." Then his two grown children stepped aside. So he could take her in with his eyes, from head to foot. Abigail was standing in front of him, without a scar. Without a tear. Without a worry. "I wouldn't have believed it," Joshua said, gathering Abigail gently into his arms.

"Believe what, my precious soul mate?" she asked.

"That you could ever have been more beautiful than you were down there — and yet, here you are."

"I know what you did in the last moments," she said quietly, as she pulled him close to whisper it in his ear. "To rescue us. And to protect us." She laid her hand on his heart. "And our Lord knows it well too. There is no greater love," she said, "than to lay down your life for another. And you did it, Joshua, for us."

"I had a great teacher," Joshua said. "A great Savior."

Suddenly, the figure in the light, who was the light that illuminated everything, was coming closer. The multiple millions of saved souls now fell to their knees. Princes and commanders, knights and peasants, men and women of power, as well as the powerless and the forgotten of the world, all of those who had staked their souls and their eternities on the perfect blood that had been shed on an ugly, Roman cross, and who had now been gathered together from throughout the millennia, all of them were worshiping and singing to the One who had ransomed them. Their Champion. Their Lord.

Not far away from Joshua, Abigail, Cal, and Deborah, Phil Rankowitz was kneeling with several other members of the Roundtable. Every head of every person was bowed for the same reason.

Walking in the apex of the light, now clearly seen, was Jesus Christ, the King of Kings. And He was approaching.

SIXTY-FIVE

The Next Day, New Babylon, Iraq

Alexander Coliquin was in his two-thousand-square-foot suite. He seemed oblivious to the multiple catastrophes across the globe. From the windows of the top floor of the white-stoned U.N. building, he could see palm trees swaying in the wind and the gardens stretching for a half mile out to the gated entrance.

But his two closest associates, Deputy Secretary Ho Zhu and Bishop Dibold Kora, were transfixed in front of the wall of web TVs, clicking through screen after screen to collect the global coverage of the stunning events of the day.

In San Francisco, a record earthquake toppled a portion of the Golden Gate Bridge on the Sausalito side and sent cars tumbling into the bay. Quakes off the eastern seaboard created a tsunami that swept into Charleston, South Carolina, and carried off more than eighteen hundred people. There were tremors in Istanbul, Moscow, Tangiers, and Wellington. In Perth, a third of the downtown towers collapsed into the sea as massive tectonic plates deep in the earth shifted violently beneath that part of Australia's coast.

But more amazing were the "unexplained phenomena," as the press called it. Jet liners veering off course. Traffic jams caused by driverless cars. Judges disappearing from courtrooms. Churches vacant. People vanishing in the middle of meetings. Television anchors in Biloxi, Richmond, and Omaha evaporating during live broadcasts. Missing persons reports flooded into every metropolitan police department in every city. Those disappearances caused more than a dozen near crashes of airliners as copilots were forced to take over the planes when pilots evaporated from cockpits. An ocean liner that suddenly had no captain or first mate plowed into three other cruise ships in the Port of Miami and sank two of them. A 240-car pileup occurred on the 101 outside of Los Angeles when drivers were no longer behind their steering wheels. Financial experts on the television coverage were already predicting that a few insurance companies could go bankrupt just from the automobile collision claims alone.

Bishop Kora spoke first, wagging his finger at the two dozen television screens. "Now the conspiracy theories will come. The fanatics. The lunatic fringe. They will call this the judgment of God ..."

"No, they won't," Coliquin replied effortlessly, turning from the window to address him. "The dangerous ones will call it the rapture."

"You will need to issue a statement," Ho Zhu said in his usual perfunctory tone. "And if possible, announce a joint effort with President Tulrude. An international plan to restore order. She needs more help."

"More help?" Kora bulleted back. "It isn't enough that you had Hewbright's Allfone hacked and handed Tulrude that five-point economic plan on a silver platter?"

"No, not enough," Ho Zhu stated in a matter-of-fact tone. "She needs a boost in the polls. Hewbright is closing the gap. And Secretary Coliquin, the world needs to hear from you."

"Yes, a statement," Coliquin said. "Don't worry. I have that well in hand."

Two hours later, Coliquin gave an address in a live global broadcast from his new Iraq headquarters. It was covered by every Internet news agency on the planet.

"Ladies and gentlemen," he began as he looked out from behind his mahogany desk directly into the camera linked to an international satellite multi-feed. His handsome face wore an expression of weighty concern. "Today we face a great quandary. So many questions abound. Natural disasters. Tragic loss of life. Why, we ask ourselves. And in the midst of it — perhaps the saddest thing of all — the death of millions of people. But we may have a partial answer. For unknown reasons, countless people have apparently, and suddenly, abandoned their homes, their places of work, their cars, and retreated to remote areas. Reports are coming in slowly that many of these people were known to be radical, fundamentalist Christian extremists, and theories are surfacing that they may have committed mass suicide in distant, wilderness areas. It may take a long time to locate and recover all the bodies. Perhaps we never will. And we may never know all the reasons for their irrational, delusional actions. In the darkness of their confused dogma, they may have thought that the end of the world was approaching. They may have taken the last, desperate leap because of their rigid, frenzied beliefs about Jesus, thinking that they could somehow hasten His coming. And so as a result, my friends, they are gone. My heart goes out to all those who mourn today."

Coliquin gave a half shake of his head and pursed his lips, in a posture of sad regret.

"But there is a light in the darkness. I have commissioned Bishop Dibold Kora, my special envoy, to commence talks with President Tulrude, in conjunction with the G-7 and the European Union and nearly a hundred international relief agencies, to commence a massive effort to meet the needs of those around the world who are suffering. Equally important," Coliquin said, "is our global plan to complete our project for unity, the One Movement, to prevent the spread of dangerous religious ideas like the ones that seem to have caused this terrible act of self-annihilation. After all, my friends, can we truly say that we love our neighbor if we allow our neighbor to suffer under the evil spell of hateful, harmful, religious propaganda? There is a better way. And you can be confident that if we follow that way, it will lead us to a better world."

Israel

The disappearance of millions of people around the world had a magnifying effect on those who had been left behind. Bart Kingston had read confirmations, which continued to pour in worldwide, that those who disappeared had indeed been Christians, and this tended to multiply exponentially the attitudes that many had already been harboring about religion, or God, or more particularly about Jesus and the book that detailed His story. Some had remained suspicious, and others seemed to consider the idea that Jesus had come to redeem the human race.

Kingston was still in Jerusalem when it all happened. He had tried to make contact with Peter Campbell, but the man was nowhere to be found. Kingston even trudged into the Old City section, making his way through the crowds that had gathered in the streets. He had checked Campbell's office and even his apartment.

Kingston had planned to fly back to New York, but he had cancelled his flight. He needed to stay in Israel for the time being. First, because he had journalistic responsibility. And second, because he had to sort out some things in his own head. If that was possible. And he wasn't sure it was.

◻◻◻

In Tel Aviv, Ethan was now approaching Joshua's high-rise apartment. He was so deep in thought he had momentarily forgotten which street he was on. He had to stop and look around. Then he reoriented himself. The apartment building was a half block away.

His Allfone rang. It was Rivka. She sounded subdued. "Hello, friend."

"Hi."

"How are you feeling? Confused, I bet."

"Confused? That doesn't begin to explain it. I'm a mess, Riv."

"I know," she said with a soft kind of regret, "I am so sorry about losing Josh."

"Yeah, well, I can't think straight right now. But what you said — 'losing Josh'? I'm not sure about that ... not exactly."

"Ethan ..."

"Well, did he die? Or didn't he? What happened, really?"

"Ethan, Josh's fighter plane was struck by a missile."

"I'm a pilot, Rivka. I know some things about flying. The sensors in the cockpit of Josh's F-35 LV indicated that his body had evacuated the cabin — yet the canopy on that jet was never blown. The ejection seat was never activated. The ground crew found bits of his flight suit in the wreckage. But no signs of human remains. Not a single trace of his DNA. You explain that ..."

"You know what happens when a jet explodes," she said. There was regret in her voice, certainly, but also persistence. "Everything burns up. Everything."

"Not everything. There's always a human trace. Even a small one. But here, there was nothing. Zero. Zilch."

"Okay, Ethan, I know you're upset," she said.

He could tell she was placating him. Maybe that was okay, but he wasn't in the mood. Ethan was not going to let it drop. "Then what about Abby and Cal and Deborah? The IDF rounded up the terror cell that was responsible for tying them up in that school in the Negev and making them the target for the bio-warhead. But then the Israeli special ops guys located the school — you know what they found? Three empty chairs, some loose rope, and a pile of clothes. Whoosh. The rest of the Jordan family had disappeared. And then there are all those reports about the millions of other people who disappeared ..."

Rivka changed topics abruptly. "I thought maybe we could catch some dinner together. Give you a chance to talk."

"I'm talking right now," he said, as he stood in front of Joshua's apartment tower. "But you're not listening." After a pause, Ethan settled down. "Sorry. Don't mean to make you the bad guy."

"That's okay. Anyway, you're right. I'm *not* one of the bad guys. Those would be the guys who were trying to blow your head off while you were driving an armored car down the streets in Nablus."

"Right," Ethan replied, trying to stay focused. "And I guess I never got the chance to thank you for shooting straight and keeping me alive back there. So thanks."

"Don't mention it. Besides, you had the tougher job. You had to play the sitting duck. Not me."

Ethan strode up the steps to the front door of the residential tower. "Listen, I'll get back to you. We'll make plans, okay?" he said to Rivka, tenderly, before they ended the call. "I want to sit down with you. Have a long talk. But only after I've cleared some things up in my own head first."

They said good-bye and agreed to meet the next day.

Ethan stood at the front door of Joshua's apartment tower and pushed the security pad. After it buzzed, he identified himself. The security guard at the desk let him in.

"Morning, Mr. March. So sorry about Colonel Jordan."

Ethan gave a slow shrug. "Me too."

"You would like to see, maybe, his personal effects?"

"I thought maybe I'd check out his place. I'm really not sure why I'm here."

"I think that Colonel Jordan must have figured you out pretty well, yes?"

"Why's that?"

"He left instructions."

"What kind?"

"A sealed note. Left with manager. Some time ago. To be opened in the event of 'unexplained absence or suspicious disappearance.' His orders. So, with what happened yesterday, we decided that . . . hope you don't mind, but we felt we should open the envelope."

Ethan bristled. *Man, these guys didn't even wait forty-eight hours.*

He waited for the rest of the story.

"So," the desk manager said, "he left this." And with that he handed him a small key.

"What's this for?"

"Safety deposit box of Colonel Jordan. Here in the building. His note said to give this to you. That's all."

Ethan fingered the key, then asked where the box was. The desk manager led him to the second floor and into the room with the safety-deposit boxes. Ethan inserted the key and opened the little metal door. There was only one thing waiting for him. A DVD player.

The manager gave him the key to Joshua's apartment, and Ethan walked inside with the portable video pad. It was a strange feeling, knowing that Joshua was gone. But where? That was the question. He noticed that there was a half-filled cup of coffee on the kitchen counter that Joshua hadn't finished. Probably fixed himself some coffee pre-dawn, just before heading out to the airbase for what would be his last mission.

Ethan chuckled a little at that. *Hey, Josh, I thought Abby got you off coffee and onto tea.*

But the smile faded quickly as Ethan plunked down on the couch. He had never felt so utterly alone. A jumble of crazy thoughts ran through his head. For a guy who always felt he needed to control his future, Ethan was facing a bizarre, uncertain life ahead. Josh, who was not just his boss and mentor, but who had also become his friend, had just vanished into thin air. Along with his entire family. They had become a second family to him. Though he never expected things to turn out like this, especially after Deborah had broken things off.

Suddenly, Ethan was aware of the vibration of his Allfone. He plucked it out of his pocket. It was an incoming email. He touched the screen and opened it up. A text message from "Jimmy Louder."

"Huh," Ethan mumbled. He hadn't heard from the Air Force captain since the aftermath of his rescue from North Korea. Ethan had the chance to greet him at South Korean HQ after the mission. But only very briefly. Then the Air Force whisked him back to the United States for debriefing and a return to his wife and kids.

But Ethan wasn't in a mood to read it. Not now. He had something much more important to do. He waved his finger over the On tab of Joshua's video player. The screen lit up. He touched the Forward button.

What he saw next made him jump a little.

It was Joshua's face filling up the screen, looking straight at him.

"Ethan, if you're looking at this right now, I'm off the planet, my friend. And you've been left behind. I didn't want that for you. But that's the way it is. I told you that I felt that the timeline was short, that Jesus would be mustering his army of followers pretty soon, that world events were rushing to a climax. So, I'm up there. And you're still down here."

"Whoa," Ethan muttered. This was heavy. Ethan immediately hit

Pause on the video pad and caught his breath. He waited several minutes before he hit Resume on the control.

When Ethan started the video again, Joshua walked him through what he called the "half-time coach's chalk-talk." Starting with the basics, once again, about who Jesus was, why He came to earth, why He died, what His death accomplished for the sins of mankind, the proof of His divinity by rising from the grave. And how Ethan needed to confess and believe those things and personally receive the person of Christ as Savior and Lord.

Ethan had heard it all before. Ever since his "salvation event," as Joshua called his Iranian jail experience, he would drum it into Ethan every chance he got. But now, it was different. Ethan couldn't avoid it. Couldn't dismiss it either. Too much had happened for him to play games. Like the miraculous disappearance of Josh and his entire family — raptured away from the earth, it seemed — just like Josh had said, the way the Bible had predicted it would happen.

Joshua's face on the screen leaned forward just a bit. Ethan stared back. For that instant, it seemed almost as if a holographic, three-dimensional image of Joshua was there in the room with him.

No, Ethan thought to himself, *even more real than that.* As Joshua spoke, Ethan sensed that what he was hearing now was the truest thing that ever existed.

"Let's start with the facts," Joshua said. "Jesus died on a cross in Jerusalem. Now Ethan, I don't know where you are right now as you are listening and watching this, but maybe you are still in Israel. The landmarks of the miraculous life of Jesus the Christ, the Promised One, are all over the Galilee and Jerusalem. I've shown you many of them myself. But just knowing that isn't enough. You need to face up to your status as a sinner, a man who has fallen short of God's design for you, just as I had to do. You and I are alike in many ways, you know. Including this — when we measure up our lives with the specs of God's moral plan for us, we know that we've blown it. Time and time again."

Ethan nodded at that, even though he was humbled to think of himself in the same category as his mentor. But there it was, the plain fact that Ethan — headstrong, both ruthlessly sure of himself at times and yet, beneath it all, also insecure as well — now had to face up to the same reality that Joshua had.

"Okay," Ethan said. "I got it. I guess I can't deny it. Proud. Selfish. Arrogant at times. Always looking out for myself. I could go on and on ... yeah ..."

But then something happened. Ethan was no longer addressing the image on the screen. He knew that what he had to say had to be said to God Himself, and to His Son Jesus.

Ethan's voice trembled. "Okay, God, yes. I admit I'm a sinner."

On the screen, Joshua kept talking, "Jesus didn't just die on the cross, Ethan. He was the sinless Son of God, willingly dying on the cross for your sins. Yours, Ethan. The same as mine. As the perfect sacrifice — the only sacrifice that would satisfy God's perfect sense of justice."

"Yes, God," Ethan murmured. "I know that's true. For some time I've been convinced of that, down deep, but I just didn't want to come out with it ... until now ... which I guess makes me a kind of coward ..." Ethan's voice was beginning to crack.

"And then," Joshua continued, "to prove to the whole world that He was God in the flesh, Jesus defied the grave and walked out of that tomb three days later ..."

"Yes," Ethan said. His eyes were cloudy now. Moist with tears. "I remember the stories. Jesus raised others from death. He was God. Walking around, right here in Israel. Looking out for other folks. Never for Himself ... Perfect ... Of course Jesus rose from the grave ..."

Joshua added, "And the only remaining thing, after acknowledging all of that, is to open your heart, invite Christ in, as Lord and Savior ..."

"Don't know why," Ethan said, breaking down once more, "why, oh God, why You'd want Your Son to live inside of a guy like me, selfish, scheming, lying ..."

Ethan was weeping, his head in his hands. "But God, I'm asking if Jesus could come into my heart. Right now ... Savior and Lord. No more escape plans for me ... no more dodging it, trying to weasel out of it ... no, Sir. Please, Jesus, come into me ..."

Reaching out through his tears, Ethan hit the Pause button once again. He sat for a while in silence, not knowing how much time had passed.

Finally he asked a question out loud.

"Okay, Ethan ... now what?"

He found himself staring at the ugly shag carpet on the floor of Joshua's little Tel Aviv apartment, and he couldn't help but laugh loudly at Joshua's bad taste in carpeting.

That's why you needed Abby — she always was a better interior decorator.

Right then, sitting on the couch in Josh's apartment, Ethan was able to reflect. He was beginning to figure something out. Like why Joshua had invested so much into him. Keeping him close. Talking endlessly about preparation. Yes, as it turned out, Joshua had figured Ethan out pretty well. Joshua must have known he would probably miss the first train when it came roaring past, and after the rapture he would be left back on the platform of the station with the rest of the human race.

He hit Resume.

Joshua's face appeared again. And what he had to say was hard and tough to hear. But Ethan wanted it all, the good and the bad. And that's what he got.

"Ethan, I hope you've accepted Jesus Christ into your heart. If so, you've been born again. So now, what you have to do next will be up to you. The world is about to start exploding around you. The forces of hell are going to be mounted against you. I guarantee it. That's what you're up against."

Then the image of Joshua's face on the screen broke into the kind of smile that Ethan recognized. Some people might even think it was a look that was a little brash on the surface. But Ethan knew better. Deep down Joshua had been a man who simply knew who he was and what he had to do.

"In the beginning you'll feel pretty much alone, Ethan. You'll have to stand strong." Joshua said, "I'll walk you through things in this video log as much as I can. But that's just the start. After a while you'll be able to handle things on your own. You'll be able to decipher for yourself what God has already described about the last dark night of the world that is coming, even if you can't see it yet, because you'll have His road map. So when the very worst comes — when the enemy tries to cripple you and destroy you, there won't be any surprises."

Ethan had been bracing himself, but now he muttered back to the screen, "Hey, Josh, thanks for the good news."

On the screen, an ever-widening grin spread over Joshua's face. It was the look of a man who had been gripped with an amazing story, and because he knew down to his soul that it was all true, he couldn't wait to tell it.

"But listen, Ethan, it's not all gloom and doom. There's the rest of the story, and it's magnificent. I'm going to share that with you too. Just wait until I tell you exactly what's going to happen at the end. But I don't want to get ahead of myself. I'm going to lay this out for you. The same as if you were being given a pre-mission flight check. But, Ethan, this is going to require that you take each step as a walk of faith."

Ethan found himself nodding at the screen. "Okay, Josh. What you got for me?"

Joshua's image continued to speak. "You need to know two things. First, I believe in my heart that God has picked you to shake things up down there on earth. To help lead an incredible, worldwide spiritual revival. There's still hope for folks down there. And you're the one to tell them that."

Ethan shook his head. "Oh, man. Are you sure you've got the right guy, Josh?"

"Second thing, Ethan," Joshua continued. "You may feel alone, but you're not. God will bring you into contact with an army of people who are ready to claim Christ for themselves — and to stand fast against the darkness. Against the Evil One. The hideous force that will temporarily be running things down there. You need to start searching for fellow compatriots to help you with this mission."

Ethan hit the Pause button, shook his head, and spoke out loud. "And where am I supposed to find them?" He thought about that for a few minutes. Joshua's words *walk of faith* rang in his ears.

"Okay, God," Ethan said. "Where do I start?" Then there was another minute of thinking. That is when Ethan became aware of his Allfone that he had put back in his pocket. He pulled it out and flipped it open. Then he hit the Display button for Captain Louder's email that he had received just minutes earlier. Ethan began to read it. It said:

Ethan — Captain Jimmy Louder here. I wanted to connect with Joshua Jordan. But things being as they are — I guess that isn't in the cards now. So I'd like to talk to you. If you're still here, that is. It's about something that Josh had told me during the rescue over in North Korea. And a few things too that my grandfather used to tell me. Why do I get the feeling that things in this old world are never going to be the same? I think I know what is going on, and I want to make sure that I line up with the right side on all of this. Time to make some mission-critical decisions. Can we talk? Here's my cell number, and you've already got my email ..."

Ethan March smiled. Then he laughed out loud and kept laughing. It felt good to let loose. Yes, Ethan decided, in a little while, right after finishing the video message from Joshua, he would make contact with Jimmy Louder. Maybe he would be his very first partner in his new mission.

Things were already happening quickly. For a guy who had always maintained an outward bravado while inwardly grappling with the fear of losing control — whether it was pitching a fastball, keeping a girlfriend, or flying the newest Air Force fighter — Ethan realized that he had now chosen a different path. A few minutes ago he had just told God that it would be God, not Ethan, who would be in charge of his life and directing the trajectory. If that was true, then his future was strangely settled, even if he didn't know exactly what that meant or what his life was going to look like.

Yet somewhere inside, Ethan already felt a newfound sense of certainty, as if he were about to launch a flight into the turbulent center of something dark, dangerous, and unfamiliar. But he was okay with that. Only this time there would be no computerized flight deck in front of him. And while it might be his hand grasping the side-stick in the cockpit, Ethan was already sensing that it would be the power of God within him that would have to control the flight pattern.

So he returned to the video player and hit the Resume button again. The image of Joshua's face came to life again on the screen. When that happened, Ethan spoke out loud from a heart that had been humbled, yet his voice was also decisive and immovable, like chiseled rock.

"All right. I'm here. And I'm listening now. I'm ready for my orders."

DISCUSSION QUESTIONS FOR *BRINK OF CHAOS*

by Craig Parshall

1. Joshua has been separated from his country, his wife, and his children, for two years since the end of the preceding novel, *Thunder of Heaven*. He has been living in exile, primarily in Israel, a nation that has given him sanctuary while unjust criminal charges are being pursued against him by a corrupt White House administration. His wife, Abigail, has counseled him to stay abroad — out of the jurisdiction of the U.S. courts until she can prove his innocence. Do you think that was good advice?

2. In *Thunder of Heaven*, and the preceding novel, *Edge of Apocalypse*, the risks of nuclear weapons in the hands of terrorists or rogue nations is presented. Now, in *Brink of Chaos*, we see the threat of a horrendous biological weapon under the control of a terror cell. Which threat do you believe is a greater risk?

3. The lives of Ethan March and Rivka, the Israeli spy, keep intersecting. Where do you envision their relationship going in the future? What impediments would there be to a romantic relationship?

4. In the futuristic view of America in this novel, the government is exercising a surprising amount of electronic surveillance over its citizens. How close, or far away, are we from that kind of scenario actually happening? What are both the arguments for and those against this kind of electronic surveillance of citizens that are mentioned in the novel?

5. *Brink of Chaos* presents one possible picture of a future rapture of Christians off the earth. If God were to remove His church from

TIM LaHAYE AND CRAIG PARSHALL

the world today, what kinds of repercussions do you think would occur for those "left behind" on the earth?

6. Alexander Coliquin's ambition for global power is expanding in *Brink of Chaos*. Do you see any roadblocks to his goal?

7. *Brink of Chaos* begins with a startling dream. Do you think that God speaks to his followers today in dreams? Has He done so in the past? Is there any support in the Bible for this to occur in the future?

8. Was Abigail Jordan wise or unwise, right or wrong, in refusing to receive the government mandated BIDTag? How does that square with the Bible's mandate for Christians to obey the government? Does the Bible give examples of exceptions to the general rule of obedience to rulers?

9. Of the five main characters in the novel, Joshua Jordan, Abigail Jordan, Deborah Jordan, Cal Jordan, and Ethan March, with which character do you most closely associate? Why?

10. How do you visualize God's "heavenly realm" now, before the coming of Christ to the earth? What parts of the Bible would support that image?

The End Series

Edge of Apocalypse

#1 New York Times *Bestselling Author*
Tim LaHaye and Craig Parshall

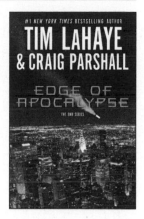

The End Series by *New York Times* bestselling author Tim LaHaye and Craig Parshall
is an epic thrill ride ripped from today's
headlines and filtered through Scriptural
prophecy.

In this adrenaline-fueled political thriller laced with end times prophecy, Joshua Jordan, former U.S. spy-plane-hero-turned-weapons-
designer, creates the world's most sophisticated missile defense
system. But global forces conspire to steal the defense weapon,
and U.S. government leaders will do anything to stop the nation's
impending economic catastrophe — including selling out Jordan and
his weapon.

As world events set the stage for the "end of days" foretold in
Revelation, Jordan must consider not only the biblical prophecies
preached by his wife's pastor, but the personal price he must pay if
he is to save the nation he loves.

Available in stores and online!

Thunder of Heaven

A Joshua Jordan Novel

#1 New York Times *Bestselling Author* *Tim LaHaye and Craig Parshall*

The End Series by *New York Times* bestselling author Tim LaHaye and Craig Parshall is an epic thrill ride ripped from today's headlines and filtered through Scriptural prophecy. As world events begin setting the stage for the "end of days" foretold in Revelation, Joshua Jordan must weigh the personal price he must pay to save the nation he loves.

Thunder of Heaven will appeal to the tens of millions of readers who have already made Tim LaHaye a household name and one of the bestselling authors of all time. This book is a return to form for Tim LaHaye whose previous prophetic fiction series, Left Behind, has sold roughly 70 million copies. Those who have read Left Behind and are eager for more highly charged fiction based on biblical prophesies will embrace *Thunder of Heaven* for the same reasons that turned Left Behind into the world's most celebrated publishing phenomenon of the last two decades.

Available in stores and online!

Revelation Unveiled

Tim LaHaye,
coauthor of the bestselling
Left Behind Series

The biblical foundation for the bestselling Left Behind Series ... In *Revelation Unveiled*, Dr. Tim LaHaye, coauthor with Jerry Jenkins of the bestselling novels *Left Behind* and *Tribulation Force*, reveals the scriptural foundation of this series. *Revelation Unveiled* explains such critical topics as: the Rapture of the Church, the Return of Christ, the Great Tribulation, the Final Battle against Satan and His Hosts, the Seven Seals, the Millennial Reign, the Seven Trumpets, the Seven Bowls of Wrath, the Great White Throne, the Destruction of Babylon, the New Heaven, and the New Earth. Previously titled *Revelation Illustrated and Made Plain*, this revised and updated commentary includes numerous charts. With simple and accessible language, *Revelation Unveiled* will help you better understand this mysterious, final book of the Bible and its implications.

Prophecy Books by Tim LaHaye

Are We Living in the End Times?

Charting the End Times

Charting the End Times Study Guide

Revelation Unveiled

The Popular Bible Prophecy Commentary

*The Popular Encyclopedia of Bible Prophecy The Rapture:
Who Will Face the Tribulation?*

Tim LaHaye Prophecy Study Bible

Understanding Bible Prophecy for Yourself

*These and other LaHaye resources are available at:
www.timlahaye.com*

Share Your Thoughts

With the Author: Your comments will be forwarded to the author when you send them to *zauthor@zondervan.com*.

With Zondervan: Submit your review of this book by writing to *zreview@zondervan.com*.

Free Online Resources at

www.zondervan.com

Zondervan AuthorTracker: Be notified whenever your favorite authors publish new books, go on tour, or post an update about what's happening in their lives at www.zondervan.com/authortracker.

Daily Bible Verses and Devotions: Enrich your life with daily Bible verses or devotions that help you start every morning focused on God. Visit www.zondervan.com/newsletters.

Free Email Publications: Sign up for newsletters on Christian living, academic resources, church ministry, fiction, children's resources, and more. Visit www.zondervan.com/newsletters.

Zondervan Bible Search: Find and compare Bible passages in a variety of translations at www.zondervanbiblesearch.com.

Other Benefits: Register to receive online benefits like coupons and special offers, or to participate in research.

ZONDERVAN®

ZONDERVAN.com/
AUTHORTRACKER
follow your favorite authors